THE WILTED TULIP

A Critique of Calvinism

JERALD L. MANLEY

The Wilted Tulip was written after over five decades of study and interaction as a Baptist pastor with the practical impact of doctrinal beliefs on churches and in the lives of believers and non-believers. The innumerable articles and books that have been read over those decades undoubtedly have influenced my choices for wording, as have the uncountable conversations and discussions on this topic that have occurred over these years. A diligent effort has been made to provide the proper and deserved credit for thoughts and quotes that are known to have originated with someone else. It is not my intention to claim originality for that labor which others have given.

All cited web addresses were active at the time of the writing of *The Wilted TULIP*.

The Authorized Version, commonly called the King James Version, is the source for all of my Biblical quotations.

Biblical references in citations from other authors are their choices and must be their responsibility.

Second Edition, Revised

ISBN: 1493577387
ISBN-13: 978-1493577385

DEDICATION

The Wilted TULIP is dedicated to those men of God—laymen, teachers, professors, missionaries, preachers, and pastors that with enormous patience and great love have so willingly given of their time to impart to me their knowledge of Scripture and to share the wisdom they gained through the experiences of their ministries. God in His goodness allowed me to walk in the company of giants of the faith; many of whom are now Home with Him. These all have earnestly contended to keep the path of doctrine and practice perspicuous. *The Wilted TULIP* is an effort to be faithful to them.

CONTENTS

ACKNOWLEDGMENTS

The LORD was merciful in giving me godly parents who placed a Bible in my hands at an early age and encouraged my reading of *the Book written by God*. He graciously provided me with a personal library of several thousand volumes that have allowed me access to the good and wise guidance from generations of godly counselors. In His kindness, the LORD also intersected my path with men of the Book from whom I have been privileged to glean knowledge through these decades of ministry. The years with these varied resources and conversations regarding the Scriptures have produced this book.

For this revised second printing of *The Wilted TULIP*, I am especially grateful for the encouragement and the corrective suggestions given by Julie Hudson Manley, Dr. Bob Wallace, Pastor Jody Wolf, Gary Roland, and John Timothy Manley.

INTRODUCTION

The TULIP of Calvinist theology is being planted in new Baptist gardens every day. While the intellectual beauty found in the logical philosophical system expressed by the TULIP has a strong appeal to many Christians, each of the five petals of the TULIP expresses a Point of doctrine that I believe, when weighed in the balance of Scripture, is found wanting.

The Wilted TULIP is written in the language of the person in the pew and is published with the prayer that it might serve for inquiring minds as a precautionary exposure to the shrouded errors of Calvinism. The changing of the mind of the ardent Calvinist is not anticipated, but it is prayerfully sought.

While I must oppose the doctrines of Calvinism and the Calvinistic definitions that support them, I do not desire to attack the Calvinist. In spite of what I understand to be the distortions made by the Calvinistic definitions of simple Biblical words and the falseness of those doctrines that compose the TULIP, I do not question the sincerity or the salvation of the Calvinist; and, it should not be inferred that I do.

By comparing the writings of Calvinists with the wording as it is found in Scripture, this book will challenge the validity of the Five Points of the TULIP of Calvinism and will contest the definitions that TULIP imposes upon Bible words. I believe that the confrontation reveals that those five doctrines with the special definitions of Calvinism that are *forced* upon Bible words in order to make them *palatable* are throughly defective biblically. Calvinism appears to be logical; however, Calvinism is unscriptural. Calvinism is **only** made logical when Scripture is altered to fit Calvinism by the acceptance and the application of the unique word meanings manufactured by Calvinism.

I believe that the TULIP exists in much the same manner as a flower does that has been severed from its root, but which looks vibrant and healthy in the vase *while* it is being artificially sustained; yet, that same flower is doomed to fade and wilt, dropping its petals one-by-one.

Jerald L. Manley

CHAPTER 1

THE TULIP

I have labored since childhood under the mistaken impression that the tulip is a flower that is native to the Netherlands. My mental image of that land is one of dikes, windmills, wooden shoes, and tulips. However, tulips, were unknown in the Netherlands until the 16th Century, strangely coinciding with the appearance of the Reformation.

> Tulips originated in Turkey getting their name from the Turkish word "tulbend" which means turban. Tulips were thought to look like the turbans. ... Tulips were introduced to Holland from Persia.[1]
>
> To many minds, the tulip and the windmill are virtually synonymous with the Netherlands. Most historians would agree that the windmill in Europe made its first appearance in the Low Countries, sometime before the twelfth century and the tulip is not a native of Holland, being unknown in that country until the sixteenth century.

[1]http://gardeningtips.org/Tulip.shtml

The colorful, cup-shaped flower, long popular among gardeners, is actually a native of the western Mediterranean and the steppes of Central Asia, and some species can be found growing wild in northern Africa, southern Europe, and in Japan. The empire of the Ottoman Turks once included much of the tulip's natural habitat, and it was through Turkey that most tulips reached Western Europe and the Netherlands.

The Turks prized the tulip, and were cultivating that flower on a large scale by the mid-sixteenth century when the Austrian ambassador to the Turkish Empire brought some tulip bulbs from Constantinople to his garden in Vienna. From Austria, the flower found its way to the Low Countries. In 1562, the first large shipment of Turkish tulips reached Antwerp, then part of the Dutch nation.

The tulip quickly became a favorite among European gardeners, and the Netherlands soon took the lead in producing prized specimens.

In the 1630's *[sic]*, a rage of tulip speculation, called tulipomania, gripped much of Holland, and farmers rich and poor began speculating in the tulip trade. Single bulbs of prized varieties sold for as much as $1,000, one particular bulb for $4,000, a small fortune at the time.

Alas, the tulip rage tapered off within a few years, leaving thousands of Dutchmen penniless. The economic scars of the tulipomania were felt in Holland for decades.[2]

---

[2]http://www.bigsiteofamazingfacts.com/the-history-of-tulipshttp://www.investopedia.com/features/crashes/crashes2.asp

Even as I mistakenly identified the tulip as a flower that is native to Holland,[3] I had also assumed that the Five Points of the acronym TULIP were connected with, if not actually devised by, the Synod of Dort.[4] Indeed, it is from that Synod that the TULIP's Five Points may be traced as they be-come the defining doctrinal foundation of Calvinism. However, the Canons of Dort, which the Synod composed as the answer to the five articles of the 1610 Remonstrance presented by the followers of Jacob Arminius. Since their writing, the Canons have been used to define Calvinism, were not originally presented in the form of the Five Points of the TULIP.

Moreover, as the following paragraphs explain, the Synod of Dort did not construct the Canons of Dort to follow the arranged order of the Points of the TULIP. In fact, the TULIP never appears in any writings that John Calvin or the Synod of Dort produced. The TULIP acronym was not originated by or introduced by John Calvin, by the Council of Dort, or by any other Reformer.

> *The Decision of the Synod of Dordt on the Five Main Points of Doctrine in Dispute in the Netherlands* is popularly known as the Canons of Dordt. It consists of statements of doctrine adopted by the great Synod of Dordt which met in the city of Dordrecht in 1618–19. Although this was a national synod of the Reformed churches of the Netherlands, it had an international character, since it was composed not only of Dutch delegates but also of twenty-six delegates from eight foreign countries.

---

[3]While we Americans often use *Holland* to identify the entire country, Holland is actually a region of the Netherlands and is not the proper name for the country. The Netherlands has providences. Noord (North) Holland and Zuid (South) Holland are two of the twelve providences.

[4]While also found spelled as Dordt, the proper name for the city is Dordrecht.

The Synod of Dordt was held in order to settle a serious controversy in the Dutch churches initiated by the rise of Arminianism. Jacob Arminius, a theological professor at Leiden University, questioned the teaching of Calvin and his followers on a number of important points. After Arminius's death, his own followers presented their views on five of these points in the Remonstrance of 1610. In this document, or in later more explicit writings, the Arminians taught election based on foreseen faith, universal atonement, partial depravity, resistible grace, and the possibility of a lapse from grace. In the Canons the Synod of Dordt rejected these views and set forth the Reformed doctrine on these points, namely, unconditional election, limited atonement, total depravity, irresistible grace, and the perseverance of saints.

The Canons have a special character because of their original purpose as a judicial decision on the doctrinal points in dispute during the Arminian controversy. The original preface called them a "judgment, in which both the true view, agreeing with God's Word, concerning the aforesaid five points of doctrine is explained, and the false view, disagreeing with God's Word, is rejected." The Canons also have a limited character in that they do not cover the whole range of doctrine, but focus on the five points of doctrine in dispute.

Each of the main points consists of a positive and a negative part, the former being an exposition of the Reformed doctrine on the subject, the latter a repudiation of the corresponding errors ... Although in form there are only four points, we speak properly of five points, because the Can-

> ons[5] were structured to correspond to the five articles of the 1610 Remonstrance. Main Points 3 and 4 were combined into one, always designated as Main Point III/IV.[6]
>
> The First Main Point of Doctrine: *Divine Election and Reprobation*
>
> The Judgment Concerning Divine Predestination which the Synod Declares to Be in Agreement with the Word of God and Accepted till now in the Reformed Churches, Set Forth in Several Articles
>
> The Second Main Point of Doctrine: Christ's Death and Human Redemption through It
>
> The Third and Fourth Main Points of Doctrine: Human Corruption, Conversion to God, and the Way It Occurs
>
> The Fifth Main Point of Doctrine: The Perseverance of the Saints[7]

The use of the TULIP to describe Calvinism was not inspired by the tulips of Holland, though the tulips arrived in Holland almost concurrently with the events that precipitated the Synod of Dort. The development and introduction of the TULIP has been erroneously attributed by some directly to John Calvin.[8] Speculation has been offered that since the early Calvinist theologians were familiar with Aristo-

---

[5]The English translation of the Canons has over 12,000 words.

[6]http://www.reformed.org/documents/index.html?maiframe=http://www.reformed.org/documents/canons_of_Dordt.ht ml

[7]http://www.reformed.org/documents/index.html?maiframe=http://www.reformed.org/documents/canons_of_dordt.ht ml

[8]"John Calvin is one of the Reformed Theologians, and in trying to help people understand his theology developed the mnemonic device TULIP. Each letter of TULIP teaches people one lesson of how to live and how much God loves us. This way people could better understand who God was in their life and how their salvation was already planned and fully in God's hands. The TULIP mnemonic helped people in Geneva understand and remember that God is sovereign over all of us, a doctrine that John Calvin fully believed in and taught." http://rev-akins.hubpages.com/hub/John-Calvins-TULIP-for-the-novice-theologian

tle's five categories for cause, as a natural act, they would have formed their own reasoning into Five Points.[9] Therefore, it is argued that if Calvin did not use the TULIP, then some other Reformer, perhaps William Ames, Theodore Beza, Kaspar Olevianus, or Zacharias Ursinus would have organized the Five Points.

Some have even fantasized that the critics and the detractors of Calvin developed the term in derision.

> It's important to appreciate the geo-socio-politico *[sic]* conditions at the time of the Reformation. This was the time when John Calvin, Martin Luther, Ulrich Zwingli, and others dared to defend the Biblical revelation against a militant Papal Church which had previously executed similar voices ... for daring to defy the teaching of the Papacy. ... In penning what he [Calvin] saw as the teaching of Scripture on matters of doctrine, he published his volumnous *[sic] The Institutes of the Christian Religion.* Rather than stressing the goodness of man, and therefore man's ability to earn favour with God and His eternal acceptance, Calvin saw Scripture emphasising *[sic]* something quite different. Some time *[sic]* later Calvin's ideas were mocked by his opponents who derisively coined the English acronym: *TULIP* to sum up Calvin's teaching. Those who agreed with Calvin used this acronym for their own purposes (the promotion of what they saw Scripture teaching about mankind's true condiiton, *[sic]* need for God, and God's solution to man's problem.[10]

Actually, the use of the acronym TULIP is entirely modern. The TULIP has no ancient lineage; it has

---

[9]http://theconventicle.blogspot.com/2006/10/five-solas.htm
[10]http://findingtruthmatters.org/articles/tulip.html

no connection to any Reformer; it did not arise in either Geneva or Dort. Perhaps most surprisingly, the *indispensable* TULIP does not appear in the literature of Calvinism until the 20th Century.

The website http://www.theopedia.com/TULIP provided the following research regarding the first appearance of the TULIP.

> There is no certainty regarding the origin of the acronym TULIP. However, the five points of Calvinism were discussed, as such, before the popular rise of this acronym, for example in R. L. Dabney's work, *The Five Points of Calvinism*, circa 1878. Dabney's five headings are total depravity, effectual calling, God's election, particular redemption, and perseverance of the saints.[11]
>
> The earliest use of TULIP in this regard appears to be in 1905 by Rev. Cleland Boyd McAfee, in a lecture before the Presbyterian Union, Newark, NJ, as recorded by William H. Vail, writing in *The New Outlook*, (1913).[12]
>
> The popular use of TULIP as a teaching device was stimulated by Loraine Boettner in *The Reformed Doctrine of Predestination* first published in 1932.[13]
>
>> The Five Points may be more easily remembered if they are associated with the word T-U-L-I-P; T, Total Inability; U, Unconditional Election; L,

---

[11]Robert Lewis Dabney, *The Five Points of Calvinism*, Richmond, VA: Presbyterian Committee of Publications, 1895.

[12]William H. Vail, *The Five Points of Calvinism Historically Considered*, The New Outlook, Vol. 104 (1913), p. 394.

[13]"Ever since the appearance of Loraine Boettner's magistrial *[sic]* *The Reformed Doctrine of Predestination*, it has been customary to refer to the five points according to the acrostic TULIP." Steele, David N., Curtis C. Thomas, and S. Lance Quinn, *The Five Points of Calvinism: Defined, Defended, Documented*, 2nd ed. Phillipsburg, NJ: P & R Publishing; 2004, xiv.
The TULIP acronym undeniably is of modern origination.

> Limited Atonement; I, Irresistible (Efficacious) Grace; and P, Perseverance of the Saints.[14]

Tulips did not originate in the Netherlands. The TULIP did not originate with John Calvin or during the Reformation. The tulip arrived in the Netherlands from Persia through Turkey and via Austria. The doctrines of Calvinism came to Europe from North Africa, where it was promoted by the Roman Bishop Augustine, and through Switzerland by the Frenchman, John Calvin.

I am not the first to be intrigued by the resemblance between the fatalism of Islam and the fatalism contained in Calvinism. The parallels of the course of the journeys of the tulips and the TULIP are merely an eerie symbol of that correspondence.

Though the appearance of the acronym TULIP has not been verified prior to its appearance in 1905 and it is therefore an anachronism, for the sake of brevity and continuity, TULIP will be used as a synonym for the doctrines of Calvinism in this publication.

As the horticulturalist or the backyard flower gardener would confirm, the tulip actually has *six petals, not five.*[15]

The tulip flower is as misrepresented and misused by the acronym TULIP as are the Scriptures by the doctrines of Calvinism. Both the flower and the Scriptures have been strategically altered to fit a philosophical and theological system, with whatever does not support that system simply being ignored and discarded.

---

[14]This statement is found between Chapters 9 and 10 of *The Reformed Doctrine of Predestination.*

[15]I am aware that double tulips, which have multiple petals, do exist; however, the common tulip has six.

When the TULIP of Calvinism is carefully examined under the piercing light of Scripture, it becomes apparent that the five petals of the TULIP simply do not exist in Scripture.

THE FIVE POINTS OF CALVINISM	
T	Total Depravity meaning Total Inability
U	Unconditional Election
L	Limited Atonement
I	Irresistible Grace meaning Irresistible Calling
P	Perseverance of the Saints

CHAPTER 2

PURPOSE

I sought a straightforward, uncomplicated, authoritative defense of Calvinism that I might use to represent that system of doctrine reasonably and fairly. My desire in writing this book is to challenge what Calvinism actually teaches and not to construct a theoretical *straw man* for the sole purpose of its destruction. The booklet, *The Five Points of Calvinism,*[16] written by Elder W. J. Seaton,[17] was chosen to establish the doctrinal distinctives of Calvinism because of its style of presentation as much as for its ease of accessibility. This attractive and well-written booklet of only twenty-four pages provides a succinct summary of the identifying

---

[16]W. J. Seaton, *The Five Points of Calvinism*, The Banner of Truth Trust, East Peoria, IL, 2007. The booklet may be accessed on several websites, among which are:

(1) http://rediscoveringthebible.com/Fivepoints.pdf
(2) www.nicenecouncil.com;
(3) www.monergism.com;
(4) inlibrislibertas.word-press.com;
(5) www.graceonlinelibrary.org.
(6) www.the-highway.com.

[17]An internet search revealed that W. J. Seaton is the elder of the Inverness Reformed Baptist Church, Inverness, Scotland.

doctrines of Calvinism, while avoiding the customary technical vocabulary of the theologians. The author conveys a pastor's desire to communicate to the person in the pew rather than to impress the scholar in the seminary.

The Five Points of Calvinism,[18] available in printed form since 1970 through The Banner of Truth Trust,[19] has obviously established a reputation for being highly regarded among the Reformed audience for its accurate presentation and resolute defense of Calvinism as evidenced by the booklet having been reprinted twelve times as of 2007, the date of my copy.

The plan and purpose of the author is provided on the back cover.

> By an accident of history[20] in the 17th Century five great Christian truths, formulated by successors of the reformers at the Synod of Dort to counter a drift[21] from

---

[18]When I refer to the booklet, *The Five Points of Calvinism,* I will use italics, otherwise the term Five Points of Calvinism will be synonymous with TULIP.

[19]The Banner of Truth Trust is recognized as a publisher of Reformed materials. The unswerving advocacy of the Trust for the doctrines of Calvinism cannot be questioned. The Trust is to be commended for keeping in print many great treasures of the Puritans and other Reformed writers from past centuries and many gems from contemporary writers.

[20]Forgive me for finding this statement to be an occasion of humor as I find a Calvinist speaking of "an accident of history" producing the Five Points of Calvinism. History has no accidents for the Calvinist, as Michael Bremmer writes, "In other words, no occurrence, large *or* small, occurs outside the sovereignty of God—from the number of rain drops falling on your lawn during an afternoon thunder storm *[sic]*, to the dramatic events of the Desert Storm war, all are within, and part of, God's divine decree. As often commented, even if one molecule is roaming 'free' in the universe, God is not sovereign." http://www.mbrem123./calvinism/free-will.php
See more of the context for this statement in APPENDIX 5.

[21]The drift was the growing dissatisfaction stirred primarily by the teachings of Jacob Arminius that questioned certain aspects of the doctrines taught by the Nederlandse Hervormde Kerk, the national Church of Holland, which was known in this country as the Dutch Reformed Church. The Synod of Dort convened as a response for *The Articles of the Remonstrants,* which was framed under five points or headings. The

> the Gospel, became linked with the name of the Genevan Reformer who had died half a century earlier. The label 'Calvinism' was at first a propaganda tactic on the part of the opponents, but while defenders of the Reformation Faith recognize that it could well be called by another name they came to accept the term as denoting those doctrines which placed man in entire dependence upon the free grace of God in salvation. Since the Reformation, there have been eras when Calvinism, apparently discredited and forgotten, has risen again with vital force and evangelical power. If that is happening, as it appears today, then it means that biblical teaching is once more coming to the fore. This present booklet is written to explain that teaching, and the author's standpoint is the same as that of C. H. Spurgeon who once wrote, "We believe in the five great points commonly known as Calvinistic *[sic]*;[22] but we do not regard these five points as being barbed shafts which we are to thrust between the ribs of our fellow-Christians. We look upon them as being five great lamps which help to irradiate the cross; or, rather, five bright emanations springing from the glorious covenant of our Triune God, and illustrating the great doctrine of Jesus crucified."

Seaton's motivation for writing his booklet is clearly presented in the PREFACE of his booklet.

Synod met in 154 sessions over seven months in 1618 concluding that no accommodation or reconciliation was possible. The response correspondingly arranged to answer the five points raised by the Arminians established the teachings of Calvinism into that logically systematic structure that centuries later would be best known by the acrostic TULIP.

[22]I have attempted to restrict the use of *[sic]* to those incidents in the works of others that I wish to be certain are not attributed to misprinting on my part.

> There is scarcely another word that arouses such suspicion, mistrust, and even animosity among professing Christians as the word Calvinism. And yet much of the zeal that is levelled *[sic]* against the system and those who hold and preach it is most certainly a zeal which is not according to knowledge. The following articles are written in the hope that much of the abuse that is hurled at the Calvinistic system of theology will be withdrawn, and that the truth of that great teaching, which was the backbone of our fathers in the faith, and the strength of the church and therefore more glorious era than our own, will be clearly seen.

Seaton advanced his arguments without vitriolic attack upon those with opposing viewpoints and did so in a moderate and Christian manner. I intend my comments to be as direct as were his and to be as moderate and Christian in my rebuttal of Calvinism as he was in his advocacy for the TULIP. My opposition to Calvinism does not preclude civil discourse or Christian fellowship. Opposition may be direct and even may be pointed, without becoming personal.

Many Calvinists are transparent in their beliefs. They identify themselves openly without camouflaging their system of particular doctrinal distinctions. While I disagree with their position, I respect and appreciate their candor and integrity.

When reading avowed Calvinists such as Charles Haddon Spurgeon, John Gill, and others, I approach their commentaries and sermons as if I were the prospector panning for gold in a cold Alaskan stream. I dip my pan into the sediment at the bottom of the stream and then *pan* away, swirling and skimming at the surface of rippling water, until only the bright nuggets remain. Panning requires some shaking, considerable sifting, and a good supply of clear, clean running water. When I read these men, I keep my Bible open, sifting their comments through the clear, clean flowing water of the word of God[23] until the nuggets appear.

It is true that I have found certain writers (non-Calvinist as well as Calvinist) to have so few flakes of gold that the effort of panning is not profitable labor. Several of the contemporary writers fall into this last category. Discernment is required to read any human publication or to listen to any preacher or teacher. *I include myself in this stipulation.*

The necessity for the confrontation with Calvinism and for the open refutation of Calvinism is not because of transparent confessed Calvinists such as the Gills and the Spurgeons of the world, but it is with those Calvinists that will covertly infiltrate non-Calvinist churches and institutions with the designed intention to subvert the doctrinal position of the congregation or the students. Subversion is not a fruit of the Spirit; moreover, seditions are the work of the flesh.[24]

My purpose in presenting this work is to inoculate believers in non-Calvinist churches and institutions against Calvinism. I purpose to expose the readers to sufficient presentation of the doctrines of Calvinism to develop a resistance to the possibility of infection, but not to inject such a heavy dose that it causes the development of the syndrome.

Preventative medication is always more pleasant than the curative surgery that will be required when Calvinism is diagnosed. The last resort of amputation may become the only solution to saving the life

---

[23]My practice is to restrict the use of the phrase "Word of God" as a name for the LORD Jesus and to restrict the phrase "word of God" as a title for Scripture.

[24]Galatians 5:19–21 Now the works of the flesh are manifest, which are *these*; Adultery, fornication, uncleanness, lasciviousness, Idolatry, witchcraft, hatred, variance, emulations, wrath, strife, seditions, heresies, Envyings, murders, drunkenness, revellings, and such like: of the which I tell you before, as I have also told *you* in time past, that they which do such things shall not inherit the kingdom of God.

of a church or institution, but that surgical removal is always a drastic operation that produces considerable pain to all members of that body. The prognosis in such cases is always grim and tentative. A full recovery is never assured.

The *Merriam-Webster Dictionary*[25] [*M-WD*] defines Calvinism as "the theological system of Calvin and his followers marked by strong emphasis on the sovereignty of God, the depravity of mankind, and the doctrine of predestination." This description would imply that these three central principles adequately define Calvinism.

While these Three Points might serve sufficiently for the purpose of the dictionary, Calvinism logically requires a minimum of five essential doctrines. There are strict Calvinists that hold to more than Five Points.[26] While some individuals consider themselves to be Calvinists and not to hold to all five, I stress that the Five Points are *the minimum* for the philosophical theological system of Calvinism to sustain its logic. This will be discussed in more detail in chapter 15.

The TULIP of Calvinism has been effectively summarized in one paragraph:

> Man is totally unable to save himself on account of the Fall in the Garden of Eden being a *total* fall. If unable to save himself, then God must save. If God must save, then God must be free to save whom He will. If God has decreed to save whom He will, then it is for those that Christ made atonement on the Cross. If Christ died for them, then the Holy Spirit will effectually

---

[25]The Merriam-Webster Dictionary, published by Merriam-Webster, Inc. will be used as the reliable neutral authority for all definitions.

[26]Dr. John Piper has stated that he is a Seven Point Calvinist, adding Point 6 as "double predestination" and Point 7 "the best of all possible worlds." http://www.desiringgod.org/resourcelibrary/articles/what-does-\piper-mean-when-he-says-hes-a-seven-point-calvinist

> call them into that salvation. If salvation then from the beginning has been of God, the end will also be of God and the saints will persevere to eternal joy.[27]

That paragraph is an excellent example of simplicity and straightforwardness. It provides the very essence of Calvinism in uncomplicated and understandable terminology that allows for no confusion of intent for the *discerning* reader. Each of the Five Points of Calvinism is identified in one paragraph for those that know the Calvinistic *code words*. The writer was even candid enough to identify the first of those *code words* by placing the word *total* in italics. For the Calvinist, that word has a particular definition; for the Calvinist, the word *total* indicates a spiritual condition of complete inability.

In *The Wilted TULIP*, when I refer to these five doctrines, I will capitalize the words, e.g. Total Depravity. When I am describing the spiritual condition implied by that doctrine, the words will be in the lower case, e.g. total depravity.

---

[27]Seaton, *The Five Points of Calvinism*, 8. In all citations from this work, the italics and other marks of emphasis are his *except where specifically identified.*

CHAPTER 3

NECESSITY

Increasingly, the doctrines that have become identified by the titles of Reformed or Protestant,[28] Sovereign Grace, Augustinian, and, most

---

[28]My use of Protestant as a synonym for Reformed does not rise from personal Baptist prejudice. That the two words are synonyms is established by the *M-WD*: "Reformed: 2 capitalized: PROTESTANT; specifically: of or relating to the chiefly Calvinist Protestant churches formed in various continental European countries."
Because some might choose to use a particular word indifferently, carelessly, or improperly does not alter the definition of that word. Baptists are not properly identified as Protestants as they are not lineal descendants of the Reformed movement. A Reformed Baptist is therefore a merger of two separate streams flowing from different doctrinal fountains. An individual may indeed have come out from the Roman Catholic Church [RCC] and identified himself with Baptists; however, the doctrines and practices of Baptists did not come out from the RCC, because those following Baptists distinctives were never a part of the RCC. It is a proverbial statement, as well as a historical fact, that the only agreement between Luther and the Pope was that of persecuting Baptists. Confirmation for this assertion will be found in APPENDIX 10. Calvin had the same distaste for Anabaptists. The common recipients of the hatred of both the RCC and the Protestant Reformers were those who refused infant baptism or baptism for the removal of original sin. The following support for this statement is from a decidedly non-Baptist source:

> "But the Anabaptists were given little opportunity of building up a complete pattern of church life and order. The Diet of Speier in 1529 decreed immediate death for any who did not present their

commonly, Calvinism are being received as acceptable by Baptist churches and educational institutions that historically have resisted and opposed those same doctrines. In particular, pastors and professors having allegiance to the Second London Confession of 1689 (whether openly or with varying degrees of covertness) are increasingly found within the Southern Baptist Convention, other non-convention Baptist associations and fellowships, and in Independent Baptist churches. The Second London Confession of 1689 is throughly a Calvinist document that was compiled to be the doctrinal statement for Particular Baptist churches in England and Wales. The 1689 Confession is based upon the Reformed 1646 Westminster Confession of Faith. The Philadelphia Confession of Faith (1742) is nearly identical to the 1689 Confession with two chapters added, Singing Praise and Laying on of Hands.

The apparent patriotism of the proponents of Dominion Theology and Christian Reconstructionism often serves to make their Calvinism acceptable to Baptists. Reformed Baptists have revived to the extent that they have constructed active fellowships, conferences, and associations. In recent years, several publishing companies have been formed specifically to identify with this burgeoning resurgent market of Calvinist Baptists.

It is a sad, but recognized, fact that the infiltration of Calvinists within Baptist churches and educational institutions is most often identified during

---

children for baptism. The Emperor, the Roman hierarchy and most of the Protestant leaders agreed together in this drastic policy. The main motives behind it were probably fear of social unrest and desire to preserve the authority of the clergy, rather than any clearly thought out theology or ecclesiology. But official theory was committed to a belief in original sin, from the penalties of which baptism provided the only way of escape. The Anabaptists held a different view both of sin and of baptism. The Edict of Speier was ruthlessly enforced." Ernest A. Payne, Senior Tutor, Regent's, Park College, Oxford; *The Anabaptists Of The 16th Century;* London: 1949; The Carey Kingsgate Press, Ltd.; 6 Southampton Row, W.C.I.

the postmortem after an unexpected seismic event with its accompanying volcanic eruption. Sometimes a specific individual already in residency within the congregation discovers the TULIP through some exterior influence and begins to seek others with whom to share the discovery of this deeper truth. This is nearly always undertaken surreptitiously. At other times, a new pastor, a new staff hire, a new member, a new student, or a new faculty member arrives and, having quietly established a following, begins sowing the seeds of the TULIP. Proselytizing by infiltration is less than honesty on parade.

With the increasing emphasis upon advanced academic degrees for pastors and church staff, individuals are obtaining their postgraduate education from Calvinist or Calvinistic schools solely because of their alleged or recognized academic status. Many of these graduates will then return to the churches with more than the degree from the institution; they also bring the doctrines of Calvinism, sometimes, perhaps, without realizing how greatly they have actually been influenced. Calvinism, because of its self-proclaimed dependency on logic and its self-styled ability to provide special or advanced insight, has a strong attraction for those with an intellectual inclination. That is a rather precise description of individuals seeking advanced degrees and many of them do become adherents of Calvinism after attending a Calvinist or Calvinistic institution.

While I fully approve of, and strongly advocate for, an educated ministry, I am a stronger proponent of and a more fervent promoter for receiving that education from an institution that has a consistent reputation as being biblically sound in doctrine and practice as well as being sound in academics.

To surrender separation from error in the pursuit of an advanced degree is to invite doctrinal disaster.

It is worthy of note that the followers of the LORD Jesus were more recognized for His influence than for their educational attainments.[29] To attend any institution solely for the market value of the prestige of the projected degree is not a spiritual motivation.

Multiplied Christian Colleges and Seminaries are continuously combating the rise of Calvinism within the faculty and among the student body. In the course of proper academic instruction, error must be presented and, then, it must be carefully and adequately shown to be false. However, in that process, certain individuals will become intrigued with Calvinism and will persuade themselves or they will

---

[29]Acts 4:13 Now when they saw the boldness of Peter and John, and perceived that they were unlearned and ignorant men, they marvelled; and they took knowledge of them, that they had been with Jesus.
While modern scholarship dismisses Peter and John as educationally deprived fishermen from the hills of Galilee, there can be no mistake that Paul was exceptionally well educated; however, Paul did not use his scholastic attainment to persuade others to receive the Gospel. I also remind my readers that Peter and John were successful businessmen.
Acts 22:3 I am verily a man *which am* a Jew, born in Tarsus, *a city* in Cilicia, yet brought up in this city at the feet of Gamaliel, *and* taught according to the perfect manner of the law of the fathers, and was zealous toward God, as ye all are this day.
1 Corinthians 2:4 And my speech and my preaching *was* not with enticing words of man's wisdom, but in demonstration of the Spirit and of power: 5 That your faith should not stand in the wisdom of men, but in the power of God. 6 Howbeit we speak wisdom among them that are perfect: yet not the wisdom of this world, nor of the princes of this world, that come to nought: 7 But we speak the wisdom of God in a mystery, *even* the hidden *wisdom*, which God ordained before the world unto our glory: 8 Which none of the princes of this world knew: for had they known *it*, they would not have crucified the Lord of glory. 9 But as it is written, Eye hath not seen, nor ear heard, neither have entered into the heart of man, the things which God hath prepared for them that love him. 10 But God hath revealed *them* unto us by his Spirit: for the Spirit searcheth all things, yea, the deep things of God. 11 For what man knoweth the things of a man, save the spirit of man which is in him? even so the things of God knoweth no man, but the Spirit of God. 12 Now we have received, not the spirit of the world, but the spirit which is of God; that we might know the things that are freely given to us of God. 13 Which things also we speak, not in the words which man's wisdom teacheth, but which the Holy Ghost teacheth; comparing spiritual things with spiritual. 14 But the natural man receiveth not the things of the Spirit of God: for they are foolishness unto him: neither can he know *them*, because they are spiritually discerned.

be persuaded that the matter must be researched further to verify that the instructor fairly and correctly presented the errors of Calvinism. Among those individuals will be a few that will become enthralled with the intellectual appeal of Calvinism, and, due to their personal immaturity in discernment, they will fail to remain simple concerning that which is evil (Romans 16:19). Accordingly, they become ensnared by what they perceive as the cerebral brilliance displayed in their Calvinist resources.

Occasionally, a professor or teacher will accept a position in an institution for the unannounced premeditated purpose of subtly enticing students. More often, the individual becomes enamored with a particular Calvinist author in the pursuit of fresh materials and wider wisdom and thereby gradually is entangled in the unrecognized snare nested within his new authoritative source. He will begin to promote that author to his students by favorable quotations or suggested or required readings. This subtle dissemination of what could not be taught openly is insidious in its design and corrupting in its consequences.

When either the students or the faculty members become attracted to Calvinism, it will take considerable time and providential exposure for the danger to be revealed. That eventual discovery always generates a battlefield with the accompanying casualties to both the combatants and the innocents.

Churches are not exempt from infiltration; every local church is the potential target for a proselytizer of some false doctrine. Those who are being considered for a position with any measure of authority should always be screened for their doctrine.

Any candidates for the office of pastor especially must be examined by someone who knows how to discern a covert Calvinist as well as multiple other errors. Individuals considered for positions on a church staff definitely need to be chosen carefully to be certain that there is no propensity for false doctrine or the naivety to introduce it unwittingly.

Teachers, youth workers, and those who work with the music are able to integrate false doctrine into their activities surreptitiously. Church officers should be elected wisely and selectively, because they are in a position to introduce, or to block, the arrival of false teaching.

Even the members can bring in false teaching. Sometimes, allowing or encouraging an individual or family to visit for a few weeks before deciding on church membership will prove to have been the preventative medicine to avoid the conflict of infiltrated error. Over the span of six to eight weeks of preaching, the Biblical pastor will almost certainly present sufficient areas of doctrine in his messages to generate a conversation, if not a reaction.

The only safety for any church is through the consistent and constant watchcare by the leadership and the membership of each church. It is far easier, certainly it is much less damaging, to prevent an error from entering the congregation than to remove that error from the membership. The one may appear abrasive, but the other is always disruptive and will never be accomplished without casualties.

CHAPTER 4

IDENTIFICATIONS

Reformed as a title identifies the theological association with those individuals who sought to reform the Roman Catholic Church [RCC] but that eventually left the RCC under the pressure of persecution or that were excommunicated by the RCC. The era of the Reformation is most commonly dated as beginning with the 95 Theses of Martin Luther in 1517 and continuing to 1648 when the Treaty of Westphalia effectively ended the religious wars in Europe. The efforts to reform the RCC obviously began before well before 1517, but that is an acceptable general beginning date for the era of the Reformation.

The word Protestant[30] describes the protestation of the Reformers against the excesses of the RCC. While retaining many of the doctrines and practices of the RCC, Luther and others voiced a call for the

[30]See footnote 26 for the definition of Protestant. It should be acknowledged that while not all Protestants are Calvinists, all Protestants are descended from the Reformers.

reform of the RCC. It was the sale of indulgences[31] (some of which were for sins that *might be* committed in the future), and other such excesses that spurred the public actions. As the RCC resisted, became intransient, and finally demanded subservient compliance, these individuals resisted the pressures and the dangers, refused to surrender their consciences, and retained their opposition. The courage required and the bravery demonstrated for those actions is undeniable; however, the divorcement was forced upon the Reformers. Separation from the RCC was certainly not their initial design or desire.

They did not reject, certainly they did not repudiate, some of the central fundamental doctrines of the RCC. They desired only to reform—keeping some of the form and much of the substance, but reshaping the structure and the application.

It is important to recognize that the disagreement was at first more against the *practices* of the RCC than it was against the *doctrines* of the RCC. However, as the move to reform failed, the movement became a division. In the process of time, the areas of doctrinal differences became a part of the rupture between the Reformers and the RCC and between the various Reformers themselves.

It should be stated that both the RCC and the Reformers wrote of individuals and groups, which were identified by various names, that were outside

---

[31]The *M-WD* gives: "remission of part or all of the temporal and especially purgatorial punishment that according to Roman Catholicism is due for sins whose eternal punishment has been remitted and whose guilt has been pardoned (as through the sacrament of reconciliation)." The practice of granting indulgences began with the RCC offering forgiveness for sins or a lessening of the penalty for sins to entice participation in the Crusades. When Pope Julius I determined to construct the *Basilica di San Pietro* (usually referred to as St. Peter's Cathedral, though the proper RCC designation is that of a Basilica, not a Cathedral), indulgences were used to raise the necessary funds. The purchased indulgence promised a reduction or even elimination of time in purgatory for the person buying the indulgence or for a person already in purgatory.

of the RCC but that were separate from and not identified with the Reformers. These individuals and groups received pressure that escalated to persecution from both the Reformers and the RCC.

Chief among the causes for the unity of the RCC and the Reformers in their pressure, which often became persecution, against those churches and individuals that were in existence prior to the Reformation, continued with a viable existence through the Reformation, remained firmly outside of the RCC, and that would not align with the Reformers, was the issue of believer's baptism. The RCC and the Reformers agreed that baptism, particularly infant baptism, was required and both the RCC and the Reformers were enraged that the validity of their common baptism would be questioned.

The Reformers consistently maintained that the baptism that they had received by the authority of the RCC was valid. No record exists of a single Reformer having repudiated his RCC baptism and receiving believer's baptism after leaving or being excommunicated by the RCC.

The commonality between all the reformers and the RCC, beyond their baptism, was a deep, bitter hatred for anyone who believed that the baptism of the RCC and the Reformers was invalid and who accordingly called for those who followed Christ to receive believer's baptism.

Both the Reformers and the RCC gave those believers that were outside the RCC the derogatory name of the *re-baptizers* or Anabaptists.[32] Those

---

[32]The term Anabaptists was used by the RCC and the Reformers to identify various groups that each considered dissidents or heretics. Historians have also used the name indiscriminately. Within those who were broadly labeled Anabaptists would have been individuals and churches that would not have an affinity for those others receiving the same brand at that time or in any other era. However, among those churches and individuals who were so labeled did exist some that retained and maintained the doctrine and practices of the apostolic

believers rejected that name[33] insisting that they did not *re-baptize* anyone; they were convinced that the baptism of infants was not Biblical, and therefore it was not a genuine baptism. These individuals and churches that were independent from both the RCC and the Reformers faithfully practiced the immersion of believers after and upon their profession of faith.

A wide range of doctrinal persuasions existed among the Reformers that would eventually divide them. The specific title of Reformed, however, has become associated exclusively with Calvinism. It is nonetheless a broad term and encompasses Calvinists of varying conformity to the TULIP.

SOVEREIGN GRACE

This title is often used by those Calvinists who wish to emphasize the Calvinist doctrines, but who seemingly do not wish to be labeled as followers of a man, even though his name is John Calvin. The use of the word *grace* in the name of a church does not necessarily designate that church as Calvinist; however, it is sometimes used for specifically for that purpose.

The word *grace* is a Bible word and while the word *sovereign* is not a word that is found in the Scriptures, the concept is assuredly there. The GOD of Heaven is sovereign.[34] He is indeed "superlative in

---

churches. Not all of those identified by the RCC and the Reformers with the Anabaptist label were sound in the faith; ***however, some were***. A similar situation exists with the name Baptist in the present age. The use of the name whether to self-identify or as a label applied by others does not guarantee either uniformity or accuracy in that application. My comments are in reference to those Anabaptists that were indeed biblically sound.

[33]http://www.pbministries.org/History/John%20T.%20Christian/vol1/history_15.htm

[34]Isaiah 43:13 Yea, before the day was I am he; and there is none that can deliver out of my hand: I will work, and who shall let it? Psalm 10:16 The LORD is King for ever and ever: the heathen are perished out of his land.

quality: EXCELLENT; of the most exalted kind; having undisputed ascendancy: PARAMOUNT; having supreme authority that is absolute and unlimited in extent and enjoying autonomy."[35]

Grace is certainly an essential Bible word. God is the God of all grace (1 Peter 5:10); however, God is not a despot. He is *the* Ruler with absolute power and authority, but He does not exercise His power tyrannically. He proclaimed His Own Name as "merciful and gracious, longsuffering, and abundant in goodness and truth."

> Exodus 34:5–7 And the LORD descended in the cloud, and stood with him there, and proclaimed the name of the LORD. And the LORD passed by before him, and proclaimed, The LORD, The LORD God, merciful and gracious, longsuffering, and abundant in goodness and truth, Keeping mercy for thousands, forgiving iniquity and transgression and sin, and that will by no means clear the guilty; visiting the iniquity of the fathers upon the children, and upon the children's children, unto the third and to the fourth generation.

It is to the throne of grace that we believers may always come unto the God of all grace in order to find mercy.

> Hebrews 4:16 Let us therefore come boldly unto the throne of grace, that we may obtain mercy, and find grace to help in time of need.

Psalm 47:2 For the LORD most high is terrible; he is a great King over all the earth.
1 Timothy 6:15–16 Which in his times he shall shew, who is the blessed and only Potentate, the King of kings, and Lord of lords; Who only hath immortality, dwelling in the light which no man can approach unto; whom no man hath seen, nor can see: to whom be honour and power everlasting. Amen.

[35]This is the *M-WD* definition of sovereign.

> Psalm 86:15 But thou, O Lord, art a God full of compassion, and gracious, longsuffering, and plenteous in mercy and truth.

> 1 Peter 5:10 But the God of all grace, who hath called us unto his eternal glory by Christ Jesus, after that ye have suffered a while, make you perfect, stablish, strengthen, settle you.

Good words, such as grace and sovereign, may be used carelessly or improperly, through ignorance, and those words may even be used somewhat deceitfully, by assigning them a special or secretive meaning that is unknown to the casual reader or listener. The latter is the approach of Calvinism. Words to the Calvinist have special assigned meanings, which are exclusive to Calvinism.

AUGUSTINIAN

These Calvinists identify themselves as followers of St. Augustine, 354–430, the Bishop of Hippo, who is conferred the exalted title of *Doctor of the Church* by both the RCC and the Church of England. He is considered by many secular and religious scholars as the most important figure in the ancient Western church. Born in North Africa to a pagan father and a Christian mother, he converted to Christianity at the age of 31. According to his contemporary Jerome, the translator of the Vulgate and who is also recognized by the RCC with the title of *church father*, Augustine "established anew the ancient Faith."[36] This designation would mark Augustine as a Reformer before the year 400.

Among his unique teachings, Augustine is considered to have developed the doctrines of *Original Sin*, *Just War*, and *Predestination*. He is remembered

---

[36]Jerome wrote to Augustine in 418: "You are known throughout the world; Catholics honour and esteem you as the one who has established anew the ancient Faith." http://www.answers.com/topic/st-augustine-of-hippo#ixzz1VNhsWyz0

as the author of *The City of God* and *Confessions*. He also wrote *On Baptism* and *Against the Donatists*, fiercely attacking these *re-baptizers*. The Donatists were only one group among those outside the RCC that were subjected to pressure and persecution for *a full millennium* before the Reformers were born.

Early in life, Augustine became a Manichean.[37] Subsequently, he was strongly influenced by Platonism,[38] being attracted to its mysticism. There was also a strong infatuation with the Stoics.[39] His concept of Christianity clearly shows these philosophical influences.

Augustine is exceptional among the so-called church fathers in that he is revered by the RCC, *all* Calvinists, and most other Protestants.[40] Calvin is generally acknowledged to have refined and explained more fully the teachings of Augustine on soteriology, the doctrine of salvation, by emphasizing election, predestination, sovereign efficacious grace, etc. Calvin also followed Augustine in advocating that Israel is replaced by the church in the plan of God.

Augustine is described by one writer as "a powerful advocate for orthodoxy and of the episcopacy (the RCC clerical system) as the sole means for the

---

[37]The *M-WD provides*: "a believer in a syncretistic religious dualism originating in Persia in the third century A.D. and teaching the release of the spirit from matter through asceticism."
Academic Dictionaries and Encyclopedias gives a wider definition of "an adherent of the dualistic religious system of Manes, a combination of Gnostic Christianity, Buddhism, Zoroastrianism, and various other elements, with a basic doctrine of a conflict between light and dark, matter being regarded as dark and evil." http://universalium.academic.ru/145736/Manichean

[38]The *M-WD*: "the philosophy of Plato stressing especially that actual things are copies of transcendent ideas and that these ideas are the objects of true knowledge apprehended by reminiscence."

[39]The *M-WD*: "a school of philosophy founded by Zeno of Citium about 300 B.C. holding that the wise man should be free from passion, unmoved by joy or grief, and submissive to natural law."

[40]http://www.newadvent.org/cathen/02091a.htm

dispensing of saving grace."[41] That accurate revelation shows the fallacy of using Augustine as a source for Biblical truth. The errors of Augustine pollute whatever truth he might include in his writings. No fountain is able to send forth both bitter and sweet water.[42] The error always comingles with and corrupts the truth.

Besides this obvious heresy of placing the "means for the dispensing of saving grace" in the hands of an earthly institution, specifically the RCC—that error alone is sufficient to remove him from the ranks of the orthodox—it is undeniable that Augustine believed many additional things that are certainly not possible to describe as orthodox, such as:[43]

1. the perpetual virginity of Mary,
2. the necessity of baptism for salvation,
3. the creation as described in Genesis is an allegory,
4. the intercession of the [dead] saints,
5. in the "real presence of Christ in the Eucharist."

Additionally, Augustine appears to be the first in history to formulate a distinction between the visible and the invisible church; this concept was largely ignored until Calvin stressed it in his writings.[44] Augustine held so determinately to the reality of the presence of Christ in the Eucharist that he wrote the incomprehensible statement that *the LORD Jesus carried Himself in His Own hands* when He broke the bread after the Passover in the Upper Room.

> *And was carried in his own hands*: how indeed this could be done in case of a

[41]http://www.ccel.org/a/augustine/

[42]James 3:11 Doth a fountain send forth at the same place sweet *water* and bitter?

[43]http://www.americancatholictruthsociety.comarticles/augustinecatholic.htm http://www.willcoxson.net/faith/augprot.htm

[44]http://www.newgenevacenter.org/09_Biography/09a_In-Depth-Biographiesaugustine2.htm

> man, who, Brethren, can understand? For who is carried in 'his own hands?' In the hands of others *can a* man be carried, in his own hands is no man carry, how this may be understood of David according to the letter, we cannot find; but in Christ we find. For Christ was carried in His Own Hands, when commending His Own Body, He said, This is *My Body.* For That Body He carried in His Own Hands.[45]

The following is a quotation from another of the 350 surviving sermons of Augustine. This particular discourse was addressed to new Christians:

> "I promised you [new Christians], who have now been baptized, a sermon in which I would explain the sacrament of the Lord's Table ... That bread which you see on the altar, having been sanctified by the word of God, is the body of Christ. That chalice, or rather, what is in that chalice, having been sanctified by the word of God, is the blood of Christ. What you see is the bread and the chalice; that is what your own eyes report to you. But what your faith obliges you to accept is that the bread is the body of Christ and the chalice is the blood of Christ. This has been said very briefly, which may perhaps be sufficient for faith; yet faith does not desire instruction."[46]

Augustine was also a firm believer in amillennialism.[47] Amillennialism by its nature requires an

---

[45]*A Library of Fathers of the Holy Catholic Church*, Expositions on the Book of Psalms by St. Augustine, Bishop of Hippo, Oxford, John Henry Parker, London, 1847, 350.

This incoherent strangeness is found in his introductory notes on Psalm 34 (quite frequently mistakenly identified on the internet as being from Psalm 33—proof that copyists duplicate errors) in which Augustine seemingly quotes from the Septuagint; however I have found no translation of the Septuagint reading as does his citation from 1 Samuel 21:13.

[46]http://www.catholic.com/library/Real_Presence.asp

[47]Amillennialism is the perspective that there will not be a future literal 1000-year reign of Christ upon the earth. Amillennialists do in

allegorical interpretation of Scripture. While not a determining factor in the definition of orthodoxy, it is intriguing to take note that *all* of the Reformers, when they withdrew, or were expelled from the RCC, retained Augustine's utilization of the allegorical interpretation of Scripture. An allegorical interpretation of the Scriptures widely opens the door to disregard the literal meaning of any passage at the personal whim of the interpreter.

It takes only a minimum effort in research to discover that even otherwise doctrinally sound, good men are able to overlook the blatant heterodoxy of Augustine (that he propagated in direct opposition to orthodoxy, often intentionally attempting to refute orthodoxy), to proclaim that Augustine re-established the doctrine of the apostle Paul.

---

fact believe in a millennium; what they reject, though, is the idea of a future literal 1000-year reign of Christ on earth after the second coming of Christ. According to Amillennialism, the millennium of Revelation 20:1–6 is being fulfilled spiritually in the present age. Thus, the millennium or kingdom of Christ is in existence now. Amillennialists affirm that the millennium began with the resurrection or ascension of Christ and will be consummated when Jesus returns to establish the Eternal Kingdom that is discussed in Revelation 21–22. For amillennialists, Satan is presently bound and Christians are now enjoying the benefits of the millennium. Some amillennialists claim that the millennium also involves the reigning of saints who are now in heaven. Amillennialists claim that the 1000-year period that is mentioned in Revelation 20:1–6 refers to a long indefinite period between the two comings of Christ and is not a literal 1000-year period that occurs after Jesus' return. They do not believe in a Rapture. Because amillennialists believe that Christ is currently reigning in the millennium, some, like Jay Adams, believe the title Realized Millennialism (Jay Adams, *Realized Millennialism: A Study in Biblical Eschatology)* is a more appropriate title than Amillennialism. In regard to the end times, Amillennialism affirms the following chronological scenario:

1. Christ is now ruling in His kingdom while Satan is bound and unable to deceive the nations.
2. Tribulation is experienced in the present age even though Christ is ruling.
3. Jesus will return again to earth.
4. After Jesus returns there will be a general bodily resurrection of all the righteous people and a general judgment of all unbelievers.
5. The Eternal Kingdom will begin.

http://www.theologicalstudies.org/amillennialism.html

There is no Biblical or extra-Biblical evidence that would support any consideration of the proposition that the Gospel of the LORD Jesus or the existence of the New Testament church ever universally disappeared. The light of Biblical truth was never completely dimmed to extinguishment by the advancement of heresy and error.

Moreover, the apostle Paul and Augustine, whom the RCC, Reformationists, and most Protestants generally identify as *Saint* Augustine, have nothing in common on the matters of the faith and practice once delivered to the saints.

Augustine was not orthodox in his doctrine; he advocated heretical doctrine. He was not *a Reformer*, as Jerome described him; on the contrary, Augustine was a Distorter and a Perverter of "the faith, which was once delivered unto the saints." One has to set aside the substance of what the man personally wrote that he believed in order to transform him into a faithful follower of Christ. As to his salvation, if he believed what he wrote that he believed, then Augustine died lost and apart from salvation. I do hope that he was spiritually wiser than his writings were.

CALVINIST

Those individuals that use this name directly identify with the belief system of John Calvin (1509–1564). The name was originally used by the RCC and the followers of Jacob Arminius as a pejorative, but was gradually accepted as an honorific by the followers of John Calvin.

Calvin, though a Frenchman, is most often associated with the city of Geneva, Switzerland. He resided in Geneva twice. The first time, as pastor of the parish, he insisted on the separation of the church—*his church*—and the state, going so far as to refuse to allow the Eucharist to be observed by the city because of its immorality. He was compelled to leave the city due to the strong resistance of the citizens to his intrusion into their lifestyles.

When he accepted the invitation to return, both he and the citizens knew that he would rule with absolute authority. The citizens were compelled to be religious and to be under the discipline of the civil, social, and religious standards taught by Calvin. The city council met twice yearly and was incapable of any action not approved *in advance* by the Council of Two Hundred, which in turn could do nothing not approved *in advance* by the Council of Sixty, which was dominated *by* Calvin. Violations of religious laws were prosecuted by the civil authorities. There was no separation of church and state.

Calvinists maintain that Calvin is maligned by any accusations of abusing his position and imposing his moral and religious standards on the residents of Geneva. While religious historians divide as to the interpretation of his actions, his conduct is recorded for any student of history to discover. Contemporary followers of Reconstructionism and of Dominion Theology are lineal theological descendents of the governance beliefs of John Calvin.

Calvin banished *perpetually* Anabaptists from the city. He personally had Servetus burned at the stake for heresy after denying Servetus any counsel and by the use of obscure laws. Among the charges brought against Servetus was that he blasphemed when he said that the land of Israel in the 1500s was a barren land. This was declared to contradict Moses who wrote that it was a land of milk and honey.[48]

Calvin's most important work is the *Institutes of the Christian Religion.* He also produced multiple

---

[48]http://www.entheology.org/library/winters/LUTHER.TXT

commentaries covering nearly every Book of the Bible.[49]

CALVINISTIC (NOMINAL CALVINIST)

One often hears an individual express a *feeling* that is worded something along the line of "I must be a Calvinist, because I am not an Arminian." These are sincere individuals; but unfortunately, they have no accurate understanding of what the Five Points of Calvinism actually involve. They have only a vague idea that the Calvinist teaches that salvation is not based upon works either in the obtaining or in the keeping. They do not comprehend the doctrines of Total Inability that requires Unconditional Election or the Perseverance of the Saints that necessities perpetual faithfulness.

They understand only that man[50] cannot save himself and must have salvation as the gift of God.

They accept that salvation is by grace and that no one would be able to keep himself saved through his own efforts; therefore, security must be entirely in the hands of God.

They presume from what they have heard that Calvinists believe (1) that humanity is lost and is in need of a Saviour, (2) in salvation by grace and not by works, and (3) in the security of the believer. They therefore assume that they must be at least a Three-Point Calvinist. However, that is a misconception of what really constitutes the Five Points of Calvinism. Actually, their three confessed beliefs are not included within any of the Points of Calvinism.

Moreover, the truth is that the option is not restricted to choosing between one or the other in an *either-or* dilemma. The option is not between being

---

[49]"Calvin's Latin writings fill 59 volumes of the massive *Corpus Reformatorum.* http://www.calvin500.com/john-calvin/works-by-Calvin

[50]Except where the context indicates a particular individual, the word *man* is used as the generic Biblical term for all humanity.

either a Calvinist *or* being an Arminian. Despite protestations to the contrary, both of these theological systems began during the Reformation; therefore, both systems arrived 1500 years too late to be considered as true New Testament Christianity.

The premise underlying both systems of theology is that original Christianity had been lost (as early as Augustine), needing to be rediscovered, or was corrupted, needing to be reformed and restored. That premise is contrary to Biblical statements[51] as well as to historical evidences. Both systems rose from within the Protestant movement, which in its entirety originated *within* the RCC. The one system traces its origin to Jacob Arminius, the pastor and professor of theology of Leiden,[52] the other to John Calvin, pastor of Geneva. Both systems assert descent from the apostles. Both systems present their doctrines as the reclamation of the truth. Both systems are capable of summation in five theological statements that are the antithesis of the other's five Points. Both systems are wrong.

The choice is *not* between the devised belief system of Jacob Arminius and that of John Calvin. Biblically, truth will be found only within the confines of Scripture and not through some special, new, or rediscovered truth proffered by any individual, whether human or angelic.

> Galatians 1:8–9 But though we, or an angel from heaven, preach any other gospel unto you than that which we have preach-

---

[51]From among the abundance of promises and prophecies of the continuing existence of the faithful proclamation of the Gospel and of the church, which He established, until the return of the LORD Jesus, I will cite only two. Matthew 16:18 And I say also unto thee, That thou art Peter, and upon this rock I will build my church; and the gates of hell shall not prevail against it. Then we which are alive *and* remain shall be caught up together with them in the clouds, to meet the Lord in the air: and so shall we ever be with the Lord. (1 Thessalonians 4:17)

[52]http://www.victorshepherd.on.ca/Other%20Writings/jacobarminius.htm

> ed unto you, let him be accursed. As we said before, so say I now again, If any man preach any other gospel unto you than that ye have received, let him be accursed.

From Genesis through the Revelation, there is presented only one plan of salvation and that one plan of salvation is offered by the Sovereign God of Heaven to whosoever will.[53]

In Romans, chapter four, the apostle Paul detailed how (1) before the law was given, Abraham was saved by grace through faith, (2) after the Law was given, David was saved by grace through faith, and (3) he and the Roman believers were saved by grace through faith after the death and resurrection of the LORD Jesus. The conclusion is that the same salvation received by Abraham, David, and Paul is also available and extended as a legitimate offer to all who will believe.

> Romans 4:1–25 What shall we say then that Abraham our father, as pertaining to the flesh, hath found? For if Abraham were justified by works, he hath whereof to glory; but not before God. For what saith the scripture**? Abraham believed God, and it was counted unto him for righteousness. Now to him that worketh is the reward not reckoned of grace, but of debt. But to him that worketh not, but believeth on him that justifieth the ungodly, his faith is counted for righteousness. Even as David also describeth the blessedness of the man, unto whom God imputeth righteousness without works, Saying, Blessed are they whose iniquities are forgiven, and whose sins are covered.**

---

[53]Whosoever is used with the following verbs: shall confess (Matthew 10:32; Luke 12:8; 1 John 4:15); shall receive (Mark 9:37; Luke 9:48); cometh (Luke 6:47; Romans 9:33, 10:11); believeth (John 3:15,16; Acts 10:43; 1 John 5:1); shall call (Acts 2:21; Romans 10:13); will (Revelation 22:17).

Blessed is the man to whom the Lord will not impute sin. Cometh this blessedness then upon the circumcision only, or upon the uncircumcision also? **for we say that faith was reckoned to Abraham for righteousness. How was it then reckoned? when he was in circumcision, or in uncircumcision? Not in circumcision, but in uncircumcision. And he received the sign of circumcision, a seal of the righteousness of the faith which he had yet being uncircumcised:** that he might be the father of all them that believe, though they be not circumcised; that righteousness might be imputed unto them also: And the father of circumcision to them who are not of the circumcision only, but who also walk in the steps of that faith of our father Abraham, which he had being yet uncircumcised. **For the promise, that he should be the heir of the world, was not to Abraham, or to his seed, through the law, but through the righteousness of faith. For if they which are of the law be heirs, faith is made void, and the promise made of none effect:** Because the law worketh wrath: for where no law is, there is no transgression. **Therefore it is of faith, that it might be by grace; to the end the promise might be sure to all the seed; not to that only which is of the law, but to that also which is of the faith of Abraham;** who is the father of us all, (As it is written, I have made thee a father of many nations,) before him whom he believed, even God, who quickeneth the dead, and calleth those things which be not as though they were. Who against hope believed in hope, that he might become the father of many nations; according to that which was spoken, So shall thy seed be. And being not weak in faith, he considered not his own body now dead, when he was about an hundred years old,

> neither yet the deadness of Sara's womb: He staggered not at the promise of God through unbelief; but was strong in faith, giving glory to God; And being fully persuaded that, what he had promised, he was able also to perform. **And therefore it was imputed to him for righteousness. Now it was not written for his sake alone, that it was imputed to him; But for us also, to whom it shall be imputed, if we believe on him that raised up Jesus our Lord from the dead; Who was delivered for our offences, and was raised again for our justification.** [Emphasis is added.]

Abraham was saved by faith. "Abraham believed God, and it was counted unto him for righteousness."

David was saved by faith. "Even as David also describeth the blessedness of the man, unto whom God imputeth righteousness without works."

Paul was saved by faith. "Now it was not written for his sake alone, that it was imputed to him; But for us also, to whom it shall be imputed, if we believe on him that raised up Jesus our Lord from the dead."

Salvation is by faith "for us also ... to whom it shall be imputed, if we believe on him that raised up Jesus our Lord from the dead."

The only condition attached to the invitation to salvation is "if we believe." For it is written, that this salvation is "for us also, to whom it shall be imputed, if we believe on him that raised up Jesus our Lord from the dead; Who was delivered for our offences, and was raised again for our justification."

CHAPTER 5

PROPOSITION

The Calvinist becomes an expert in lifting words and phrases from the text of Scripture and using them in ways (1) that conflict with the original context; and (2) that require a meaning that is not within the standard dictionary definition; and (3) that require special instruction.

It is only when the inquirer, student, or novice receives the proper instruction through a Calvinist that provides the special definitions for the selective terminology of Calvinism that the observed conflicts with the words of Scripture evaporate, thereby enabling the illogical to become logical. Without those stealth meanings, the logic of the Calvinist remains illogical and the conflict with Scripture continues unaffected.

In addition to utilizing the Calvinist dictionary with special meanings for words, the Calvinist bases his logic upon a series of faulty theorems and uses techniques of debate that are recognized as fallacious reasoning. The following definitions of logical fallacies is not exhaustive, but it is sufficient for the purpose of this study.[54] Though I am primarily focusing on the *if-then* fallacy in this book, each of these erroneous methods of interpretation is found consistently in presentations of Calvinism.

> *Affirming the consequent*—A fallacy of the form "if A, then B; B, therefore A." Example: "If Smith testifies against Jones in court, Jones will be found guilty. Jones was found guilty. Therefore, Smith must have testified against him." (Jones could have been found guilty without Smith's testimony.)
>
> *Argumentum ad ignorantiam* ("arguing from ignorance")—A fallacy that occurs when someone argues that because we don't know something is true, it must be false, or because we lack proof that a statement is false, it must be true. Ignorance or lack of evidence doesn't *[sic]* necessarily mean a position or claim is true or false. Common Examples: "No one has ever proven that UFOs exist. Therefore, they don't exist." (Something can exist despite the absence of confirmation. Lack of proof is justification for caution or even scepticism, *[sic]* but not dogmatic assertions.) "There is simply no proof that God exists. Therefore, God doesn't exist." (God might exist even though there is no way empirically to prove it.)
>
> *Begging the question*—Circular reasoning in which a claim is assumed to be true and is then tucked in the conclusion: e.g., "Government by the people is ideal because democracy is the least inadequate *[sic]* form of government." ("Government by the people" is the working definition of democracy; the first part of the statement

---

[54] http://www.philosophicalsociety.com/Logical%20Fallaci es.htm

needs to be proven, not reasserted in the predicate.)

Fallacy of false alternatives—A fallacy occurring when the number of alternatives is said to be fewer than the actual number. Common examples of this fallacy are statements containing either/or, nothing/but, all-or-nothing elements. Examples: "Is she a Democrat or a Republican?" (She may be a socialist, a libertarian, a Leninist, an anarchist, a feminist or any number of other things, including one who is strictly apolitical.) "If you aren't for your country, then you are against it." (One may be neither "for" nor "against" but may occupy a position of strict neutrality or be affirmative sometimes and critical at others.)

Fallacies of interrogation—There are two forms of this particular fallacy. One is asking two or more questions and demanding a single answer when, in fact, each question might require separate treatment. The other form is asking a question whose answer would necessitate acceptance of a presupposition, one which the answerer might separately deny. The famous example of this second form is asking, "Do you still beat your wife?" Answering "no" legitimates *[sic]* the question and does nothing to contradict the presupposition that the husband once did beat his wife. Asking a question with presuppositions is fine so long as a narrow answer is not demanded.

If-then fallacies —

1. Affirming the consequent (If P, then Q. Q. Therefore P.).
2. Denying the antecedent (If P, then Q. Not P. Therefore not Q.)
3. Converting a conditional (If P, then Q. Therefore if Q, then P.)
4. Negating antecedent and consequent (If P, then Q. Therefore if not P, then not Q.)

The use of the *if-then* argument does not guarantee the introduction of a fallacy. Its use mandates that both phrases of the *if-then* statements must be carefully examined individually and cautiously verified separately as to whether or not it is true. Should the suggested *if* prove to be fallacious, the subsequent *then* cannot be accepted as either accurate or true.

A proper understanding of how to detect faulty methodology and the thoughtful application of that understanding will greatly aid in the avoidance of doctrinal error. Recognizing the problematic pattern of reasoning that is required for Calvinism to be logical is the first step in avoiding the acceptance of that error.

Calvinism is built on the foundation of the Five Points of the TULIP. Every Point of the TULIP is essential to Calvinism and each Point must be retain-ed in the specific positional placement of the TULIP for Calvinism *to be logical*. The first proposition must be valid, for the second to be acceptable. This is also mandatory for each of the subsequent Points.

Furthermore, the five points of the TULIP must be defined by the precise definitions of Calvinism for Calvinism *to be reasonable*. Only when those meanings are imposed upon Bible words is Calvinism reasonably supported by Scripture. Remove those assigned designations and Calvinism is both perceptibly illogical and discernibly unscriptural.

Since these five premises are the foundation of Calvinism *and* since each individual assertion must be accepted in the exactly precise order as it is logically and sequentially arranged in the TULIP acrostic, should a single petal of the TULIP be proven faulty, then all five petals of the TULIP simultaneously fall.

It is the proposition of *The Wilted TULIP* that under the pressure of Scriptural examination the structure named for Calvin will crumble from the weakness of its alleged logically constructed foundation having been found illogical.

CHAPTER 6

APPLICATION

I have previously cited the following paragraph as a masterful job of summarizing Calvinism in a single brief paragraph. First, I call your attention to the multiple uses of the word *if* in that paragraph. Each occurrence has been set in bold type to focus your attention on that word.

> Man is totally unable to save himself on account of the Fall in the Garden of Eden being a *total* fall. **If** unable to save himself, then God must save. **If** God must save, then God must be free to save whom He will. **If** God has decreed to save whom He will, then it is for those that Christ made atonement on the Cross. **If** Christ died for them, then the Holy Spirit will effectually call them into that salvation. **If** salvation then from the beginning has been of God, the end will also be of God and the saints will persevere to eternal joy.[55]

[55]Seaton, *The Five Points of Calvinism*, 8

The *M-WD*[56] provides the primary uses for the word *if* as being *in the event that, allowing that, on the assumption that,* or *on condition that.* The common usage of the word *if* is as an indefinite word. The word introduces a proposition and, by its use, requires a conclusion as to the validity of that proposition. Each *if* is followed by a *then.* To help emphasize this, I am placing each *if* and each *then* in bold type.

> Man is totally unable to save himself on account of the Fall in the Garden of Eden being a *total* fall. **If** unable to save himself, **then** God must save. **If** God must save, **then** God must be free to save whom He will. **If** God has decreed to save whom He will, **then** it is for those that Christ made atonement on the Cross. **If** Christ died for them, **then** the Holy Spirit will effectually call them into that salvation. **If** salvation **then** from the beginning has been of God, the end will [**then**] also be of God and [**then**] the saints will persevere to eternal joy.

The Calvinist presents these *if* statements as *absolutes* that are to be received as true and unquestionable; therewith, the *then* conclusion by the Calvinist is mandated and unchangeable. This begs

---

[56]Full definition entry for the word *if* from the *M-WD*:

1 a: in the event that b: allowing that c: on the assumption that d: on condition that

2 WHETHER "asked if the mail had come," "I doubt if I'll pass the course"

3 used as a function word to introduce an exclamation expressing a wish "if it would only rain"

4 even though: although perhaps "an interesting if untenable argument"

5 and perhaps not even "few if any changes are expected"—often used with not "difficult if not impossible"—if anything: on the contrary even: perhaps even "if anything, you ought to apologize"

Notice should be taken that the word *if* never introduces a certainty; it always proposes a possibility with an uncertain outcome.

the question, "Are the *if-then* arguments of Calvinism inescapably required by Scripture?"

The word *if* is not a declaration of fact; it is the introduction of an assumption, a conjecture, a postulation, a hypothesis, or a supposition. That assertion must be examined and accepted as either true or rejected as false.

The word *then* presents a conclusion that flows from the assertion contained in the word *if.* That *then* conclusion must be evaluated and accepted as proven legitimately and irrefutably to be true or it must be rejected as unsustainable and untrue.

The use of the word *if* does not guarantee the validity of the assertion (assumption, conjecture, postulation, hypothesis, or supposition). An *if* does not automatically verify, legitimatize, or sanctify a *then*—not even in Scripture.

Notice the use of the *if-then* argument in the following verse.

> Galatians 2:21 I do not frustrate the grace of God: for if righteousness *come* by the law, then Christ is dead in vain.

The statement "if righteousness come by the law" is presented as an assumption to be weighed as to its validity, because if that *if* of assertion is true, then the consequence is "then Christ is dead in vain." The use of the conjunction *if,* which means *in the event that, allowing that, on the assumption that, on condition that,* only introduces the consideration of a possibility to be considered for acceptance or rejection. The use of the adverb *then* draws a conclusion that requires a judgment as to the validity of the assumption presented by the *if.* In Galatians 2:21, the assumption of the *if* is clearly false; therefore, the conclusion suggested in the *then* is also false. Righteousness does not come by the law and Christ did not die in vain.

Second, I believe that this summary paragraph of Calvinism unwittingly reveals that the Five Points established by the Synod of Dort are based upon a series of *if's* that must all be favorably assumed for the system to hold together. Disprove or even raise a fault with even one *then* and the entirety of Calvinism falls.

Though the Calvinist always speaks with authority,[57] claims the strength of superiority as to adherents,[58] and asserts the infallibility of his logic,[59] the system is nothing more than speculation based upon five interconnected assumptions.

> (1) If man cannot save himself, then God must save him. (2) If all are not saved, then God has not saved all. (3) If Christ has made satisfaction for sins, then, it is for the sins of those who are saved. (4) If God intends to reveal their salvation in Christ to the hearts of those whom he chooses to save, then, God will provide the means of effectually doing so. (5) If, therefore, having *ordained* to save, *died* to save, and *called* to salvation those who could never save themselves, [then] He will also

---

[57]"It is no novelty, then, that I am preaching, no new doctrine. I love to proclaim those strong old doctrines that are nicknamed Calvinism, but which are surely and verily the revealed truth of God as it is in Christ Jesus." Attributed to Charles Haddon Spurgeon, Seaton, *The Five Points of Calvinism*, 9.
"These are the so-called Five Points of Calvinism. We shall now proceed to examine them in more detail, firmly based as they are upon the Word of God, and held tenaciously by our forebears in 'the faith once delivered to the saints.'" Seaton, *The Five Points of Calvinism*, 8.

[58]In two paragraphs on pages 22 and 23, Elder Seaton lists the following names: William Carey, Andrew Fuller, David Brainerd, George Whitefield, Robert Murray M'Cheyne, Andrew Bonar, William Burns, Luther, Calvin, Tyndale, Latimer, Knox, Wishart, Perkins, Rutherford, Bunyan, Owen, Charnock, Goodwin, Flavel, Watson, Henry, Watts, Edwards, Whitefield, Newton, Spurgeon, and finishes with the statement that these men "are but a few of God's noble army of witnesses to the truth of sovereign grace."

[59]"And again, let us recognize the fact that all that the men at the Synod of Dort (and those who teach likewise) were doing, was putting into small compass in a systematic form, the teaching of God's gospel of free and sovereign grace." Seaton, *The Five Points of Calvinism*, 21.

> *preserve* those saved ones on to eternal life to the glory of his Name.[60]

The Calvinist is revealed as nothing more or less than a spiritual speculator even when his system is presented in the best possible light. Every tenet of Calvinism, *of necessity,* must be phrased in assumptive terms using theoretical conclusions.

The seducing spirit of Calvinism is so strong that, while the Calvinist appeals to logic, priding himself on his intellectual reasoning ability, he never discerns the illogical position in which he has placed himself. The Calvinist succumbs so completely to his system of reasoning that he describes his own confidence of the assurance of his personal security in terms that betray his insecurity.

> This is the believer's hallmark, that he belongs to Christ; that he is persevering in the things of Christ, that he is 'giving all diligence to make his calling and election sure.' The believer in Christ may fall into temptation, but the Lord will 'not suffer him to be tempted above that which he is able, but will with the temptation also make a way to escape,' so that the believer comes forth, and goes forth again in the things pertaining to his salvation to the glory of Christ. Those matchless verses of Romans 8.28–39 *[sic]* show the Divine logic in God's eternal salvation; the logic that Calvinism simply states.[61]

Please take note that the responsibility is placed entirely upon the believer in the above paragraph: "he is persevering," "he is 'giving all diligence to make his calling and election sure,'" and the believer must come forth and go forth again. The believer must not only give "all diligence," but that same

---

[60]Seaton, *The Five Points of Calvinism,* 21.
[61]Seaton, *The Five Points of Calvinism,* 22.

believer must himself "make his calling and election sure."

The Calvinist is preserved because he perseveres; the Calvinist must give all diligence to "make his calling and election sure." Calvinism teaches that the believer will arrive in Heaven because he perseveres. Should he not persevere, that failure *on his part* is considered the unimpeachable evidence that he was neither called nor elected, but that he only *thought* that he was one of the elect. Thus, the Calvinist is always trying, enduring, holding out, for he must be persevering. If he is one of the elect, he has the ability to persevere; but until he enters Heaven, the Calvinist can have no settled assurance that he is persevering and not struggling in the strength of the carnal nature *or* that he will ultimately persevere.

In practical reality, the hope of the Calvinist for a home in Heaven is as much of a *hope-so* salvation as that of the full-fledged Arminian. Read the following excerpt from the testimony of Dr. R. C. Sproul,[62] a leading contemporary Calvinist, as he reveals his lack of assurance that he is actually one of the elect.

> There are people in this world who are not saved, but who are convinced that they are. The presence of such people causes genuine Christians to doubt their salvation. After all, we wonder, suppose I am in that category? Suppose I am mistaken about my salvation and am really going to hell? How can I know that I am a real Christian?

---

[62]Dr. R. C. Sproul is president of Ligonier Academy of Biblical and Theological Studies, ordained as a teaching elder in the Presbyterian Church in America, the author of more than seventy books, and holds degrees from Westminster College, Pittsburgh Theological Seminary, and the Free University of Amsterdam. http://www.ligonier.org/about/rc-sproul/

> A while back I had one of those moments of acute self-awareness that we have from time to time, and suddenly the question hit me: "R. C., what if you are not one of the redeemed? What if your destiny is not heaven after all, but hell?" Let me tell you that I was flooded in my body with a chill that went from my head to the bottom of my spine. I was terrified.
>
> I tried to grab hold of myself. I thought, "Well, it's a good sign that I'm worried about this. Only true Christians really care about salvation." But then I began to take stock of my life, and I looked at my performance. My sins came pouring into my mind, and the more I looked at myself, the worse I felt. I thought, "Maybe it's really true. Maybe I'm not saved after all."
>
> I went to my room and began to read the Bible. On my knees I said, "Well, here I am. I can't point to my obedience. There's nothing I can offer. I can only rely on Your atonement for my sins. I can only throw myself on Your mercy." Even then I knew that some people only flee to the Cross to escape hell, not out of a real turning to God. I could not be sure about my own heart and motivation. Then I remembered John 6:68. Jesus had been giving out hard teaching, and many of His former followers had left Him. When He asked Peter if he was also going to leave, Peter said, "Where else can I go? Only You have the words of eternal life." In other words, Peter was also uncomfortable, but he realized that being uncomfortable with Jesus was better than any other option! [63]

It is tragic that a man with the theological training and the Biblical exposure that Sproul has would

---

[63]R. C. Sproul, *Assurance of Salvation*, Tabletalk, Ligionier Ministries, Inc., November 1989.

be compelled to express his hope of Heaven in the meager terms of "being uncomfortable with Jesus."

In Calvinism, all of the *elect* have security and the Calvinist will forsake family and friendships, split a church, or destroy a school defending the doctrine of election; however, he will also forsake family and friendships, split a church, or destroy a school fighting against the doctrine of the security of the *believer*.

The assurance of the individual Calvinist is always contingent upon his personal perseverance. The very concept of personal assurance is contrary to the logic of the system of Calvinism. The Calvinistic doctrine of the Perseverance of the Saints declares the absolute unalterable security of the *elect*; however, that same doctrine refuses to give assurance of security to any individual for the unavoidable reason that no individual is ever confident that he has persevered to the end until he has actually done so.

The evidence of the election of saints to the Calvinist is the perseverance of the saints.

> ... the believer's hallmark that he belongs to Christ; that he is persevering in the things of Christ, that he is 'giving all diligence to make his calling and election sure.'[64]

Perseverance, however, by its very definition, is never complete until the individual passes from this life into the life to come. Election is evidenced by perseverance; therefore, the elect will persevere. The Calvinist cannot proclaim with integrity the security of the believer; he must rest on the Perseverance of the Saints and continue to hope that he is one of the elect and that he will persevere until the moment of death.

---

[64]Seaton, *The Five Points of Calvinism*, 22.

The persistent nagging questions for Sproul and for all Calvinists are "Am I one of the elect? Am I numbered among the saints? On the other hand, am I only a suffering from a delusion? Am I only a believer and not one of the elect?"

To me, the saddest witness to this aspect of Calvinism is the document that contains the final recorded words of John Calvin. Reading the Last Will and Testament of John Calvin should raise issues that would be sufficient reasons to cause anyone tempted to become a Calvinist to have a pause to reconsider doing so.

Dictated and signed while Calvin was on his deathbed, his Will reveals that John Calvin did not seem to know with certainty that he was one of the elect. As he lay dying, he could only pray with the hope that "since God is a Father of mercy, he will show himself a Father to me, who confess myself a miserable sinner." The English translation of the full will is provided in APPENDIX 9. The statements in the will to which I particularly desire to call attention have been printed with **bold font.**

> I, John Calvin, minister of the word of God in the church of Geneva, finding myself so much oppressed and afflicted with various diseases, that I think the Lord God has determined speedily to remove me out of this world, have ordered to be made and written, my testament, and declaration of my last will, in form and manner following:
>
> First, I give thanks to God, that taking compassion on me whom he had created and placed in this world, he not only delivered me by his power out of the deep darkness of idolatry, into which I was plunged, that he might bring me into the light of his gospel, and make me a partaker of the doctrine of salvation, of which I was most unworthy; that with the same goodness and mercy he has graciously

> and kindly borne with my multiplied transgressions and sins, for which I deserved to be rejected and cut off by him; and has also exercised towards me such great compassion and clemency, that he has condescended to use my labor in preaching and publishing the truth of his gospel.

Calvin is thankful for being "made a partaker of the doctrine of salvation" and for being used to preach and to publish "the truth of his *[sic]* gospel." He acknowledges only that he had knowledge of the doctrine of salvation; he is not able to say that he is trusting in that doctrine of salvation. In his Will, Calvin does not mention *trust* or *faith* as something that he possesses. Instead, he speaks of his *intention.*

> I also testify and declare, that it is **my full intention to pass the remainder of my life** in the same faith and religion, which he has delivered to me by his gospel; having no other defense or refuge of salvation than his gratuitous adoption, on which alone my safety depends.

He intends to persevere through the remainder of his life in "the same faith and religion, which he *[sic]* has delivered to me by his *[sic]* gospel." On his deathbed, Calvin could not rest in faith; he must labor to persevere. Dying, Calvin speaks of *intention*; he does not speak of *assurance*.

> I also embrace with my whole heart the mercy which he exercises towards me for the sake of Jesus Christ, atoning for my crimes by the merits of his death and passion, **that in this way satisfaction may be made for all my transgressions and offenses, and the remembrance of them blotted out.**
>
> I further testify and declare that, as a suppliant, I humbly **implore** of him to grant me **to be** so washed and purified by the blood of that sovereign Redeemer, sited *[sic]* for the

> sins of the human race, that I **may be** permitted to stand before his tribunal in the image of the Redeemer himself.

Calvin is couches his prayer in the future tense: "to be so washed" and "that I may be permitted." It seems that he has no witness of the Holy Spirit bearings witness with his spirit that he is a child of God.[65]

> I likewise declare, that according to the measure of grace and mercy which God has **vouchsafed** me, **I have diligently made it my endeavor,** both in my sermons, writings, and commentaries, purely and uncorruptly *[sic]* to preach his word, and faithfully to interpret his sacred Scriptures.

Diligently endeavoring would be an appropriate and accurate description of the life of John Calvin; and, true to his doctrinal system, he attributed his endeavoring diligently to the measure of grace and mercy that God had extended him. Even so, John Calvin, on the very doorstep of eternity, could only testify that he *intended* to *persevere* the rest of his life and to *implore* God that He would grant that John Calvin might be one of the elect.

The final words of John Calvin are certainly very different from the closing written testimony of the Apostle Paul.

> 2 Timothy 1:12 For the which cause I also suffer these things: nevertheless I am not ashamed: for I know whom I have believed, and am persuaded that he is able to keep that which I have committed unto him against that day. ... 4:6–8 For I am now ready to be offered, and the time of my departure is at hand. I have fought a good fight, I have finished *my* course, I have kept the faith: Henceforth there is

---

[65]Romans 8:16

> laid up for me a crown of righteousness, which the Lord, the righteous judge, shall give me at that day: and not to me only, but unto all them also that love his appearing.

The apostle rested in the solid confidence that he was on the way to Heaven. Paul's hope was securely anchored in the *Person and Work* of the LORD Jesus. Paul knew *Whom* he had believed. Paul's confidence was not in *his* diligent endeavors, but in the One in Whom he believed. The apostle could write, "I count all things *but* loss for the excellency of the knowledge of Christ Jesus"; continuing that though "touching the righteousness which is in the law," he was blameless; nonetheless, the apostle counted "them but dung." (Philippians 3:3–7)

Diligent efforts never produce assurance; but the penitent may draw near to God, "*[i]n full assurance of faith*" (Hebrews 10:22), which Matthew Poole, in his *Commentary on the Holy Bible,* defines as "believing in, and being fully assured and confident of, Christ's merits and God's promise."

However, John Calvin makes no such affirmation. He seems to seek spiritual comfort based upon his *diligent endeavors.*

> I testify and declare that in all the controversies and disputes, which I have conducted with the enemies of the gospel, I have made use of no craftiness, nor corrupt and sophistical arts, but have been engaged in defending the truth with candor and sincerity.
>
> But, alas! my study, and my zeal, if they deserve the name, have been so remiss and languid, that I confess innumerable things have been wanting in me to discharge the duties of my office in all excellent manner; and unless the infinite bounty of God had been present, all my study would have been vain and transient.

> I also acknowledge that unless the same goodness had accompanied me, the **endowments** of mind bestowed upon me by God, must have made me more and more chargeable with guilt and inactivity before his tribunal.
>
> And on these grounds I witness and declare, that I **hope** for no other refuge of salvation than this alone—that since God is a Father of mercy, he **will show** himself a Father to me, who confess myself a miserable sinner.

Based upon his word choice, it appears that John Calvin did not have the confidence that God was his Father, but had only some **hope** that God *would show Himself to be* his Father. I take note that, as the words stand in the last paragraph, Calvin concluded his ***hope of refuge of salvation*** [his word choices] with his confession of being a miserable sinner and the ***hope*** that God "will show himself *[sic]* a Father to me." It surely appears that his basis for this ***hope*** *of salvation* was not unconditional election, not irresistible grace, and not perseverance, but was in his confession that he was a sinner.

I make no suggestion that Calvin abandoned the doctrines for which he is famous. I only take notice of the legitimate meaning of the words which this brilliant man chose to use to express his thoughts.

As I finished reading those final words of John Calvin, I thought of the great learning of this theologian, his vast exposure to the word of God, and his complicated presentation of the Gospel, it seemed overwhelming to consider that *all of his endowments, his study, and his zeal provided him with no amount of deathbed assurance.*

It was then that I remembered reading the unusual salvation testimony of the author of the words of the hymn *I Know Whom I Have Believed.*

Daniel Webster Whittle (1840–1901) was named after American politician Daniel Webster. Whittle reached the rank of major in the American civil war, and for the rest of his life was known as "Major" Whittle. During the war, Whittle lost his right arm, and ended up in a prisoner of war camp. Recovering from his wounds in the hospital, he looked for something to read, and found a New Testament. Though its words resonated with him, he was still not ready to accept Christ. Shortly after, a hospital orderly woke him and said a dying prisoner wanted someone to pray with him. Whittle demurred, but the orderly said, "But I thought you were a Christian; I have seen you reading your Bible." Whittle then agreed to go. He recorded what took place at the dying youth's bed side *[sic]*:

I dropped on my knees and held the boy's hand in mine. In a few broken words I confessed my sins and asked Christ to forgive me. I believed right there that He did forgive me. I then prayed earnestly for the boy. He became quiet and pressed my hand as I prayed and pleaded God's promises. When I arose from my knees, he was dead. A look of peace had come over his troubled face, and I cannot but believe that God who used him to bring me to the Savior, used me to lead him to trust Christ's precious blood and find pardon. I hope to meet him in heaven.

After the war, Whittle became treasurer of the Elgin Watch Company in Chicago, Illinois. In less than 10 years, though, he entered the evangelism field. During this period, he worked with musicians Phillip Bliss and James McGranahan.[66]

---

[66]http://www.cyberhymnal.org/htm/i/k/ikwihb.htm

The memory of the most unusual setting of his own salvation experience and his involvement in the conversion of the dying soldier would later move Whittle to pen the simple poem for which James McGranahan then wrote the music. The result has provided the treasured Gospel song that has given comfort to the hearts of many saints in the darkened hours.

The simplistic tune was not due to lack of talent to produce the complex; it was a deliberate choice. McGranahan trained for the opera; however, when he wrote music for congregations, he seems to have labored to provide what the untrained voice could sing and the average person could understand as he listened.

I Know Whom I Have Believed.[67]

I know not why God's wondrous grace
To me He hath made known,
Nor why, unworthy, Christ in love
Redeemed me for His own.

I know not how this saving faith
To me He did impart,
Nor how believing in His Word
Wrought peace within my heart.

I know not how the Spirit moves,
Convincing us of sin,
Revealing Jesus through the Word,
Creating faith in Him.

I know not what of good or ill
May be reserved for me,
Of weary ways or golden days,
Before His face I see.

I know not when my Lord may come,
At night or noonday fair,
Nor if I walk the vale with Him,
Or meet Him in the air.

---

[67]In Public Domain.

Refrain:

> But I know Whom I have believed,
> And am persuaded that He is able
> To keep that which I've committed
> Unto Him against that day.

As you read the words, surely you remembered the moving scene that lies behind this song. The need of that dying soldier was not to hear the nebulous message from John Calvin that "if you are one of the elect, then you will be regenerated so that you may be given the faith to believe; otherwise you are predestined to die lost." That man, who was about to move into eternity without salvation, needed to hear "the simplicity that is in Christ,"[68] exactly as Daniel Whittle confessed that he did.

Scripture as written, has no place for the *if-then* Calvinist presentation of salvation.

> John 3:14–15 And as Moses lifted up the serpent in the wilderness, even so must the Son of man be lifted up: That whosoever believeth in him should not perish, but have eternal life.

> Numbers 21:6–9 And the LORD sent fiery serpents among the people, and they bit the people; and much people of Israel died. Therefore the people came to Moses, and said, We have sinned, for we have spoken against the LORD, and against thee; pray unto the LORD, that he take away the serpents from us. And Moses prayed for the people. And the LORD said unto Moses, Make thee a fiery serpent, and set it upon a pole: and it shall come to pass, that every one that is bitten,

---

[68]2 Corinthians 11:3–4 But I fear, lest by any means, as the serpent beguiled Eve through his subtilty, so your minds should be corrupted from the simplicity that is in Christ. For if he that cometh preacheth another Jesus, whom we have not preached, or *if* ye receive another spirit, which ye have not received, or another gospel, which ye have not accepted, ye might well bear with *him*.

> when he looketh upon it, shall live. And Moses made a serpent of brass, and put it upon a pole, and it came to pass, that if a serpent had bitten any man, when he beheld the serpent of brass, he lived.
>
> Isaiah 45:22 Look unto me, and be ye saved, all the ends of the earth: for I *am* God, and *there is* none else.

I acknowledge that I do not understand how it is that simply looking at a brazen serpent lifted on a pole gave life to the snake-bitten Israelite who turned his eyes upon that type (Numbers 21:8; John 3:14–15) any more than I understand how "looking unto Jesus the Author and Finisher of our faith" (Hebrews 12:2) gives eternal life to the sin-bitten sinner. I do not understand how "faith cometh by hearing and hearing by the word of God" (Romans 10:17). I do not understand how eternal life is given to those that believe. However, John testified that the words that he wrote were written "that ye might believe that Jesus is the Christ, the Son of God; and that believing ye might have life through his name" (John 20:31). I do not understand why "Christ Jesus came into the world to save sinners" (1 Timothy 1:15). Even so, "Thus saith the Scriptures."

Placing myself in agreement with the Apostle Paul, Daniel Webster Whittle, and innumerable others, I will gratefully sing: "But I know Whom I have believed, and am persuaded that He is able to keep that which I've committed unto Him against that day."

> 2 Timothy 1:12 ... for I know whom I have believed, and am persuaded that he is able to keep that which I have committed unto him against that day.

I fervently anticipate having fellowship in eternity in my Heavenly Father's House with Calvinists such as Charles Haddon Spurgeon, Adoniram Judson, John Gill, Matthew Poole, William Carey, John Newton, and uncountable individuals.

Despite their written testimonies of not having personal assurance of being one of the redeemed, I do hope to see R. C. Sproul and John Calvin in heaven. I write this notwithstanding the hatred of John Calvin for my spiritual ancestors and their bloody persecutions at his direction.

I deeply regret that the erroneous and odious depiction of God and of His grace as presented by Calvin has been, and will continue to be, a stumbling block to so many others, perhaps, dooming them to eternal damnation.

CHAPTER 7

TOTAL INABILITY

> Man is totally unable to save himself on account of the Fall in the Garden of Eden being a *total* fall. If unable to save himself, then God must save. If God must save, then God must be free to save whom He will. If God has decreed to save whom He will, then it is for those that Christ made atonement on the Cross. If Christ died for them, then the Holy Spirit will effectually call them into that salvation. If salvation then from the beginning has been of God, the end will also be of God and the saints will persevere to eternal joy.[69]

I call attention to the word *total* that the author placed in italics to set that word apart to emphasize that particular word with a dose of special attention. In that sentence, the word *total* is used as the adjective for the word *fall.* The totality of the fall is given as the reason why man is unable to save himself. The Calvinist defines Total Inability as the spiritual condition in which every person enters the

[69]Seaton, *The Five Points of Calvinism*, 7.

world, that of being completely incapable of doing any good of any kind and without possessing any ability whatsoever to respond to God.[70] The word depravity is intermingled in use with the word inability in the writings of Calvinists so that those two words are full synonyms within that system.

Dr. John Piper[71] is recognized as one of the leading proponents of Calvinism. He is a prolific writer. The following excerpts from an article that he wrote entitled *Total Depravity*[72] provide a straightforward illustration of the Calvinist's definition of the term Total Depravity. His writings ought to be read carefully: always remembering that he is an advocate for Calvinism. The reader ought to evaluate the marked propensity of Piper to choose translations based upon their particular verse wordings.

While I believe he is promoting error, I do not challenge his sincerity. I do caution the reader that his evident skill as a wordsmith requires reading with discernment what is written to avoiding being drawn into that error. The subtle nature of the gradual bending of Biblical statements is deceptive.

The error that makes an immediate 90-degree departure from truth is never the great danger, because its falseness is readily apparent. The error that is most dangerous is the error that begins with only a small 5-degree or so of subtle departure from the truth, but which begins a determined gradual drift that is connected to a continual curve toward the 90-degree departure into heresy.

---

[70]"Since responding to God is a good act, and man is unable to accomplish a good act, man is unable to respond to God, i.e. a=b, b=c, therefore a=c." Pastor Jody Wolf, The Heritage Baptist Church of Pensacola, FL, personal correspondence.

[71]"John Piper is the Pastor for Preaching at Bethlehem Baptist Church in Minneapolis, Minnesota ... studied at Wheaton College ... Fuller Theological Seminary, and the University of Munich (D.theol.)." http://www.desiringgod.org/about/john-piper

[72]http://www.monergism.com/thethreshold/articles/piper/depravity.html

One certainly arrives at the 180-degree doctrinal error in a wide gradual arc and not in a sudden horseshoe curve. Therefore, read, but be aware of what it is that is being read. To support the special Calvinist definition of Total Depravity, Piper uses the words *total, totality,* or *totally* repeatedly. The *totality* of the *total* must be *totally* emphasized.

> When we speak of man's depravity we mean man's natural condition apart from any grace exerted by God to restrain or transform man. There is no doubt that man could perform more evil acts toward his fellow man than he does. But if he is restrained from performing more evil acts by motives that are not owing to his glad submission to God, then even his "virtue" is evil in the sight of God.

The word *exert* is important to the argument of Piper. Calvinism teaches that God must *exert* grace in order that an individual man or the whole of corporate man may be restrained or transformed. To exert, according to the *M-WD* is "to put forth" or "to bring to bear." Keep in mind that while Titus 2:11 plainly declares, "For the grace of God that bringeth salvation hath appeared to all men," the Calvinist contends that grace is *brought to bear or put forth only to the elect.*

Moreover, when Piper speaks of "his glad submission to God," he is speaking of a quality that the non-elect can *never* exercise, because the non-elect will *never* receive the ability to do so. This unpleasant issue of the non-elect being responsible and accountable to do what he cannot do is always just under the surface of the writings of the Calvinist.

I think that in this next citation Piper misappropriates a verse and gives it an application that is not within the context of the passage of Scripture from which it was lifted. While the context is that of the life choices of a believer, Piper applies the verse to the non-elect in his rejection of salvation.

Setting aside that aspect, though not ignoring it, I must call attention to the undeniable reality that the Calvinist doctrine being promoted by Piper continues to lay guilt upon the non-elect for not doing what he is *totally* incapable of doing.

> Romans 14:23 says, "Whatever does not proceed from faith is sin." This is a radical indictment of all natural "virtue" that does not flow from a heart humbly relying on God's grace.

Since the person that is among the non-elect does not have faith, he cannot have any process or course of action that proceeds *from* faith, because he does not and cannot possess faith. The teaching of Calvinism is that faith is the gift of God that the elect receive *after* regeneration. Piper confidently affirms this position in another article.[73]

All emphasis and all of the parentheses of whatever nature found in the next three paragraphs were placed there by Dr. Piper.

> ... Ephesians 2:8–9 where Paul stresses that saving faith is a gift: "By grace you have been saved through faith; and *that not of yourselves, it is the gift of God*; not by works, so *that no one may boast.*" (emphasis added) Faith is a gift from God, *so that no one may boast.* Or, as Romans 12:3 says, so that we will not think too highly of ourselves. The last bastion of pride is the belief that we are the originators of our faith.
>
> Paul knew that the abundant grace of God was the source of his own faith. He said in 1 Timothy 1:13–14, "I was formerly a blasphemer and a persecutor and a violent aggressor. Yet I was shown mercy because I acted ignorantly in *unbelief;* but the grace

---

[73]http://www.monergism.com/thethreshold/articles/piper/faith01.html

> of our Lord overflowed [for me] with the *faith* and love which are in Christ Jesus." (author's translation, emphasis added). He was an unbeliever, But then grace over-flowed to him with faith.
>
> So he knew this was the case with every other believer too. He said to the Philippi-ans, "To you it *has been given* for Christ's sake, not only *to believe on Him,* but also to suffer for His sake." (Philippians 1:29, emphasis added).

This necessity of regeneration first so that man has the capability of exercising faith is central to the philosophy of Calvinism. It is the natural *logical* application of the doctrine of Total Inability. ***If*** Total Inability is Scriptural, ***then*** regeneration must pre-cede faith; however, ***if*** Total Inability is not Scrip-tural, ***then*** regeneration does not precede faith.

The doctrine of Total Inability, which is essential to Calvinism, presents man as unable to respond in any fashion to God other than in rebellion and removes from every man the capacity to please God. It would *logically* seem that one who is *totally* unable would not even have the desire to please God. Cal-vinist maintains that God must regenerate a person before that person can "do anything to please God."

> Saving faith must be a gift from God be-cause those dead in their trespasses and sins are incapable of obeying God or doing anything to please God. Therefore it is necessary for all whom God is going to save to regenerate them first.[74]

Piper continues this emphasis of the totality of the total depravity of humanity.

> Man's depravity is total in at least four senses.

---

[74] https://mikeratliff.wordpress.com/2013/07/28/faith-is-a-gift-fro m-god-part-3/

> (1) Our rebellion against God is total. Apart from the grace of God there is no delight in the holiness of God, and there is no glad submission to the sovereign authority of God.

That last paragraph assert that unless God extends grace to a man, *which is received only by the elect* ... "there is no glad submission to the sovereign authority of God." However, this ignores the doctrinal declaration of Calvinism that the possibility that the non-elect might ever be in submission to God does not exist; the non-elect *cannot ever be in submission* because God has decreed that he will never receive grace. Nevertheless, the non-elect individual is required to accept his damnation, *because it is an action of the sovereign God.*

> Of course totally depraved men can be very religious and very philanthropic. They can pray and give alms and fast, as Jesus said (Matthew 6:1–18). But their very religion is rebellion against the rights of their Creator, if it does not come from a childlike heart of trust in the free grace of God. Religion is one of the chief ways that man conceals his unwillingness to forsake self-reliance and bank all his hopes on the unmerited mercy of God (Luke 18:9–14; Colossians 2:20–23).

According to the Calvinist doctrine of Total Depravity, "the heart of trust" is only possible after the individual is regenerated; but, the Calvinist is boldly and coldly speaks of the *unwillingness* of the non-elect.

Do not be lulled to sleepiness by the use of the phrase "the free grace of God."[75] This is not meant

---

[75]The Calvinist often, almost habitually, adds an adjective, such as atoning, elective, irresistible, persevering, preventative, regenerative, or saving, as a description or modification of the word grace; none of which are found in scripture, but all of which are required for the doctrines of Calvinism to be palatable.

to suggest that grace is freely available to all or that it is administered to all. In Calvinism, this *free grace* of which he speaks is only *free* for the elect. It is eternally unavailable for the non-elect.

> It is a myth that man in his natural state is genuinely seeking God. Men do seek God. But they do not seek him for who he is. They seek him in a pinch as one who might preserve them from death or enhance their worldly enjoyments. Apart from conversion, no one comes to the light of God.

Calvinism teaches that no one comes to God until he has been regenerated and is converted. The non-elect constitutionally cannot come, because he does not have the ability to do so. As this Calvinist continues to argue for the cardinal doctrine of Calvinism, it is necessary for him to manipulate the text of Scripture so as to alter the wording to fit the doctrine. Read carefully to observe how one preposition is skillfully changed so that what is needed to be said to support the teaching may be found in the text.

> Some do come to the light. But listen to what John 3:20–21 says about them. "Every one who does evil hates the light, and does not come to the light, lest his deeds should be exposed. But he who does what is true comes to the light, that it may be clearly seen that his deeds have been wrought in God."
>
> Yes there are those who come to the light—namely those whose deeds are the work of God. "Wrought in God" means worked by God. Apart from this gracious work of God all men hate the light of God and will not come to him lest their evil be exposed—this is total rebellion. "No one seeks for God ... There is no fear of God before their eyes!"

The AV text for John 3:20–21 reads, "For every one that doeth evil hateth the light, neither cometh to the light, lest his deeds should be reproved. But he that doeth truth cometh to the light, that his deeds may be made manifest, that they are wrought in God."

The last phrase "wrought in God," holds the preposition that, I believe Piper chooses to manipulate. He begins by changing the phrase to read "those deeds are the work of God." This completely alters the meaning from *the deeds* of a man being *wrought in* God to having *the deed* become the work of God. Take notice that he no longer uses the plural word *deeds*, but that the plural word of Scripture has been transformed into the singular word *deed*—and that deed has changed from being the work of a man to become the work *of* God. He writes boldly, "Wrought in God" means worked by God."

The prepositional phrase "wrought in God" is redesigned and restated as meaning "worked *by* God. The sentence now says something entirely different from how it is written. The plural deeds of a man have been manipulated into a singular deed of God.

I understand Piper to have changed the phrase "his deeds ... they are wrought in God" to the approximation of "God has worked the gracious work of God in causing the man to perform the deeds." The sentence is proper Calvinist doctrine as he alters it; however, I know of no rule of language that would permit this radical modification of the subjects (*man* to *God*) and the actions (*wrought in* to *worked by*). By the end of the maneuver, the sentence as reconstructed to conform to Calvinism bears no resemblance to the sentence as it was given by inspiration.

May I suggest that there exists a major difference in my work being produced—wrought—*in God* and in that work being produced—worked—*by God*. Whether used as a preposition or an adverb, the word *by* does not seem to be a legitimate synonym for the word *in*.

I believe that this transference of responsibility from man to God is valid evidence of exploitation of the text. I also believe that the evidence is overwhelming that this level of manipulation is required for Calvinism to explain verses like John 3:20–21. The doctrine purporting to be taught from the text does not exist in the text until the text is altered so that it might fit the doctrine. That is an unacceptable circle of reasoning.

The argument for regeneration *before* the exercise of faith continues with this reasoning:

> (2) In his total rebellion everything man does is sin.
>
> In Romans 14:23 Paul says, "Whatever is not from faith is sin." Therefore, if all men are in total rebellion, everything they do is the product of rebellion and cannot be an honor to God, but only part of their sinful rebellion. If a king teaches his subjects how to fight well and then those subjects rebel against their king and use the very skill he taught them to resist him, then even those skills become evil.

This is the second translation or paraphrasing of Romans 14:23 in the same article: "of faith" has been "proceeds from faith" and now becomes "from faith." All three are legitimate understandings of the underlying Greek word in this instance; however, two observations are proper: (1) The continual adjusting of the text makes acceptance of the eventual dramatic manipulation of the words possible. (2) The concept conveyed is that there is no settled text as the authority.

Different wordings are necessary to validate particular doctrines of Calvinism. The translation will be chosen as to how it best fits the doctrine. I believe this further indicates that Calvinism is imposed on the Scriptures and that it does not rise from within the word of God.

While the passage in Romans is addressing differences among fellow believers and how those conflicts are to be addressed by those particular believers, Piper usurps this statement and makes it an indictment of every individual, *including the non-elect.* He then charges that until a person is saved, that person is incapable of doing anything but sin.

The difficulty with his indictment is that, in Calvinism, the non-elect individual has no potential of ever doing anything but to commit sin, and yet that non-elect person is held fully accountable for his inescapable sin. This continues to be amplified in his next statement.

> (3) Man's inability to submit to God and do good is total. ... natural man has a mindset that does not and cannot submit to God. Man cannot reform himself.
>
> Ephesians 2:1 says that we Christians were all once "dead in trespasses and sins." The point of deadness is that we were incapable of any life with God. Our hearts were like a stone toward God (Ephesians 4:18; Ezekiel 36:26). Our hearts were blind and incapable of seeing the glory of God in Christ (2 Corinthians 4:4–6). We were totally unable to reform ourselves.

Recall and consider the strength of the words used: *inability to submit to God and do good is total ... cannot submit to God ... cannot reform ... incapable of any life ... incapable of seeing the glory of God ... totally unable to reform.* Calvinism teaches that the elect must be regenerated in order that they might be given faith so that they will have the ability to believe.

However, Calvinism also teaches that God has willed that He will not regenerate the non-elect and that He will never give the non-elect faith. Therefore, the non-elect are forever unable to please God. The non-elect are non-elect because God has chosen it to be so.

Piper proceeds to apply this definition of total inability as the moral justification for the eternal punishment of the non-elect.

> (4) Our rebellion is totally deserving of eternal punishment.
>
> Ephesians 2:3 goes on to say that in our deadness we were "children of wrath." That is, we were under God's wrath because of the corruption of our hearts that made us as good as dead before God.
>
> The reality of hell is God's clear indictment of the infiniteness of our guilt. If our corruption were not deserving of an eternal punishment God would be unjust to threaten us with a punishment so severe as eternal torment. But the Scriptures teach that **God is just in condemning unbelievers to eternal hell** (2 Thessalonians 1:6–9; Matthew 5:29f; 10:28; 13:49f; 18:8f; 25:46; Revelation 14:9–11; 20:10). Therefore, to the extent that hell is a total sentence of condemnation, to that extent must we think of ourselves as totally blameworthy apart from the saving grace of God.

Though he uses the term *unbelievers*, Piper intends us to understand that he means the *non-elect*. The non-elect have not chosen that they will reject the Gospel; the non-elect have not decided that they will not receive salvation. The non-elect are those individuals that God has chosen to never regenerate. The non-elect are those individuals that God has decided will never be given faith in order that they might believe. It is not that the unbeliever did not believe or that he will not believe; it is that he cannot believe. I fail to understand how it is rational to use the disingenuous term *unbeliever* for the person that has no capacity for believing.

In the philosophy of Calvinism, God is said to condemn the non-elect because they do not believe, *even though those non-elect are not able to believe because of the decree of God.*

The Calvinist often uses words that the non-Calvinist will read and simply accept those words as being right and true, without hesitation, because the Calvinist's definitions of those words are not recognized. Ignorance of the glossary of Calvinism is dangerous.

For example, it is a true and right statement that the Scriptures teach that God is just in His condemning unbelievers to eternal hell. However, the Calvinist has a *totally* different and *totally* incorrect definition of the word *unbelievers*. In Calvinism, unbelievers are the non-elect, who are *totally* incapable of believing.

Piper explains this in his summary paragraph.

> In summary, total depravity means that our rebellion against God is total, everything we do in this rebellion is sin, our inability to submit to God or reform ourselves is total, and we are therefore totally deserving of eternal punishment.

Piper has encapsulated the essence of the underpinnings of Calvinism in his sentence.

(1.) The descendent of Adam is *totally* depraved and exists in *total* rebellion; every activity of this child of Adam is a *totally* sinful act; therefore, each of Adam's descendents is *totally* incapable of submitting to God.

(2). This *total* rebellion for which the individual has no potential to escape or to cease, nonetheless, makes the child of Adam *totally* deserving of eternal punishment.

(3). This condemnation extends equally to the elect prior to regeneration and forever to the non-elect.

Calvinism teaches that God adjudicates full culpability to each of the non-elect and sentences those non-elected individuals to eternal punishment even though God alone is the Dispenser of regeneration and faith. Under Calvinism, God judges a man for not having what he cannot obtain, because God denies him access.

The doctrine of Total Depravity, as uniquely defined by the Calvinist is a foundation for the entire philosophy of Calvinism. Therefore, this doctrine needs careful evaluation and refutation. I acknowledge that I can-not match Piper intellectually. The issue, however, is one that is Scriptural and not intellectual. All of the claims of Calvinism must be weighed against the declarations of Scripture and not to be given value because of the brilliance of the intellectual shrewdness demonstrated.

> Isaiah 8:20 To the law and to the testimony: if they speak not according to this word, it is because there is no light in them.

I believe that the doctrine of Total Depravity as proposed by the Calvinist does not conform to the Scriptures.

The issue is not personal; I do not challenge the character of the advocate of Calvinism, his sincerity, or even his salvation. The only challenge that I am making is to the doctrine being taught.

Total Inability as advocated by Calvinism is not a Bible based doctrine. As a philosophical system, it is logical *only* with the provision that each premise is accepted as true. Invalidate this one Point and the entire TULIP must collapse.

I believe that the Gospel invitation deals a death-blow to the doctrine of Total Inability. Until in the final preparations for this chapter, I had forgotten an episode from long years ago. My maternal grandfather was a Baptist deacon in southeastern Kentucky. The only other established church in that little community near his farm was a Dutch Reformed Church. Though my grandmother had been raised in the Primitive Baptists (the Calvinists of the Calvinists), the Calvinism of the Dutch Reformed was something against which my grandfather had very strong convictions. They could be good neighbors, but their doctrine was unacceptable.

Whenever I spent time on the farm with him, he had me reading American histories, Baptist histories, and Baptist doctrine books. He introduced me to Orchard, Carroll, Walker, Kazee, and James M. Pendleton.

Sometime after entering the ministry, while reading *Christian Doctrines*, written by Pendleton, I was struck with the forcefulness of a particular passage. These paragraphs found lodging in my heart. They presented a simple, but solid logic that the smooth syllogistic *logic* of Calvinism cannot silence.

It should be understand that Pendleton would have described himself as a Calvinist and he quotes Andrew Fuller, who also labeled himself a Calvinist. However, what Pendleton wrote and what he quoted from Fuller in his discussion of *The Extent of the Atonement* destroys the feasibility of the doctrines of Calvinism identified as Total Inability, Unconditional Election, Limited Atonement, and Irresistible Grace.

The reasoning presented by Pendleton is unanswerable *when only the Scriptures are consulted.* For a book on doctrines, *Christian Doctrines* is written in practical understandable language. Under the topic of The Extent of the Atonement in his chapter on *The Atonement of Christ*, Pendleton wrote of the responsibility that every man has to accept the Gospel invitation.

> This topic, if considered in all its amplitude, would embrace the atonement in its relations to the universe. That it sustains such relations is entirely credible, but *we* are specially concerned with its relation

to God and men. In this view, the subject is one of deep personal interest to all the human race. **As to the sufficiency of the provisions of the atonement for the salvation of the world, there can be no doubt and there need be no controversy.** If, as has been shown, the value of the atonement arises chiefly from the dignity of Christ's person, and if his *[sic]* dignity results by a sublime necessity from his *[sic]* divinity, **it is a grand impertinence to attempt to limit its sufficiency. So far as the claims of law and justice are concerned, the atonement has obviated every difficulty in the way of any sinner's salvation.** In supplying a basis for the exercise of mercy in one instance, it supplies a basis for the exercise of mercy in innumerable instances. It places the world, to use the language of Robert Hall, "in a salvable state." It makes salvation an attainable object. That is, all men, in consequence of the atonement, occupy a position where saving influences can reach them. **There is no natural impossibility in the way of their salvation. If it be asked why all men are not saved, I reply, The** *[sic]* **answer is not to be sought in the atonement, but in the culpable unwillingness of sinners to be saved. Here the question is to be left, and here it ought always to have been left.**

The sufficiency of the provisions of the atonement for the world's salvation, is the only basis on which can consistently rest the universal invitations of the gospel. On this point, I cannot express my views so well as Andrew Fuller has done in the following language:

"It is a fact that the Scriptures rest the general invitations of the gospel upon the atonement of Christ. But if there were not a sufficiency in the atonement for the salvation of sinners without distinction, how could the ambassadors of Christ beseech them to be reconciled to God, and that from the consideration of his, *[sic]* having been made sin for us who knew no sin, that we might he made the righteousness of God in him? *[sic]* What would you think of the fallen angels being invited to be reconciled to God from the consideration of an atonement having been made for fallen men? You would say, It *[sic]* is inviting them to partake of a benefit which *has no existence,* the obtaining of which, therefore, is *naturally impossible.* Upon the supposition of the atonement being insufficient for the salvation of any more than are actually saved, the non-elect, however, with respect to a being reconciled to God through it, are in the same state as the fallen angels; that is, the thing is not only morally, but *naturally impossible.* But if there be an objective fulness *[sic]* in the atonement of Christ, sufficient for any number of sinners, were they to believe in him, there is no other impossibility in the way of any man's salvation, to whom the gospel comes at least, than what arises from the state of his own mind ...

"I do not deny that there is *difficulty* in these statements, but it belongs to the general subject of reconciling the purposes of God with the agency of man; whereas in the other case God is represented as inviting sinners to partake of what has no existence, and which, therefore, is physically impossible. The one, while it ascribes the salvation of the believer in every stage of it to mere grace, renders the unbeliever inexcusable; which the other, I conceive, does not. **In short, we must either acknowledge an objective fulness** *[sic]* **in**

Christ's atonement for the salvation of the whole world, were the whole world to believe in him, or, in opposition to Scripture and common sense, confine our invitations to believe to such persons as have believed already."

This extract from the writings of Mr. Fuller is commended to candid and earnest consideration, especially that part of it which presents **the absurdity of offering salvation to fallen angels because an atonement has been made for fallen men. The absurdity arises from the fact that the atonement has no reference to fallen angels; and if there are sinners of Adam's race to whom it has no more reference than to fallen angels, the offer of salvation to those sinners would be a repetition of the absurdity.**

The sufficiency of the provisions of the atonement for the salvation of all the world is the only doctrine which harmonizes with the commission of Christ to the apostles: "Go ye into all the world, and preach the gospel to every creature: he that believeth and is baptized shall be saved; but he that believeth not shall be damned." Mark xvi.15, 16. **According to this commission, salvation is to be offered to the whole human family. Language could be neither more general nor more specific—"into all the world," "to every creature."** But the fearful intimation is that some will not believe, and through unbelief will incur damnation. It must then be the duty of all to believe. Believe what? The gospel. And what is it to believe the gospel? It is so to credit its facts and its truths as to trust in Christ for salvation. Faith is said to be "in his blood"; that is, it involves reliance on the atonement made by his *[sic]* blood. If, then, it is the duty of all men to believe, and if faith implies reliance on the atonement, and if the atonement was made for a part of the race only, it follows that it is the duty of those for whom no atonement was made to rely on that which has no existence. This is an absurdity. **The more the point is considered, the more evident it will appear that the duty of all men to believe the gospel is inseparable from the "objective fulness"** *[sic]* **of the provisions of the atonement for the salvation of all men.**

Again, in believing in Christ we not only believe, primarily, that he *[sic]* died for sinners, but, secondarily, that he *[sic]* died for us as included among sinners. The latter belief is by no means to be made so prominent as the former, but it is essential to a joyous appropriation of the blessings of salvation. **Now, if Christ did not die for all, and if it is the duty of all to believe in him,** ***[sic]*** **it is the duty of some—those for whom he** ***[sic]*****did not die—to believe an untruth.** This also reduces the matter to an absurdity, for it cannot be the duty of any one to believe what is not true. We must either give up the position that it is the duty of all men to believe the gospel, or admit that the atonement of Christ has reference to all men.

Much more might be said on this point, but there is not room for more in the narrow limits of a compendium of theology. Such is the extent of the atonement, that salvation is offered to all men; nor dare we question God's sincerity in making the offer. While the atoning merit of the blood of Christ is infinite, its saving efficacy is restricted to its application. We may therefore say of the atonement that it is so general that all are saved who "come to God" by Christ, and so limited that none are saved who do not "come to God" through the Me-

> diator, "the man Christ Jesus who gave himself a ransom for all." 1 Tim. ii. 5, 6. [Emphasis is added.]

Pendleton, with Fuller's assistance, has presented reasoning that damages Total Inability beyond redemption in an intelligible and comprehensible manner. Their comments need no addendum.

The TULIP holds that the atonement secured by Jesus of Nazareth on the cross of Calvary has no more reference to the non-elect sinners of Adam's race than it does to fallen angels. Pendleton and Fuller equates the act of extending the invitation to the non-elect to that of giving that same invitation to the fallen angels. Their term for doing so is "absurdity" and that is not excessive.

One simply cannot believe the following paragraphs to be true and sincerely maintain the viability of Total Inability, Unconditional Election, Limited Atonement, and Irresistible Grace.

> The sufficiency of the provisions of the atonement for the world's salvation, is the only basis on which can consistently rest the universal invitations of the gospel.
>
> If it be asked why all men are not saved, I reply, "The answer is not to be sought in the atonement, but in the culpable unwillingness of sinners to be saved."
>
> It must then be the duty of all to believe.
>
> We must either give up the position that it is the duty of all men to believe the gospel, or admit that the atonement of Christ has reference to all men.
>
> The absurdity arises from the fact that the atonement has no reference to fallen angels ; and if there are sinners of Adam's race to whom it has no more reference than to fallen angels, the offer of salvation to those sinners would be a repetition of the absurdity.

How hard it must be for the Bible reading Calvinist to kick against such pricks of Scriptures as these!

> 1 Timothy 2:3–6 For this *is* good and acceptable in the sight of God our Saviour; Who will have all men to be saved, and to come unto the knowledge of the truth. For *there is* one God, and one mediator between God and men, the man Christ Jesus; Who gave himself a ransom for all, to be testified in due time.

> 1 John 2:2 And he is the propitiation for our sins: and not for ours only, but also for *the sins of* the whole world.

> Mark 16:15 And he said unto them, Go ye into all the world, and preach the gospel to every creature.

CHAPTER 8

UNCONDITIONAL

The materials of Calvinism must be read carefully and knowledgeably. It cannot be overemphasized that the language of Calvinism is a specialized tongue that must be interpreted. The words of Calvinism have specialized definitions. The article referenced in the last chapter is an excellent example of the necessity of knowing the vocabulary of the Calvinist. The first sentence will be misunderstood without the application of that knowledge.

> When we speak of man's depravity we mean man's natural condition apart from any grace exerted by God to restrain or transform man. There is no doubt that man could perform more evil acts toward his fellow man than he does. But if he is restrained from performing more evil acts by motives that are not owing to his glad submission to God, then even his "virtue" is evil in the sight of God.

Unless one already knows that *depravity* is defined by the Calvinist as *inability* and unless he carefully reads with that understanding in mind so that he interprets the sentence in that light, he will likely miss the assertion that God has to *exert* grace before anyone can or will be restrained or transformed.

The precise word choice required by Calvinism is not *extend*, but *exert*. The *M-WD* defines *exert* as "to put forth," or "to bring to bear especially with sustained effort or lasting effect." The selection of that particular word reveals, with forceful clarity, the deep irreconcilable, incompatible, and impassible divide that exists between Calvinism and the plain meaning of the straightforward statements of Scripture. That difference between insisting that grace will be *exerted* (forced) upon the elect only and proclaiming that grace will be *extended* (offered) to all men sets Calvinism apart. [76]

That difference must not be minimized; it is that specific distinction that identifies and separates Calvinism. The inability of man to respond to God until God specifically exerts grace to that particular man identifies and distinguishes the unique theological philosophy of Calvinism.

The first sentence, unmistakably and emphatically, states that God must exert grace in order to restrain or to transform man. The reader is to understand by this statement that without this act of the exertion of grace by God, man is unrestrained and untransformed; moreover, man has no possibility or hope of such restraint or transformation. God must *impose* grace.

Piper's opening sentence is a straightforward, two-edged assertion that:

---

[76]Titus 2:11–15 For the grace of God that bringeth salvation hath appeared to all men, Teaching us that, denying ungodliness and worldly lusts, we should live soberly, righteously, and godly, in this present world; Looking for that blessed hope, and the glorious appearing of the great God and our Saviour Jesus Christ; Who gave himself for us, that he might redeem us from all iniquity, and purify unto himself a peculiar people, zealous of good works. These things speak, and exhort, and rebuke with all authority. Let no man despise thee.

(1) No individual man has any ability to restrain himself from any action that is sinful, which is implied by the use of the word depravity, or to transform himself to do anything good.

(2) Unless or until God exerts grace to or upon that individual man, he will not be restrained from any act of sinfulness and he will have no ability to respond to God in any way whatsoever or to transform himself in any fashion from his state of total inability.

Unless and until God has willed it to be so, every man would remain in this state of total inability. God must exert grace to restrain or to transform. Some men, God only restrains: while others, He transforms. Whether a particular Calvinist will acknowledge it or not, this is the doctrine of Double Predestination; that is, one person is predestined to salvation and another person is predestined to reprobation or damnation. The doctrine of Double Predestination is required for the system of Calvinism to be consistent. To deny Double Predestination and claim to be a Calvinist is either inconsistency or hypocrisy.

Acknowledged Calvinist, Dr. R. C. Sproul agrees with the statement that the doctrine of Double Predestination cannot be removed from Calvinism without destroying the entire system through the resultant conflicting contradiction.

> If particular election is to be maintained and if the notion that all salvation is ultimately based upon that particular election is to be maintained, then we must speak of double predestination.[77]

Having conceded the necessity of defending Double Predestination, Sproul quickly sets about to *redefine* the terms to fit his approach to Double

---

[77]http://www.the-highway.com/DoublePredestination_Sproul.html

Predestination. Undoubtedly, the persistent Calvinistic *if* and *then* will be recognized. In fact, in the sentence cited above, he was compelled to double the *if.* Sproul attempts, with eloquent logic, to defend the proposition that God allows some to spend eternity in the Lake of Fire by the process of His choice of *not* predestining them to be one of the elect.

Sproul gallantly devotes considerable effort in, what is to me, the vain attempt to make God not responsible for those that He did not choose to be numbered among the elect and, who are thereby *allowed* to reject what they never had the opportunity or the ability to receive. He attempts to accomplish this by the use of the legalistic contrast between the logic of categorical syllogism's arguments of *positive-positive* and *positive-negative.* Additional context for these statements by Sproul is found in APPENDIX 3.

In the first proposition that he discusses, *positive-positive,* which he firmly rejects, God is said to select actively some to salvation, which is a *positive action,* and to select actively some to reprobation, which is also a *positive action.*

In the second proposition, *positive-negative,* which he firmly promotes, God actively chooses to elect, to call, to regenerate, and to give salvation to some, which is a *positive action,* and simply does not choose actively to elect, to call, to regenerate, and to give salvation to others, allowing them to receive what they deserve, which is therefore considered a *negative action.*

The *logic* for the difference in the two propositions is that God is not obligated to save any at all and He may disburse His mercy to as few or to as many as He chooses. Therefore, by this maneuver, in exercising a negative selection of *not predestining* a person to spend eternity in the Heaven, God is able to be held blameless in the logic of *positive-negative* Calvinism.

Somehow, viewed with this *positive-negative* Calvinist *logic*, the act of *not predestinating* a person to Heaven is *not seen* as also predestinating that person to the Lake of Fire, but *is only seen* as *not* predestinating that person to the Lake of Fire. *Positive-negative* predestination may be able to be debated logically, but it is not logically reasonable.

> In sharp contrast to the caricature of double predestination seen in the positive-positive schema is the classic position of Reformed theology on predestination. In this view predestination is double in that it involves both election and reprobation but is not symmetrical with respect to the mode of divine activity. A strict parallelism of operation is denied. Rather we view predestination in terms of a positive-negative relationship.[78]

The technicality of the strained logic of *positive-negative* may comfort the heart of a Calvinist; however, the practicality of the illogical logic of *positive-negative* is identical in consequences to that of *positive-positive.* Those who spend eternity in the Lake of Fire will do so, *under any form of Calvinistic logic,* because they never had the possibility of any other destiny.

Suppose a lifeguard (1) knows a given individual is drowning and will drown without his direct intervention in the rescue of that person, (2) has the capability to rescue that individual, (3) chooses purposely not to do so, and (4) remains seated in his life-saving tower watching as the individual drowns. Would that lifeguard attempt to use the *positive-negative logic* in his defense?

---

[78]http://www.the-highway.com/DoublePredestination_Sproul.html

If he did, I fear that he would be arrested, indicted, and tried for manslaughter, if not murder. Even though the lifeguard describes his conduct as a negative action of *not rescuing the drowning person* rather than the positive act of *causing the drowning of the person*, I seriously doubt that he could find a sympathetic jury to accept the defense argument of "I did not cause his drowning; I simply did not chose to save him from drowning." The lifeguard because he is the lifeguard cannot escape the guilt of his actions of not exercising his power and ability to rescue the victim. As to the drowned victim, the difference between the *positive-positive logic* versus the *positive-negative logic* is immaterial—he is dead by either exploitation of terms.

This compels me to recall the first sentence that I cited by Dr. Piper:

> When we speak of man's depravity we mean man's natural condition apart from any grace exerted by God to restrain or transform man.

Calvinism boldly proclaims that without the engaged exertion of grace by God, no individual will be either restrained or transformed. Therefore, unregenerated man has *no capability* for doing righteousness, *no capacity* for being good, *no ability* to overcome sin, *no aptitude* for serving God, *no power* to repent, *no potential* for change, *no possibility* of forgiveness, *no help* extended by the God of grace and mercy, *and no hope* in either time or eternity. The elect will, at the appointed hour, be regenerated; however, the non-elect will never exit that pit of decreed impotency.

Should God exert His grace, a particular man is one of the elect; however, if God does not exert His grace, that same man is one of the non-elect and is eternally damned. The man is isolated from the decision, but not from the destiny.

However, this concept engages more areas than that of eternal salvation. Unless God exerts grace, man cannot be restrained in doing as he pleases nor can he be transformed to do as God pleases. Therefore, man has no ability to do anything other than to be a sinner totally immersed in sin and there is no limitation to the extent of that ability to sin, unless and until grace is exerted by God.

Think through this concept and consider the allegations that are made and the conclusions that must be derived from those very specific affirmations. The non-elect has an impotency that is imposed upon him by God but for which he is condemned by God. Moreover, each of his sins is committed because he cannot restrain himself for the sole reason the God did not exert grace to restrain him. I find that concept is repulsive. I believe that it slanders God.

However, this condition of inability is also true for the elect before God regenerates him. Both the elect and the non-elect are what they are and neither can be otherwise. They both have a sinful nature that has no restraint until God *exerts* restraining grace. Yet, through the exercise of the *positive-negative* approach, the God that could exert grace to restrain but chooses not do so has no responsibility for what His undispensed indispensable grace did not restrain.

It will likely take more than one reading to follow the convolutions of the example that Sproul uses to clarify the differences between *positive-positive* and *positive-negative.*

> If God foreordains anything, it is absolutely certain that what He foreordains will come to pass. The purpose of God can never be frustrated. Even God's foreknowledge or prescience makes future events certain with respect to time. That is to say, if God knows on Tuesday that I will drive to Pittsburgh on Friday, then there is

> no doubt that, come Friday, I will drive to Pittsburgh. Otherwise God's knowledge would have been in error. Yet, there is a significant difference between God's knowing that I would drive to Pittsburgh and God's ordaining that I would do so. Theoretically He could know of a future act without ordaining it, but He could not ordain it without knowing what it is that He is ordaining. But in either case, the future event would be certain with respect to time and the knowledge of God. ... We see then, that what God knows in advance comes to pass by necessity or *[sic]* infallibly or necessity of immutability. But what about His foreordaining or predestinating what comes to pass? If God foreordains reprobation does this not obliterate the distinction between positive-negative and involve a *necessity of force*? If God foreordains reprobation does this not mean that God forces, compels, or coerces the reprobate to sin? Again the answer must be negative. If God, when He is decreeing reprobation, does so in consideration of the reprobate's being already fallen, then He does not coerce him to sin. To be reprobate is to be left in sin, not pushed or forced to sin.[79]

This is a brilliant use of language attempting to make the impossible possible, the untenable acceptable, and the repulsive delightful.

It is repugnant to Sproul to consider that God is responsible for any soul being a reprobate; thus, he labels that unconscionable possibility as *positive-positive predestination.* His precise statement is "Only in a positive-positive schema of predestination does double predestination leave us with a capri-

[79]http://www.the-highway.com/DoublePredestination_Sproul.html

cious deity whose sovereign decrees manifest a divine tyranny."[80]

Yet, if God alone has the ability, the power, and the position to prevent damnation by His gift of salvation and God chooses not to do so, then, by every meaning of the equivalent words of any language, God alone has the responsibility for the reprobation of any and of every lost soul.

Moreover, the same logic must be applied to every individual sin. In the Calvinist's concept, God alone has the ability, the power, and the position to prevent any sin. "When we speak of man's depravity we mean man's natural condition apart from any grace exerted by God to restrain or transform man." The statement requires the following conclusions.

1. Unless God exerts grace no man has the capacity to be transformed, changed, or to do anything but to sin—certainly, under this concept, no one could be saved, which is the ultimate transformation. Thus, God by choosing to exert grace or by choosing not to exert grace determines who will be and who will *not* be saved entirely without any cooperation or responsibility on the part of the individuals chosen or not chosen.
2. Unless God exerts grace, no person can be restrained, withheld, from any act of sin. Therefore, when any act of sin is committed by anyone, it is because God did not exert grace to restrain that person from committing the sin. Unless God exerts grace, no person is able not to sin; the person has no capacity to do otherwise, because, his sin nature is beyond any other restraint.

I insist that this describes doctrine that has an error of the highest degree. At once, God is made *the*

---

[80]http://www.the-highway.com/DoublePredestination_Sproul.html

Author of Confusion in the name of making Him the *God of Absolute Order*. Every action of every individual is determined by the choice that is made solely by God to exert grace or by the choice that is made solely by God not to exert grace. Calvinism is absolute determinism. Full responsibility for the actions of every individual rests upon God, and absolutely none rests upon any individual.

Arbitrarily, the God described by the Calvinist determined all things before there was anything to be determined. Concurrently, by that doctrine, God is made *the Author of Sin*. Most of the Calvinists that I have read are extreme with their carefulness in their maneuvering of words to absolve God of the responsibility for sin. They do this while, at the same time, they are defending the position that God has decreed all that actually occurs, *even sin*. This requires exceptional skill in the art of verbal gymnastics. An excellent example of the way that words are manipulated to achieve this linguistic contortion is the effort of Michael Bremmer.

> God's sovereignty encompasses all that comes to pass, even sin; however, God never forces anyone to act contrary their will; therefore, He is not the author of sin. When we sin, we do so because we choose to sin. That God has even ordained sin will not sit well with everyone. Yet, if Jesus is in fact the "Lamb slain before the foundation of the world" (Rev. 13.8) then sins *[sic]* appearance into the world and our redemption through the atonement, were decreed by God before creation and the fall; however, Scripture is clear that God is not the author of sin (Ja. 1.13).[81]

This paragraph states that God "ordained sin" and "decreed" "sin's appearance" and yet insists that God is not the "author of sin" *because all men act in*

[81]http://www.mbrem123.com/calvinism/freewill.php

accord with their will. However, that will is also ordained and decreed by God, according to Calvinism.

In the attempt to avoid the dilemma of Double Predestination, there are those within the ranks of the Calvinists that will assign the entire responsibility to every man for his personal eternal destiny; however, no Calvinist, whether single or double predestinarian, will grant to any man even a measure of ability to choose to believe. It is silliness to grant, or to imply, the ability *not* to believe while at the same time, emphatically denying any man the ability to believe.

With that background for the first sentence, much of the rest of the article seems to me to be doublespeak. Piper proceeds to discuss Total Depravity with a series of statements that have a progressive curvature into a false doctrine. The concluding paragraphs are just as deceptive as the first sentence. They contain enough of the truth to be believable and have enough curvature to become full-blown error.

> The reality of hell is God's clear indictment of the infiniteness of our guilt. If our corruption were not deserving of an eternal punishment God would be unjust to threaten us with a punishment so severe as eternal torment.[82]

I submit that the issue is not *the deserving* of eternal punishment; it is instead the *inability* to respond to the Gospel. It would seem to require a sadist to *threaten* a person, when the person being threatened has no ability to respond to the threat.

> But the Scriptures teach that God is just in condemning unbelievers to eternal hell (2 Thessalonians 1:6–9; Matthew 5:29f;

---

[82]http://www.monergism.com/thethreshold/articles/piper/depravity.html

> 10:28; 13:49f; 18:8f; 25:46; Revelation 14:9–11; 20:10). Therefore, to the extent that hell is a total sentence of condemnation, to that extent must we think of ourselves as totally blameworthy apart from the saving grace of God.[83]

Remember, the person who is not one of the elect has no potentiality of receiving that *saving grace* from God, because God has not exerted the grace to transform the person. How then, can the person be blameworthy?

> In summary, total depravity means that our rebellion against God is total, everything we do in this rebellion is sin, our inability to submit to God or reform ourselves is total, and we are therefore totally deserving of eternal punishment.[84]

If Calvinism is true, this is the ultimate paradox: we are *totally* unable to do right, yet we are *totally* deserving of the penalty for doing wrong.

> It is hard to exaggerate the importance of admitting our condition to be this bad. If we think of ourselves as basically good or even less than totally at odds with God, our grasp of the work of God in redemption will be defective. But if we humble ourselves under this terrible truth of our total depravity, we will be in a position to see and appreciate the glory and wonder of the work of God discussed in the next four points.[85]

Exactly what value is there in "admitting our condition," humbling "ourselves under this terrible truth of Total Depravity," or even in our appreciation

---

[83] http://www.monergism.com/thethreshold/articles/piper/depravity.html

[84] http://www.monergism.com/thethreshold/articles/piper/depravity.html

[85] http://www.monergism.com/thethreshold/articles/piper/depravity.html

of "the glory and wonder of the work of God"? There is none. To imply, by the encouragement to do these things, that there is some meritorious value in the performance is disingenuous and deceitful.

What could possibly be the value of "admitting our condition," or of humbling "ourselves under this terrible truth," or our appreciation of "the glory and wonder of the work of God," if we are not among the chosen? What does it matter what we admit or how we react if we were not elected? There could be no gain and there would be no loss related to the response or the action of any individual that was not chosen and that is, therefore, not among the elect.

The decision was made for us, according to the Calvinist, and our contrition or humility is of no effect in the matter. However, if we do not do so, it is *prima fascia* evidence to the Calvinist that we were not among the elect. Yet, to the same Calvinist, even if we are contrite and even if we are humble, we have no assurance that this did not arise entirely from our old nature, which delights in deceiving us. The Calvinist calls for us to admit, to humble, to appreciate, even while he declares that our attempt or even the accomplishment of those things has *no merit* to be recognized, has *no part* in obtaining salvation, and gives *no evidence* of being one of the elect.

The Calvinist declares that if we were chosen, it is because God exerted the grace and without any exertion on our part. We have no influence with God to persuade Him to save us. It does no good to beg Him to do so.

God does not invite us to be saved *for He has already decided whether we will be or will not be saved.* If we are to be saved, then we will be; and we cannot change that. If we are not to be saved, we will not be; we cannot change that either.

Calvinism is Christianized fatalism, regardless of the denials of those who identify themselves as

Calvinists. Fatalism is the concept that *events are fixed in advance so that human beings are powerless to change them.* No word other than fatalism explains the very first sentence of the article by Piper.

> When we speak of man's depravity we mean man's natural condition apart from any grace exerted by God to restrain or transform man.

Considering all of their magnificent effort to redeem Calvinism from any taint of assessing the responsibility upon God for the eternal damnation of the non-elect, it might seem almost as if neither Piper nor Sproul have read what John Calvin wrote in the *Institutes of the Christian Religion*, Book III, chapter xxi.

> All are not created on equal terms, but some are preordained to eternal life, others to eternal damnation; and, accordingly, as each has been created for one or other of these ends, we say that he has been predestinated to life or to death. ...
>
> We say, then, that Scripture clearly proves this much, that God by his eternal and immutable counsel determined once for all those whom it was his pleasure one day to admit to salvation, and those whom, on the other hand, it was his pleasure to doom to destruction. We maintain that this counsel, as regards the elect, is founded on his free mercy, without any respect to human worth, while those whom he dooms to destruction are excluded from access to life by a just and blameless, but at the same time incomprehensible judgment ...

Plainly, Calvin did not have a blush on his cheek when he penned the unequivocal wording of those two paragraphs. It is impossible to misunderstand or misconstrue his terminology.

> ... preordained ... to eternal damnation ... accordingly, as each has been created for

> one or the other of these ends ... predestinated ... to death ... We say, then, that Scripture clearly proves this much, that God by his eternal and immutable counsel determined once for all those whom it was his pleasure one day ... to doom to destruction ... those whom he dooms to destruction are excluded from access to life by a just and blameless, but at the same time incomprehensible judgment.

Reading the cold, harsh comments declaring that God has created some individuals solely for the purpose of having the pleasure of damning those very souls to eternal destruction, one might be tempted to believe that Calvin never read those words of Ezekiel that diametrically contradict his harsh, caustic, callous words.

> Ezekiel 18:23 Have I any pleasure at all that the wicked should die? saith the Lord GOD: and not that he should return from his ways, and live? ... 32 For I have no pleasure in the death of him that dieth, saith the Lord GOD: wherefore turn yourselves, and live ye.

> Ezekiel 33:11 Say unto them, As I live, saith the Lord GOD, I have no pleasure in the death of the wicked; but that the wicked turn from his way and live: turn ye, turn ye from your evil ways; for why will ye die, O house of Israel?

However, John Calvin did read those words, because he wrote two volumes of commentary on the Book of Ezekiel. While he only completed work on the first twenty chapters, he left detailed comments on the two verses (23, 32) of chapter eighteen that I cited. In those comments, he writes on verse 23, the following:

> If any one *[sic]* should object—then there is no election of God, by which he has predestinated a fixed number to salvation, the answer is at hand: the Prophet does

> not here speak of God's secret counsel, but only recalls miserable men from despair, that they may apprehend the hope of pardon, and repent and embrace the offered salvation. If any one *[sic]* again objects—this is making God act with duplicity, the answer is ready, that God always wishes the same thing, though by different ways, and in a manner inscrutable to us … .
>
> Now all are called to repentance, and the hope of salvation is promised them when they repent. This is true, since God rejects no returning sinner: he pardons all without exception: meanwhile, this will of God which he sets forth in his word does not prevent him from decreeing before the world was created what he would do with every individual:

Take careful note of the wording: "all are called to repentance and the hope of salvation is promised them when they repent." However, the non-elect have no possibility of repenting. "God rejects no returning sinner"; of course, he does not do so, because to Calvin, the only sinner that is capable of returning is one that God returns. This is a strained form of reasoning that only the Calvinist might understand.

He continues on verse 32:

> Here unskillful men think that God speculates on what men will do, and that the salvation or destruction of each depends on themselves, as if God had determined nothing concerning us before the foundation of the world. Hence they set him at naught, since they fancy that he is held in suspense and doubt as to the future end of every one, and that he is not so anxious for our salvation, as to wish all to be saved, but leaves it in the power of every one to perish or to be saved as he pleases. But as I have said, this would reduce God

> to a specter. But we have no need of a long dispute, because Scripture everywhere declares with sufficient clearness that God has determined what shall happen to us: for he chose his own people before the foundation of the world and passed by others. (Ephesians 1:4.) Nothing is clearer than this doctrine; for if there had been no predestination on God's part, there had been no deity, since he would be forced into order as if he were one of us: nay, men are to a certain extent provident, whenever God allows some sparks of his image to shine forth in them.

Calvin insisted that for anyone to challenge the predestination of both the elect and the non-elect was to dispute the deity of God. He is attempting to label his critics as heretics or even infidels. It should not escape our attention that many of those claiming to be Calvinists would be under the wrath of Calvin for their failure to hold to Double Predestination.

> If, therefore, the very smallest drop of foresight in men is laid hold of, how great must it be in the fountain itself? Insipid indeed is the comment, to fancy that God remains doubtful and waiting for what will happen to individuals, as if it were in their own power either to attain to salvation or to perish. But the Prophets words are plain, for God testifies with grief that he *willeth not the death of a mortal.* I answer, that there is no absurdity, as we said before, in God's undertaking a twofold character, not that he is two-faced himself, as those profane dogs[86] blurt out against us,

---

[86]The term dog(s) would seem to have a specific use in the New Testament. For examples see Matthew 7:6, Philippians 3:3, and Revelation 22:15. In his comments on Matthew 7:6, Dr. John Gill gives the definition of *dog* as "men who are violent and furious persecutors and impudent blasphemers." Calvin knowingly applies this term as a pejorative to all of those that question his teachings.

> but because his counsels are incomprehensible by us. This indeed ought to be fixed, that before the foundation of the world we were predestinated either to life or death. .... .
>
> Therefore God *delighteth not in the death of him who dieth,* if he repent at his teaching. But if we wish to penetrate to his incomprehensible counsel, this will be another objection: Oh! but in this way God is chargeable with duplicity;—but I have denied this, though he takes up a twofold character, because this was necessary for our comprehension. Meanwhile Ezekiel announces this very truly as far as doctrine is concerned, *that God wills not the death of him that perishes*: for the explanation follows directly afterwards, *be you converted and live.* Why does not God delight in the death of him who perishes? Because he invites all to repentance and rejects no one.

Calvin writes, "All are not created on equal terms, but some are preordained to eternal life, others to eternal damnation; and, accordingly, as each has been created for one or other of these ends, we say that he has been predestinated to life or to death." He then is able to place into writing within the same context and not consider it conflicting, "Why does not God delight in the death of him who perishes? Because he invites all to repentance and rejects no one."

In his commentary on Matthew, Calvin makes the following comments on 7:6 "It ought to be understood, that *dogs* and *swine* are names given not to every kind of debauched men, or to those who are destitute of the fear of God and of true godliness, but to those who, by clear evidences, have manifested a hardened contempt of God, so that their disease appears to be incurable. In another passage, Christ places the *dogs* in contrast with the elect people of God and the household of faith.
In his comments on Philippians 3:1, Calvin wrote the following description: "In the *first* place, however, he calls them *dogs;* the metaphor being grounded upon this—that, for the sake of filling their belly, they assailed true doctrine with their impure barking."

Calvin taught that God created some that are preordained to eternal death; and yet, John Calvin writes a few paragraphs later that God does not delight in that eternal damnation of him whom He had created, *because* God *invites* the non-elect to repentance. Moreover, John Calvin offers his readers the assurance that God will reject no one that does repent.

We are to understand that the invitation is legitimately extended to a given man even though God condemned that man before the world began. Furthermore, we are supposed to understand that those who were created by God for the purpose of eternal damnation and who cannot respond to the invitation to repent would not be rejected if they were to respond. I confess that the circuitous and closed reasoning of John Calvin is beyond my ability to follow.

Calvin adds to Scripture so that his system is supported. "Therefore God *delighteth not in the death of him who dieth,* if he repent at his teaching." (The italics are in the original.) Scripture as it is written does not satisfy so he changes it to meet the demands of his doctrine.

He proceeds to his summation.

> Since this is so, it follows that he is not delighted by the death of him who perishes: hence there is nothing in this passage doubtful or thorny, and we should also hold that we are led aside by speculations too deep for us. For God does not wish us to inquire into his secret.

Apparently, it matters not what the Scripture might say; the fact is settled: "This indeed ought to be fixed, that before the foundation of the world we were predestinated either to life or death." Therefore, all the words of the word of God must be conformed to that premise and whenever there is an obvious conflict, it is relegated to the department called "For

God does not wish us to inquire into his secret." This is hardly the attitude of a Berean.[87]

My premise is that the words of the word of God must be understood as they stand and not as we would like them to stand. I believe that the Scriptures require us to do this.

> Isaiah 8:20 To the law and to the testimony: if they speak not according to this word, *it is* because *there is* no light in them.
>
> Mark 7:7–9 Howbeit in vain do they worship me, teaching *for* doctrines the commandments of men. For laying aside the commandment of God, ye hold the tradition of men, *as* the washing of pots and cups: and many other such like things ye do. And he said unto them, Full well ye reject the commandment of God, that ye may keep your own tradition.
>
> 2 Peter 1:19 We have also a more sure word of prophecy; whereunto ye do well that ye take heed, as unto a light that shineth in a dark place, until the day dawn, and the day star arise in your hearts: 20 Knowing this first, that no prophecy of the scripture is of any private interpretation. 21 For the prophecy came not in old time by the will of man: but holy men of God spake as they were moved by the Holy Ghost.

---

[87]Acts17:10–11 And the brethren immediately sent away Paul and Silas by night unto Berea: who coming *thither* went into the synagogue of the Jews. These were more noble than those in Thessalonica, in that they received the word with all readiness of mind, and searched the scriptures daily, whether those things were so.

CHAPTER 9

RESPONSIBILITY

The Calvinist phrases the argument that the individual has no responsibility for his salvation in the following manner:

> We must ask, then: Can the DEAD raise themselves? Can the BOUND free themselves? Can the BLIND give themselves sight, or the DEAF hearing? Can the SLAVES redeem themselves? Can the UNINSTRUCTABLE *[sic]* teach themselves? Can the NATURALLY SINFUL change themselves? Surely not! 'Who can bring a clean thing out of an unclean?' asks Job; and he answers, 'Not one!' [Job 14.4]. 'Can the Ethiopian change his skin, or the leopard his spots?' asks Jeremiah; 'If they can,' he concludes, 'then may ye also do good, that are accustomed to do evil.' [Jer 13.23].
>
> Could the Word of God show more plainly than it does that the depravity is total? and that our inability to desire or procure salvation is also total? The picture is one of death—spiritual death. We are like Lazarus in his tomb; we are bound hand and

> foot; corruption has taken hold upon us. Just as there was no glimmer of life in the dead body of Lazarus, so there is no 'inner receptive spark' in our hearts. But the Lord performs the miracle—both with the physically dead, and the spiritually dead; for 'you hath he quickened—made alive—who were dead in trespasses and sins.' [Eph 2.1]. Salvation, by its very nature, must be 'of the Lord.'[88]

In the system of Calvinism, no man can have any part in his salvation, because that man is unable to respond to God until he has been regenerated and given faith. Secondly, God decreed who would be regenerated. Therefore, man has no responsibility in obtaining salvation.

The reasoning is that if Christ died as a substitute for a person, then that person has no choice but to be redeemed.

> Surely, if a man has been redeemed by a redeemer, then the law which he has broken must be satisfied by reason of the work of the Surety on his behalf.[89]

However, when we read the passage on redemption in the First Epistle of Peter, we find that the application of redemption is connected directly and unswervingly to the believing of the individual.

> 1 Peter 1:18–23 Forasmuch as ye know that ye were not redeemed with corruptible things, as silver and gold, from your vain conversation received by tradition from your fathers; But with the precious blood of Christ, as of a lamb without blemish and without spot: Who verily was foreordained before the foundation of the world, but was manifest in these last times for you, Who by him do believe in

---

[88]Seaton, *The Five Points of Calvinism*, 10.
[89]Seaton, *The Five Points of Calvinism*, 17.

> God, that raised him up from the dead, and gave him glory; that your faith and hope might be in God. Seeing ye have purified your souls in obeying the truth through the Spirit unto unfeigned love of the brethren, see that ye love one another with a pure heart fervently: Being born again, not of corruptible seed, but of incorruptible, by the word of God, which liveth and abideth for ever.

This is not an isolated passage in an obscure placement subject to a variety of interpretations. The words are simple and easily understood. The only action that was *foreordained* was the offering of the blood of the LORD Jesus Christ. The individuals were responsible for believing by the exercise of faith. They "purified their souls" by obeying the truth. The same truth is presented through all of Scripture from Genesis through Revelation. Responsibility rests upon the individual for all actions, and the invitation is extended to all to come to God for forgiveness.

Two examples should suffice to represent all of the passages that relate how the LORD God held the individuals of Israel accountable for their failure to believe the words of God.

> Numbers 14:11 And the LORD said unto Moses, How long will this people provoke me? and how long will it be ere they believe me, for all the signs which I have shewed among them?

> Deuteronomy 1:32 Yet in this thing ye did not believe the LORD your God,

Two other passages should serve to show the responsibility of individuals during the time of the kings.

> 2 Kings 17:14 Notwithstanding they would not hear, but hardened their necks, like to the neck of their fathers, that did not believe in the LORD their God.

> 2 Chronicles 20:20 And they rose early in the morning, and went forth into the wilderness of Tekoa: and as they went forth, Jehoshaphat stood and said, Hear me, O Judah, and ye inhabitants of Jerusalem; Believe in the LORD your God, so shall ye be established; believe his prophets, so shall ye prosper.

Leviticus 26 emphasizes both the responsibility that the individuals have to change themselves to serve the LORD and the fact that the opportunity to change is given to the individuals so that they might change themselves to serve the LORD.

> 11 And I will set my tabernacle among you: and my soul shall not abhor you. And I will walk among you, and will be your God, and ye shall be my people. I am the LORD your God, which brought you forth out of the land of Egypt, that ye should not be their bondmen; and I have broken the bands of your yoke, and made you go upright. But if ye will not hearken unto me, and will not do all these commandments; And if ye shall despise my statutes, or if your soul abhor my judgments, so that ye will not do all my commandments, but that ye break my covenant: I also will do this unto you; I will even appoint over you terror, consumption, and the burning ague, that shall consume the eyes, and cause sorrow of heart: and ye shall sow your seed in vain, for your enemies shall eat it. And I will set my face against you, and ye shall be slain before your enemies: they that hate you shall reign over you; and ye shall flee when none pursueth you. And if ye will not yet for all this hearken unto me, then I will punish you seven times more for your sins. And I will break the pride of your power; and I will make your heaven as iron, and your earth as brass: And your strength shall be spent in vain: for your land shall not yield her increase, neither

shall the trees of the land yield their fruits. And if ye walk contrary unto me, and will not hearken unto me; I will bring seven times more plagues upon you according to your sins. I will also send wild beasts among you, which shall rob you of your children, and destroy your cattle, and make you few in number; and your high ways shall be desolate. And if ye will not be reformed by me by these things, but will walk contrary unto me; Then will I also walk contrary unto you, and will punish you yet seven times for your sins. And I will bring a sword upon you, that shall avenge the quarrel of my covenant: and when ye are gathered together within your cities, I will send the pestilence among you; and ye shall be delivered into the hand of the enemy. And when I have broken the staff of your bread, ten women shall bake your bread in one oven, and they shall deliver you your bread again by weight: and ye shall eat, and not be satisfied. And if ye will not for all this hearken unto me, but walk contrary unto me; Then I will walk contrary unto you also in fury; and I, even I, will chastise you seven times for your sins. And ye shall eat the flesh of your sons, and the flesh of your daughters shall ye eat. And I will destroy your high places, and cut down your images, and cast your carcases upon the carcases of your idols, and my soul shall abhor you. And I will make your cities waste, and bring your sanctuaries unto desolation, and I will not smell the savour of your sweet odours. And I will bring the land into desolation: and your enemies which dwell therein shall be astonished at it. And I will scatter you among the heathen, and will draw out a sword after you: and your land shall be desolate, and your cities waste. Then shall the land enjoy her sabbaths, as long as it lieth desolate, and ye be in your enemies' land; even then shall the land rest, and enjoy her sabbaths. As long as it lieth desolate it shall rest; because it did not rest in your sabbaths, when ye dwelt upon it. And upon them that are left alive of you I will send a faintness into their hearts in the lands of their enemies; and the sound of a shaken leaf shall chase them; and they shall flee, as fleeing from a sword; and they shall fall when none pursueth. And they shall fall one upon another, as it were before a sword, when none pursueth: and ye shall have no power to stand before your enemies. And ye shall perish among the heathen, and the land of your enemies shall eat you up. And they that are left of you shall pine away in their iniquity in your enemies' lands; and also in the iniquities of their fathers shall they pine away with them. If they shall confess their iniquity, and the iniquity of their fathers, with their trespass which they trespassed against me, and that also they have walked contrary unto me; And that I also have walked contrary unto them, and have brought them into the land of their enemies; if then their uncircumcised hearts be humbled, and they then accept of the punishment of their iniquity: Then will I remember my covenant with Jacob, and also my covenant with Isaac, and also my covenant with Abraham will I remember; and I will remember the land. The land also shall be left of them, and shall enjoy her sabbaths, while she lieth desolate without them: and they shall accept of the punishment of their iniquity: because, even because they despised my judgments, and because their soul abhorred my statutes. And yet for all that, when they be in the land of their enemies, I will not cast them away, neither will I abhor them, to destroy them utterly, and to break my covenant with them: for I am the LORD their God. But I will for their sakes remember the

> covenant of their ancestors, whom I brought forth out of the land of Egypt in the sight of the heathen, that I might be their God: I am the LORD.

The same invitation to follow the LORD is found in the prophets, and the solemn warning that not to do so is for the individual to bear responsibility and to have accountability as to whether or not the individual does or does not respond to the invitation. Isaiah chapter 1 is an excellent example of the application of this responsibility and accountability.

> 2 Hear, O heavens, and give ear, O earth: for the LORD hath spoken, I have nourished and brought up children, and they have rebelled against me. The ox knoweth his owner, and the ass his master's crib: but Israel doth not know, my people doth not consider. Ah sinful nation, a people laden with iniquity, a seed of evildoers, children that are corrupters: they have forsaken the LORD, they have provoked the Holy One of Israel unto anger, they are gone away backward. Why should ye be stricken any more? ye will revolt more and more: the whole head is sick, and the whole heart faint. From the sole of the foot even unto the head there is no soundness in it; but wounds, and bruises, and putrifying sores: they have not been closed, neither bound up, neither mollified with ointment. Your country is desolate, your cities are burned with fire: your land, strangers devour it in your presence, and it is desolate, as overthrown by strangers. And the daughter of Zion is left as a cottage in a vineyard, as a lodge in a garden of cucumbers, as a besieged city. Except the LORD of hosts had left unto us a very small remnant, we should have been as Sodom, and we should have been like unto Gomorrah. Hear the word of the LORD, ye rulers of Sodom; give ear unto the law of our God, ye people of Gomorrah. To

> what purpose is the multitude of your sacrifices unto me? saith the LORD: I am full of the burnt offerings of rams, and the fat of fed beasts; and I delight not in the blood of bullocks, or of lambs, or of he goats. When ye come to appear before me, who hath required this at your hand, to tread my courts? Bring no more vain oblations; incense is an abomination unto me; the new moons and sabbaths, the calling of assemblies, I cannot away with; it is iniquity, even the solemn meeting. Your new moons and your appointed feasts my soul hateth: they are a trouble unto me; I am weary to bear them. And when ye spread forth your hands, I will hide mine eyes from you: yea, when ye make many prayers, I will not hear: your hands are full of blood. Wash you, make you clean; put away the evil of your doings from before mine eyes; cease to do evil; Learn to do well; seek judgment, relieve the oppressed, judge the fatherless, plead for the widow. Come now, and let us reason together, saith the LORD: though your sins be as scarlet, they shall be as white as snow; though they be red like crimson, they shall be as wool. If ye be willing and obedient, ye shall eat the good of the land: But if ye refuse and rebel, ye shall be devoured with the sword: for the mouth of the LORD hath spoken it.

The invitation extended in Isaiah 45 is obviously a universal and open invitation, or else it is a meaningless invitation.

> 22 Look unto me, and be ye saved, all the ends of the earth: for I am God, and there is none else.

To conform to Calvinism, the following verses have to be interpreted with special Calvinist meanings attached to certain words to remove the clear affirmation of the potential capability of every individual to respond to the invitation **and** to remove the responsibility of any individual for not doing so.

> John 5:39–40 Search the scriptures; for in them ye think ye have eternal life: and they are they which testify of me. And ye will not come to me, that ye might have life.
>
> Matthew 23:37 O Jerusalem, Jerusalem, thou that killest the prophets, and stonest them which are sent unto thee, how often would I have gathered thy children together, even as a hen gathereth her chickens under her wings, and ye would not!
>
> Luke 13:34 O Jerusalem, Jerusalem, which killest the prophets, and stonest them that are sent unto thee; how often would I have gathered thy children together, as a hen doth gather her brood under her wings, and ye would not!
>
> 1 Timothy 2:3–6 For this is good and acceptable in the sight of God our Saviour; Who will have all men to be saved, and to come unto the knowledge of the truth. For there is one God, and one mediator between God and men, the man Christ Jesus; Who gave himself a ransom for all, to be testified in due time.
>
> John 3:14–19 And as Moses lifted up the serpent in the wilderness, even so must the Son of man be lifted up: That whosoever believeth in him should not perish, but have eternal life. For God so loved the world, that he gave his only begotten Son, that whosoever believeth in him should not perish, but have everlasting life. For God sent not his Son into the world to condemn the world; but that the world through him might be saved. He that believeth on him is not condemned: but he that believeth not is condemned already, because he hath not believed in the name of the only begotten Son of God. And this

> is the condemnation, that light is come into the world, and men loved darkness rather than light, because their deeds were evil.
>
> John 3:36 He that believeth on the Son hath everlasting life: and he that believeth not the Son shall not see life; but the wrath of God abideth on him.

The matter of the extent of the atonement is vital to Christianity. "For whom did Christ die?" is not an idle question. The discovery of the true answer to that question establishes whether any given individual has an opportunity to be saved.

Did the LORD Jesus die for "the whole world" to pay the price of the "sin of the world"? (Yes! 1 John 2:2, John 1:29)

Is He "the Saviour of the world?" (Yes! John 4:42, 1 John 4:14)

Did the LORD Jesus shed His blood only for the particular, the chosen, the elect, as Calvinism asserts? (*No such verse is found!*)

The question is whether the Gospel is a ***salvation invitation*** that is extended to all or an ***emancipation proclamation*** that is restricted to only those who are the numbered among the elect. The answer is essential to the understanding of the Gospel[90] itself as well as understanding the "ministry of reconciliation" (2 Corinthians 5:18) that is assigned to the believer.

---

[90]Romans 1:16 For I am not ashamed of the gospel of Christ: for it is the power of God unto salvation to every one that believeth; to the Jew first, and also to the Greek.
Hebrews 4:2 For unto us was the gospel preached, as well as unto them: but the word preached did not profit them, not being mixed with faith in them that heard *it*.
Mark 16:15 And he said unto them, Go ye into all the world, and preach the gospel to every creature.

If the atonement provided by the blood of the LORD Jesus is limited in that it is sufficient only for those who are the elect, then the preaching of the Gospel into all the world to every creature (Mark 16:15) is, in fact, a formality of proclamation and not a legitimate invitation to whosoever will to come and take of the water of life freely (Revelation 22:17). Such an answer of limitation would make the following passages and many others require a special definition for the common words as *whole* and *world*, and that is precisely what the Calvinist does. He carefully defines both words as meaning *the elect* in the following passages.

> 1 John 2:2 And he [the LORD Jesus Christ] is the propitiation for our sins: and not for ours only, but also for the sins of the whole world.
>
> 1 John 4:14 And we have seen and do testify that the Father sent the Son *to be* the Saviour of the world.
>
> John 1:29 The next day John seeth Jesus coming unto him, and saith, Behold the Lamb of God, which taketh away the sin of the world.
>
> John 4:42 And said unto the woman, Now we believe, not because of thy saying: for we have heard him ourselves, and know that this is indeed the Christ, the Saviour of the world.
>
> 2 Corinthians 5:18–21 And all things are of God, who hath reconciled us to himself by Jesus Christ, and hath given to us the ministry of reconciliation; 19 To wit, that God was in Christ, reconciling the world unto himself, not imputing their trespasses unto them; and hath committed unto us the word of reconciliation. 20 Now then we are ambassadors for Christ, as though God did beseech you by us: we pray you in Christ's stead, be ye reconciled to God. 21 For he hath made him to be sin for us,

> who knew no sin; that we might be made the righteousness of God in him.

If the words *whole* and *world* mean in Scripture what they commonly mean in normal conversation and are to be understood as they are defined in the dictionary, then the atonement secured by the LORD Jesus Christ was an unlimited atonement and the invitation to receive salvation is extended to all men throughout the world. The only way to circumvent this conclusion is to introduce special definitions for those words exactly as the Calvinists do.

The same difficulty for the Calvinist presents itself again in Romans, chapter 3, and it is answered in the same fashion. The response of the Calvinist to the wording "unto all and upon all" is to provide a special definition for the word *all* in verse 22 that differs from the definition of the word all in verse 23. The two *alls* in verse 22, to the Calvinist, means only *the elect.*

The proponent of Calvinism must either change the word *all* as it is used in Scripture or alter the meaning of that word in order to prove that the atonement is limited only to the elect. When the word is allowed to be understood with its commonly accepted meaning, *and* when that text is read as it stands in the text, this passage confirms that the atonement is "unto all" and is "upon all them that believe." Any other meaning requires a special definition for the word all.

Moreover, the passage declares that God justifies those that believe.

> Romans 3:22–26 Even the righteousness of God which is by faith of Jesus Christ unto all and upon all them that believe: for there is no difference: For all have sinned, and come short of the glory of God; Being justified freely by his grace through the redemption that is in Christ Jesus: Whom God hath set forth to be a propitiation through faith in his blood, to

> declare his righteousness for the remission of sins that are past, through the forbearance of God; To declare, I say, at this time his righteousness: that he might be just, and the justifier of him which believeth in Jesus.

The difference between heaven and hell for the individual is whether that individual believes the Gospel or does not believe the Gospel. Clearly, if these verses mean as they read, then the eternal destiny is the result of the choice made by the individual.

CHAPTER 10

LIMITED ATONEMENT

As to Limited Atonement, Seaton writes, "The third Point not only brings us to the central Point of the Five, but also to the central fact of the gospel, that is, the purpose of Christ's death on the Cross. This is not accidental. ... Thus, we have the teaching of the Bible on man set under the general heading of Total Depravity, or Total Inability. Secondly, as some men and women *are* undoubtedly saved, then it must have been God Himself who had saved them in contra-distinction *[sic]* to the rest of mankind."[91]

It is only reasonable to ask at this juncture how Seaton is able to assume that "some men and women *are* undoubtedly saved," when he has not observed their entrance into Heaven as the evidence of their final perseverance?

Setting his assumption and my question aside, we return to his assertion that "it must have been God Himself who had saved them in contra-distinc-

---

[91]Seaton, *The Five Points of Calvinism*, 14.

tion *[sic]* to the rest of mankind." This is not a sustainable statement unless the assertions of Total Inability and Unconditional Election are accepted. The assertion itself assumes *facts not in evidence* and should be dismissed from consideration.

He presents his argument in this fashion.[92]

> The question now arises: whose punishment did He bear, and whose salvation He procure? There are three avenues along which we can travel with regard to this:
>
> Christ died to save all men without distinction.
>
> Christ died to save no one in particular.
>
> Christ died to save a certain number.

The argument presents as an absolute that only three possible solutions exist to the two questions and that both questions must be resolved by the *same* answer and *only* by that answer. The questions are (1) W*hose* punishment did He bear? and (2) W*hose* salvation did He procure?

While three avenues are offered as the only possible alternatives to consider as an answer to his two questions, the issue must be addressed as to the existent possibility for any additional answers. Could the two questions individually have different answers? Could the two questions together have an answer that is not included in his proposed *three avenues*? Could he have missed even one avenue? If any of these possibilities are true, then his entire argument falls.

Could it be that the LORD Jesus bore punishment for some individuals that do not receive salvation, because they do not believe on Him? If so, that possibility obviously changes the potential for an-

[92]Seaton, *The Five Points of Calvinism*, 15.

other answer and does so by providing at least one more alternative.

Additional to the three avenues that he offered, I submit that one more possibility surely exists. That fourth possibility would be:

> Christ died to save all that believe on Him.

Calvinists stop one statement of possibility too soon. Instead of only three options, there is indeed the fourth way.

> Christ died to save *all men* without distinction.
>
> Christ died to save *no one in particular.*
>
> Christ died to save *a certain number.*
>
> Christ died to save all that believe on Him.

Does this fourth suggested avenue have any basis in Scripture? If so, the first three proposals are to be rejected as errors and it would be deliberately misleading to imply that the possibility that the proposed options submitted by Calvinism exhaust the potential. Based on the following verses, it is scripturally proper to say that Christ died to save all that believe on Him.

> John 1:12 But as many as received him, to them gave he power to become the sons of God, *even* to them that believe on his name:
>
> John 3:1–21, 36 There was a man of the Pharisees, named Nicodemus, a ruler of the Jews: The same came to Jesus by night, and said unto him, Rabbi, we know that thou art a teacher come from God: for no man can do these miracles that thou doest, except God be with him. Jesus answered and said unto him, Verily, verily, I say unto thee, Except a man be born again, he cannot see the kingdom of God. Nicodemus saith unto him, How can a man be born when he is old? can he enter the second time into his mother's womb,

and be born? Jesus answered, Verily, verily, I say unto thee, Except a man be born of water and *of* the Spirit, he cannot enter into the kingdom of God. That which is born of the flesh is flesh; and that which is born of the Spirit is spirit. Marvel not that I said unto thee, Ye must be born again. The wind bloweth where it listeth, and thou hearest the sound thereof, but canst not tell whence it cometh, and whither it goeth: so is every one that is born of the Spirit. Nicodemus answered and said unto him, How can these things be? Jesus answered and said unto him, Art thou a master of Israel, and knowest not these things? Verily, verily, I say unto thee, We speak that we do know, and testify that we have seen; and ye receive not our witness. If I have told you earthly things, and ye believe not, how shall ye believe, if I tell you *of* heavenly things? And no man hath ascended up to heaven, but he that came down from heaven, *even* the Son of man which is in heaven. And as Moses lifted up the serpent in the wilderness, even so must the Son of man be lifted up: That whosoever believeth in him should not perish, but have eternal life. For God so loved the world, that he gave his only begotten Son, that whosoever believeth in him should not perish, but have everlasting life. For God sent not his Son into the world to condemn the world; but that the world through him might be saved. He that believeth on him is not condemned: but he that believeth not is condemned already, because he hath not believed in the name of the only begotten Son of God. And this is the condemnation, that light is come into the world, and men loved darkness rather than light, because their deeds were evil. For every one that doeth evil hateth the light, neither cometh to the light, lest his deeds should be reproved. But he that doeth truth cometh to the light, that his deeds may be made manifest, that they are wrought in God. … He that believeth on the Son hath everlasting life: and he that believeth not the Son shall not see life; but the wrath of God abideth on him.

John 5:24 Verily, verily, I say unto you, He that heareth my word, and believeth on him that sent me, hath everlasting life, and shall not come into condemnation; but is passed from death unto life.

John 6:35 And Jesus said unto them, I am the bread of life: he that cometh to me shall never hunger; and he that believeth on me shall never thirst.

John 6:40 And this is the will of him that sent me, that every one which seeth the Son, and believeth on him, may have everlasting life: and I will raise him up at the last day.

John 6:47 Verily, verily, I say unto you, He that believeth on me hath everlasting life.

John 11:25–26 Jesus said unto her, I am the resurrection, and the life: he that believeth in me, though he were dead, yet shall he live: And whosoever liveth and believeth in me shall never die. Believest thou this?

John 12:46 I am come a light into the world, that whosoever believeth on me should not abide in darkness.

Acts 10:43 To him give all the prophets witness, that through his name whosoever believeth in him shall receive remission of sins.

Acts 13:39 And by him all that believe are justified from all things, from which ye could not be justified by the law of Moses.

Romans 1:16 For I am not ashamed of the gospel of Christ: for it is the power of God

> unto salvation to every one that believeth; to the Jew first, and also to the Greek.
>
> Romans 3:26 To declare, *I say*, at this time his righteousness: that he might be just, and the justifier of him which believeth in Jesus.
>
> Romans 4:5 But to him that worketh not, but believeth on him that justifieth the ungodly, his faith is counted for righteousness.
>
> Romans 4:24 But for us also, to whom it shall be imputed, if we believe on him that raised up Jesus our Lord from the dead;
>
> Romans 10:4 For Christ *is* the end of the law for righteousness to every one that believeth.
>
> Romans 10:9 That if thou shalt confess with thy mouth the Lord Jesus, and shalt believe in thine heart that God hath raised him from the dead, thou shalt be saved.
>
> Philippians 1:29 For unto you it is given in the behalf of Christ, not only to believe on him, but also to suffer for his sake;
>
> Hebrews 11:6 But without faith *it is* impossible to please *him*: for he that cometh to God must believe that he is, and *that* he is a rewarder of them that diligently seek him.
>
> 1 John 5:10 He that believeth on the Son of God hath the witness in himself: he that believeth not God hath made him a liar; because he believeth not the record that God gave of his Son.

However, Calvinism presents the third view as the only possible answer.

> The third view is that which is held by the Calvinist and is generally called limited atonement, or particular redemption. Christ died to save a *particular* number of sinners; that is, those 'chosen in him be-

> fore the foundation of the world' ... This last view, we claim, does justice to the *purpose* of Christ's coming to this earth to die on the Cross. [93]

In his following comments, Seaton introduces the intention of God as the justification for the doctrine of a Limited Atonement.

> The over-riding *[sic]* question must always be the Divine intention; did God *intend* to save all men, or did He not? If He did not intend to save all men without exception but only the elect, then, the work of Christ on the Cross is a glorious success, and we right well believe: "*All* that the Father *giveth* me, *shall* come to me ...' (*John* 6:37) If, on the other hand, it was God's intention to save the entire world, then the atonement of Christ has been a great failure, for vast numbers of mankind have not been saved. [94]

By the reasoning of Calvinism, those "vast numbers of mankind have not been saved" precisely because the merciful God of all grace has *intentionally willed them into their condition.* If Calvinism is true, then vast numbers die without atonement because there was no atonement provided for them; they never had an opportunity to be saved, *because they were born to spend eternity in the Lake of Fire.* The very concept of attributing such maliciousness to the holy God of Heaven is abhorrent to all reason and logic. I believe that it slanders God to present Him as creating some souls solely for the sole purpose of having them spend eternity in the Lake of Fire.

That representation is contrary to the plain wording of the Scriptures. Should the reader wonder how the Calvinist overlooks the clarity of 2 Peter 3:9,

---

[93]Seaton, *The Five Points of Calvinism*, 16.
[94]Seaton, *The Five Points of Calvinism*, 17.

the answer is simple to discover. While the wording of the verse is uncomplicated and unambiguous, the Calvinist does not read the verse as it is written. The Scripture reads:

> The Lord is not slack concerning his promise, as some men count slackness; but is longsuffering to us-ward, not willing that any should perish, but that all should come to repentance.

The Calvinist does not read those words with the same meanings that the non-Calvinist does. The key words of the verse, *us*, *any*, and *all*, are understood by the Calvinist to have the meaning of the Calvinist dictionary, and the verse is thereby read entirely differently when *any* and *all* are code words.

One of my favorite commentaries is the multi-volume work of Matthew Poole. He is concise and succinct in his comments. I rarely read his writings without receiving a blessing and gaining insight. However, his Calvinistic propensity for redefining the words of Scripture deceives him on this verse.

> But is long-suffering *[sic]* to us-ward; to us believers, or us elect.
>
> Not willing that any should perish; any that he hath ordained to life, though not yet called.
>
> But that all should come to repentance; all whom he hath elected; he would have the whole number of them filled up, and defers the day of judgment till it be so: or this may be meant not of God's secret and effectual will, but of his revealed will, whereby he calls all to repentance promiscuously that hear the gospel preached, hath made it their duty, approves of it, hath prescribed it as the way of salvation, commanded them to seek salvation in that

> way, and is ready to receive and save them upon their repenting: see 1Ti 2:4.[95]

As rewritten with these definitions, the verse would read, with the *proper additions* indicated by bold type.

> The Lord is not slack concerning his promise, as some men count slackness; but is longsuffering to **us elect**, not willing that **any that he hath ordained to life, though not yet called** should perish, but that **all whom he hath elected; he would have the whole number of them filled up, and defers the day of judgment till it be so:** should come to repentance **or this may be meant not of God's secret and effectual will, but of his revealed will, whereby he calls all to repentance promiscuously that hear the gospel preached, hath made it their duty, approves of it, hath prescribed it as the way of salvation, commanded them to seek salvation in that way, and is ready to receive and save them upon their repenting** ***(even though only the elect are regenerated so they can have the faith to believe what has been done for them).***

That paragraph is neither Scripture nor commentary; it is a full revision Scripture based upon a strange dynamic equivalency translation of a text that is not in existence anywhere except in the vocabulary of the Calvinist. The result is a complete misrepresentation of the text.

What Poole typically does so admirably so often in his commentary, he cannot bring himself to permit here, because of the presuppositions of his Calvinism. Poole is simply unable to let the words stand as they were written; he must redefine the

---

[95]Matthew Poole, *Commentary on the Whole Bible,* SwordSearcher Bible Program.

words so that they are understood with the special definitions that are taken from the Calvinist lexicon. I thank Poole for all the helpful things that he wrote, but I charge him with adding to the words of the word of God in his commentary on 2 Peter 3:9.

When the words of this text are granted the freedom to speak for themselves, without superimposing the Calvinistic usurpation of special interpretation, the words destroy the entire system of Calvinism at one blow.

> The Lord is not slack concerning his promise, as some men count slackness; but is longsuffering to us-ward, not willing that any should perish, but that all should come to repentance.

Dwight Moody held evangelistic campaigns in London in 1875 and 1883–84. During those meetings, he conducted *Gospel Dialogues* with Marcus Rainsford, Pastor of St. John's Church in Belgrave Square, London. These discussions were platform conversations between Moody and Rainsford that occurred in the presence of those who had responded to the invitation at the close of the service.[96] The purpose was to raise questions that *inquirers* would have and to provide a Biblical response to that question. In a sense, this was an attempt to do personal work with a large group. A series of these exchanges is found in the records of those *Gospel Dialogues* is relevant to our discussion.

> Mr. Moody—Can all these friends here believe the promises?
>
> Mr. Rainsford—The promises are true, whether we believe them or not. We do not make them true by believing them. God could not charge me with being an unbeliever, or condemn me for unbelief, if the

[96]Marcus Rainsford, *Our Lord Prays For His Own,* Kregel Classics, Grand Rapids, MI, 1985, 24–25.

promises were not true for me. I could in that case turn round and say: "Great God, why did you expect me to believe a promise that was not true for me?" And yet the Scriptures set forth unbelief as the greatest sin I can continue to commit. ... .[97]

Mr. Moody—Some may say that faith is the gift of God: and that they must wait till God imparts it to them.

Mr. Rainsford—"Faith cometh by hearing." The word of God is the medium through which faith comes to us. God has given us Christ; and He has given us His Spirit, and His Word: what need is there to wait? God will give faith to the man who reads His Word and seeks for His Spirit.

Mr. Moody—What, then, should they wait for?

Mr. Rainsford—I do not know of anything they have to wait for. God says: "Come now; Believe *[sic]* now." No, no; there is nothing to wait for. He has given us all He has to give: and the sooner we take it the better.

Mr. Moody—Perhaps some of them think they have too many sins to allow their coming.

Mr. Rainsford—The Lord Jesus has put away sin by the sacrifice of Himself. "As far as the east is from the west, so far hath He removed our transgressions from us." Why do we not believe him? He says He has "made an end of sins." Why do we not believe Him? Is He a liar?

Mr. Moody—Is unbelief a sin?

Mr. Rainsford—It is the root of all sin.

---

[97]Rainsford, *Our Lord Prays For His Own*, 456.

Mr. Moody—Has a man the power to believe these things, if he will?

Mr. Rainsford—When God gives a command, it means that we are able by His grace to do it.

Mr. Moody—What do you mean by "coming" to Christ?

Mr. Rainsford—Believing in Him. If I were to prepare a great feast in this hall tomorrow *[sic]* night, and say that any man that comes to it would have a grand feast and a five-pound note besides, there would not be any question as to what "coming" meant. God has prepared a great feast. He has sent His messengers to invite all to come; and there is nothing to pay.

Mr. Moody—What is the first step.

Mr. Rainsford—To believe.

Mr. Moody—Believe what?

Mr. Rainsford—God's invitation; God's promise; God's provision. Let us believe the faithfulness of Him who calls us. Does God intend to mock us, and make game of us? If He did so to one man, it would hush all the harps in heaven ... [98]

Mr. Moody—I understand, then, that if a man rejects Christ to-night, *[sic]* he passes judgment on himself as unworthy of eternal life?

Mr. Rainsford—He is judging himself unworthy, while God does not so consider him. God says you are welcome to eternal life.

Mr. Moody—If any one *[sic]* here wants to please God to-night, *[sic]* how can he do it?

---

[98]Rainsford, *Our Lord Prays For His Own*, 462–463.

Mr. Rainsford—God delights in mercy. Come to God and claim His mercy in Christ; and you will delight His heart.

Mr. Moody—Suppose a man say he is not "elected?"

Mr. Rainsford—Do you remember the story of the woman of Canaan? Poor soul; she had come a long journey. She asked the Lord to have mercy on her afflicted child. He wanted to try her faith, and He said: "I am not sent but to the lost sheep of the house of Israel." That looked as if He Himself told her that she was not one of the elect. But she came and worshipped Him, saying, "Lord, help me!" and He helped her there and then. No; there is no election separating between the sinner and Christ.

Mr. Moody—Say that again.

Mr. Rainsford—THERE IS NO ELECTION SEPARATING BETWEEN THE SINNER AND CHRIST. [Emphasis is in the original.]

Mr. Moody—What is there between the sinner and Christ?

Mr. Rainsford—Mercy!! Mercy!!

Mr. Moody—That brings me near to Christ.

Mr. Rainsford—So near that we cannot be nearer. But we must claim it. In John we get God's teaching about election. "This is the Father's will which hath sent Me, that of all which He hath given Me I should lose *nothing*; but should raise it up again at the last day." He will do his work, you may depend upon it. Then in the next verse we read: "And this is the will of Him that sent Me, that *every one* which seeth the Son, and *believeth* on Him, may have everlasting life: and I will raise him up at the last day." That is the part I am to take:

> and when I have done so I shall know the Father's will concerning me.[99]

Let the words of the word of God stand as they are found. We need no form of Gnostic special knowledge to decipher the code hidden in the words. The LORD Jesus speaks so plainly that "the common people heard him gladly" (Mark 12:37.) It is marvelous that any would dare to suggest the need for an interpreter to stand between humanity and the One Who is the one Mediator between God and men, the Man, Christ Jesus (1 Timothy 2:5, Hebrews 8:6, 9:15, 12:24).

I believe that the Calvinist is wrong to alter the words of the word of God by assigning unique definitions to particular words that require out of the ordinary instruction from a special dictionary or lexicon so that the words of the word of God may be understood by humanity. The Bible is not written in a secretive code.

With the Psalmist, we may say:

> Psalm 119:103 How sweet are thy words unto my taste! *yea, sweeter* than honey to my mouth!

With the prophet Jeremiah, any member of humanity may say:

> Jeremiah 15:16 Thy words were found, and I did eat them; and thy word was unto me the joy and rejoicing of mine heart:

Most wonderfully, every reader who will receive the message of the words and believe on the LORD Jesus Christ for salvation may claim the last phrase of the verse as their very own:

> ... for I am called by thy name, O LORD God of hosts.

---

[99]Rainsford, *Our Lord Prays For His Own*, 473–474.

Simply let any man read the words of the LORD Jesus and those words will find lodging in the open, sincere heart.

> Luke 8:11–18 Now the parable is this: The seed is the word of God. Those by the way side are they that hear; then cometh the devil, and taketh away the word out of their hearts, lest they should believe and be saved. They on the rock *are they*, which, when they hear, receive the word with joy; and these have no root, which for a while believe, and in time of temptation fall away. And that which fell among thorns are they, which, when they have heard, go forth, and are choked with cares and riches and pleasures of *this* life, and bring no fruit to perfection. But that on the good ground are they, which in an honest and good heart, having heard the word, keep *it*, and bring forth fruit with patience. No man, when he hath lighted a candle, covereth it with a vessel, or putteth *it* under a bed; but setteth *it* on a candlestick, that they which enter in may see the light. For nothing is secret, that shall not be made manifest; neither *any thing* hid, that shall not be known and come abroad. Take heed therefore how ye hear: for whosoever hath, to him shall be given; and whosoever hath not, from him shall be taken even that which he seemeth to have.

The words of the LORD Jesus are easily understood. No special dictionary is required to comprehend what He intended.

> John 12:44–50 Jesus cried and said, He that believeth on me, believeth not on me, but on him that sent me. And he that seeth me seeth him that sent me. I am come a light into the world, that whosoever believeth on me should not abide in darkness. And if any man hear my words, and believe not, I judge him not: for I

> came not to judge the world, but to save the world. He that rejecteth me, and receiveth not my words, hath one that judgeth him: the word that I have spoken, the same shall judge him in the last day. For I have not spoken of myself; but the Father which sent me, he gave me a commandment, what I should say, and what I should speak. And I know that his commandment is life everlasting: whatsoever I speak therefore, even as the Father said unto me, so I speak.
>
> John 14:10 Believest thou not that I am in the Father, and the Father in me? the words that I speak unto you I speak not of myself: but the Father that dwelleth in me, he doeth the works.
>
> Matthew 24:35, Mark 13:31, Luke 21:33 Heaven and earth shall pass away, but my words shall not pass away.
>
> John 6:63 It is the spirit that quickeneth; the flesh profiteth nothing: the words that I speak unto you, *they* are spirit, and *they* are life.

Even the most familiar and, perhaps, the simplest words spoken by the LORD Jesus during His earthly sojourn are in need of explanation according to the Calvinist. Few Biblical scholars have ever acquired the level of knowledge that Dr. John Gill possessed or that had his ability to place that knowledge into words. His *Exposition of the Old and New Testaments* contains over ten million words and is comprehensive in touching nearly every word of each verse of Scripture. His use of the original languages and his familiarity with the writings of the Rabbis and preachers that preceded him will likely never again be equaled.

Even so, as you read the following excerpt from that Commentary, take notice of the necessity that his devotion to Calvinism compels Gill to reword

John 3:16 to cause it to conform to what it ought to say, instead of what it does say.

> For God so loved the world, The Persic *[sic]* version reads "men": but not every man in the world is here meant, or all the individuals of human nature; for all are not the objects of God's special love, which is here designed, as appears from the instance and evidence of it, the gift of his Son: nor is Christ God's gift to every one; *[sic]* for to whomsoever he gives his Son, he gives all things freely with him; which is not the case of every man. Nor is human nature here intended, in opposition to, and distinction from, the angelic nature; for though God has showed a regard to fallen men, and not to fallen angels, and has provided a Saviour for the one, and not for the other; and Christ has assumed the nature of men, and not angels; yet not for the sake of all men, but the spiritual seed of Abraham; and besides, it will not be easily proved, that human nature is ever called the world: nor is the whole body of the chosen ones, as consisting of Jews and Gentiles, here designed; for though these are called the world, Joh 6:33; and are the objects of God's special love, and to them Christ is given, and they are brought to believe in him, and shall never perish, but shall be saved with an everlasting salvation; yet rather the Gentiles particularly, and God's elect among them, are meant; who are often called "the world," and "the whole world," and "the nations of the world," as distinct from the Jews; see Ro 11:12, compared with Mt 6:32.

The Calvinism of Gill forces him to establish that the word "world" must be *interpreted* to mean exclusively "the elect" even though he has to go through the Persic version to change the word *world* to *men* and then define *men* as "*the elect.*"

The Calvinist believes that God loves the elect, but that God does not love the world. In Calvinism, Christ is indeed the gift of God for *the world*, but this is only true, because the word "world" is understood *by the Calvinist* to mean "the elect of the world." Therefore, according to Calvinism, it is a Scriptural error to tell any individual that God loves him.

The testimony of Pastor J. C. Stevens as to his own experience with Calvinism and this specific issue of the love of God for the world of lost men is quite stunning. Calvinism is cold logic; but when the words of Calvinism are applied to warm flesh and blood, the heat of the impact of those words may be keenly felt.

> As a young Christian, I was drawn in, for a short while, to many of the doctrines of Calvinism. It seemed perfectly reasonable to me that Christ would not have wasted any of His precious blood; and yet it did not (at that time) dawn on me that "Limited Atonement" meant a redemption limited to only a few. But what really stopped me cold was when one of these good men rebuked me for telling a lost man that God loved him and sent His Son to die for him. I was expressly told that it was "unscriptural to have a burden for the lost." Calvinist theology says that God does NOT love sinners, in spite of what Romans 5:8 says. I knew in my heart that I was not only a sinner, but an exceeding wicked sinner, and that it was the fact that, in spite of this, God loved me enough to sacrifice His own (and only begotten) Son for my redemption. My wickedness brought me to deep conviction (through the work of the Holy Spirit), but it was His love that drew me to Christ. I think I can honestly say that, at one time I was a Calvinist. But

> it was God's (real) sovereign grace that opened my eyes.[100] [Emphasis and parentheses are in the original.]

While this may seem to be an isolated incident, it is fully in accord with the doctrines of the TULIP. According to the Calvinist, *who is true to his doctrine*, God does not love the world. As a matter of record, the God described by John Calvin takes "pleasure" at the death and eternal destruction of the sinner.

> We say, then, that Scripture clearly proves this much, that God by his eternal and immutable counsel determined once for all those whom it was his **pleasure** one day to admit to salvation, and those whom, on the other hand, **it was his pleasure to doom to destruction**. We maintain that this counsel, as regards the elect, is founded on his free mercy, without any respect to human worth, while those whom he dooms to destruction are excluded from access to life by a just and blameless, but at the same time incomprehensible judgment.[101] [Emphasis is added.]

Yet, the Calvinist who adorningly quotes Calvin will not be embarrassed to identify the TULIP as "the doctrines of GRACE." He is able to do this because of the definition that the Calvinist gives to the word *grace*.

Dr. John MacArthur defines *grace* thusly, "Grace is God's sovereign initiative to sinners ... Grace is the power of God to fulfill our New Covenant duties."[102]

---

[100]Pastor J. C. Stevens, Grace Baptist Tabernacle, Manchester, KY, personal correspondence.

[101]John Calvin, *Institutes of the Christian Religion,* Book 3, chapter 21, section 7.

[102]http://www.gty.org/Resources/Articles/A317

Grace to the Calvinist is that power or ability that God imposes on certain individuals. That distribution of grace then enables the recipient to please God.

The text of the Authorized Version contains the English word *grace* a total of 159 times.[103] The Old Testament has the word *grace* 37 times, which is translated from the Hebrew word חֵן. Found a total of 67 times, חֵן is also translated in the other passages as *favour, gracious, well-favored,* and even *precious* and *pleasant;* however, חֵן is never translated as or used in the sense of *power* or *ability.*

In the Greek text translated into the English of the Authorized Version, the word *grace* is translated from the Greek word **χαρις.** The translators found that other words were needed to bring the word of God into English. They found places where the word **χαρις** needed to be translated as *favour, gracious, thank, thanks, thankworthy, benefit, joy,* even *liberality;* however, **χαρις** was never translated as *power* or *ability.*

Moreover, the words *power* or *ability* will not make sense as a synonym for grace in any verse of Scripture, whether that verse is in the Old Testament or in the New Testament.

The word grace is used in the Bible in the sense of "unmerited favor freely bestowed." Three key Bible words are justice, mercy, and grace. Receiving what we deserve is justice. Not receiving what we do deserve is mercy. Receiving what we do not deserve is grace.

Grace in reference to the actions of God in our salvation is *favor, unmerited favor.*

---

[103]The searches to generate the numbers were made using *Strong's* from the Bible program SwordSearcher.

CHAPTER 11

IRRESISTIBLE GRACE

> This fourth point of the Calvinistic system of belief is, once again, the logical outcome of all that has gone before it. If men are unable to save themselves on account of their fallen nature, and if God has purposed to save them, and Christ has accomplished their salvation, *then* it logically follows that God must also provide the means for calling them into the benefits of that salvation which He has procured for them.[104]

Notice in this paragraph that the dependency is again upon the *if-then* argument. All of Calvinism is built upon that foundation of *if-then.* As shown before, this is an argument from logic, but it is not necessarily the use of sound logic. Read again the material on the types of fallacies that are used in pseudo-logical arguments. While this list does not present a list of every possible fallacious proposition, it does list those that are easily observed in the arguments propounded by the Calvinist.

---

[104]Seaton, *The Five Points of Calvinism,* 17.

The next paragraph reveals that the doctrine of Irresistible Grace rises from the necessity of the logic of Calvinism and not from the study of the Scriptures. Observe the phrase: "there must be such a doctrine as the doctrine of irresistible grace."

> We believe that not only *can* men and women resist God's gospel, but they do, and *must* by their very natures, resist it. Therefore, there must be such a doctrine as the doctrine of irresistible grace. In other word, some influence greater than our natures—greater than our resistance—must be brought to bear upon our souls, or else we are doomed, for 'the natural man receiveth not the things of the Spirit of God.'[105]

In a legal proceeding, this doctrinal justification would be challenged as *arguing from facts not in evidence*. Total Inability, as the Calvinist defines it, is not provable from Scripture. Unconditional Election, which depends upon Total Inability for its existence, is therefore not proven. The consequence is that there is no need for the doctrine of Irresistible Grace to be manufactured. The foundation that is essential for the support of Irresistible Grace does not exist. However, Calvinism requires the doctrine of Irresistible Grace.

Seaton argues:

> There are three great forces at work in the matter of a man's salvation:
>
> Man's will
>
> The Devil's will
>
> God's will
>
> Which will be the victor? If God's will is not victorious in the matter of our salvation, then, the Devil's must be, for the devil is stronger that we are." ... He con-

---

[105]Seaton, *The Five Points of Calvinism,* 19.

> quers Satan, and He conquers puny man as well, to the praise of His irresistible grace.[106]

This proposal would seem to raise more questions than it would settle. Are there actually "three great forces at work" and is there a genuine question as to "[w]hich will be the victor"?

The defense of the doctrine of Calvinism is filled with these paradoxes. If Calvinism were to be true, then there could be only **one force** "at work in the matter of a man's salvation."

Should Calvinism be true, the strength that Satan has or the resistance that man could muster would be immaterial, because the "the matter of a man's salvation" was settled before the foundation of the world. The introduction of three wills in *the matter* of salvation is puzzling. How does the issue of Satan's will support the Calvinism's concept of the sovereignty of God and, in particular, the doctrine of Irresistible Grace? The first two petals of the TULIP—Total Inability and Unconditional Election—allow the will of a man no relationship to or participation in *the matter* of his salvation.

If grace is irresistible, then there must be only one force—one will—at work in "the matter of a man's salvation." The will of man would not be involved. The will of Satan could not be involved. To imply any struggle by God for victory would seem to challenge, if not repudiate, the very essence of Calvinism. Such an argument is inconsistent, illogical, and incompatible with Calvinism; yet it is presented as essential to maintain the viability of the TULIP's Irresistible Grace. The paradox is clearly with the logic of Calvinism; it is certainly not within the revelation of Scripture.

---

[106]Seaton, *The Five Points of Calvinism*, 20.

Scripture records in his rebellion and fall, that Lucifer exercised his *will* to challenge God. The text that describes his fall, Isaiah 14:9–14, specifically uses the word *will* five times.

> Hell from beneath is moved for thee to meet thee at thy coming: it stirreth up the dead for thee, even all the chief ones of the earth; it hath raised up from their thrones all the kings of the nations. All they shall speak and say unto thee, Art thou also become weak as we? art thou become like unto us? Thy pomp is brought down to the grave, and the noise of thy viols: the worm is spread under thee, and the worms cover thee. How art thou fallen from heaven, O Lucifer, son of the morning! how art thou cut down to the ground, which didst weaken the nations! For thou hast said in thine heart, I **will** ascend into heaven, I **will** exalt my throne above the stars of God: I **will** sit also upon the mount of the congregation, in the sides of the north: I **will** ascend above the heights of the clouds; I **will** be like the most High. [Emphasis is added.]

Though it is explicitly revealed that it was through the exercise of his will that Lucifer rebelled, Job chapters one and two clearly show that the will of Lucifer, who is now named Satan, is not the counterpart of the will of God. Even as God has set the bounds of the sea so that the waters cannot pass (Job 38:11, Jeremiah 5:22), so Satan is held in check by limitations established by the GOD of Heaven. The record of Scripture is clear that those limitations on Satan restrict the extent of his actions, but they do not infringe on his freewill.

> 1:1 There was a man in the land of Uz, whose name was Job; and that man was perfect and upright, and one that feared God, and eschewed evil. And there were born unto him seven sons and three daughters. His substance also was seven

thousand sheep, and three thousand camels, and five hundred yoke of oxen, and five hundred she asses, and a very great household; so that this man was the greatest of all the men of the east. And his sons went and feasted in their houses, every one his day; and sent and called for their three sisters to eat and to drink with them. And it was so, when the days of their feasting were gone about, that Job sent and sanctified them, and rose up early in the morning, and offered burnt offerings according to the number of them all: for Job said, It may be that my sons have sinned, and cursed God in their hearts. Thus did Job continually. Now there was a day when the sons of God came to present themselves before the LORD, and Satan came also among them. And the LORD said unto Satan, Whence comest thou? Then Satan answered the LORD, and said, From going to and fro in the earth, and from walking up and down in it. And the LORD said unto Satan, Hast thou considered my servant Job, that there is none like him in the earth, a perfect and an upright man, one that feareth God, and escheweth evil? Then Satan answered the LORD, and said, Doth Job fear God for nought? Hast not thou made an hedge about him, and about his house, and about all that he hath on every side? thou hast blessed the work of his hands, and his substance is increased in the land. But put forth thine hand now, and touch all that he hath, and he will curse thee to thy face. And the LORD said unto Satan, Behold, all that he hath is in thy power; only upon himself put not forth thine hand. So Satan went forth from the presence of the LORD. And there was a day when his sons and his daughters were eating and drinking wine in their eldest brother's house: And there came a messenger unto Job, and said, The oxen were plowing, and the asses feeding beside them: And the Sabeans fell upon them, and took them away; yea, they have slain the servants with the edge of the sword; and I only am escaped alone to tell thee. While he was yet speaking, there came also another, and said, The fire of God is fallen from heaven, and hath burned up the sheep, and the servants, and consumed them; and I only am escaped alone to tell thee. While he was yet speaking, there came also another, and said, The Chaldeans made out three bands, and fell upon the camels, and have carried them away, yea, and slain the servants with the edge of the sword; and I only am escaped alone to tell thee. While he was yet speaking, there came also another, and said, Thy sons and thy daughters were eating and drinking wine in their eldest brother's house: And, behold, there came a great wind from the wilderness, and smote the four corners of the house, and it fell upon the young men, and they are dead; and I only am escaped alone to tell thee. Then Job arose, and rent his mantle, and shaved his head, and fell down upon the ground, and worshipped, And said, Naked came I out of my mother's womb, and naked shall I return thither: the LORD gave, and the LORD hath taken away; blessed be the name of the LORD. In all this Job sinned not, nor charged God foolishly.

2:1 Again there was a day when the sons of God came to present themselves before the LORD, and Satan came also among them to present himself before the LORD. And the LORD said unto Satan, From whence comest thou? And Satan answered the LORD, and said, From going to and fro in the earth, and from walking up and down in it. And the LORD said unto Satan, Hast thou considered my servant Job, that there is none like him in the earth, a perfect and an upright man, one

> that feareth God, and escheweth evil? and still he holdeth fast his integrity, although thou movedst me against him, to destroy him without cause. And Satan answered the LORD, and said, Skin for skin, yea, all that a man hath will he give for his life. But put forth thine hand now, and touch his bone and his flesh, and he will curse thee to thy face. And the LORD said unto Satan, Behold, he is in thine hand; but save his life. So went Satan forth from the presence of the LORD, and smote Job with sore boils from the sole of his foot unto his crown. And he took him a potsherd to scrape himself withal; and he sat down among the ashes. Then said his wife unto him, Dost thou still retain thine integrity? curse God, and die. But he said unto her, Thou speakest as one of the foolish women speaketh. What? shall we receive good at the hand of God, and shall we not receive evil? In all this did not Job sin with his lips.

This entire episode would be meaningless if Job could only respond to the onslaught of Satan as God permitted him to respond. However, that is precisely what is required when Calvinism is applied to these events. Under the philosophy of Calvinism, God designed and decreed the actions of Satan and those of Job before the world began. Were this to be true, the story of Job would be reduced to a tragedy where the actors were following an inviolable script.

Job must have the capability of *trusting* or of *not trusting* in the LORD; otherwise, the drama would have no purpose. Denying Job that exercise of his freewill would cause God to be guilty of willing the slaughter of the sons of Job along with their families and the destruction of the wealth and the heath of Job exclusively for the sadistic pleasure of Satan. That possibility is incomprehensible.

This does not equate to the denial or the removal of spiritual warfare. Satan is surely the raging roaring lion seeking whom he may devour (1 Peter 5:8), because he understands that his time is limited (Revelation 12:12). Satan hinders, deceives, and sifts the believers and strives for an advantage over all men even to transforming himself into an angel of light. (1 Thessalonians 2:18, Revelation 12:9, Luke 22:31, 2 Corinthians 2:11, 11:14)

Scripture assuredly presents Satan as the fierce opposer of righteousness; by his name, he is the adversary. Satan has a title, the devil, which defines as *slanderer.* The LORD Jesus describes Satan as one who actively "taketh away the word that was sown" in the hearts of some of those that hear the Gospel, "lest they should believe and be saved." (Mark 4:15; Luke 8:12)

These efforts of Satan are devoted to snaring individuals in order to keep them from salvation. The apostle Paul writes to Timothy that he was to instruct those that oppose themselves so that by "repentance to the acknowledging of the truth ... they may recover themselves out of the snare of the devil, who are taken captive by him at his will."

> 2 Timothy 2:24–26 And the servant of the Lord must not strive; but be gentle unto all men, apt to teach, patient, In meekness instructing those that oppose themselves; if God peradventure will give them repentance to the acknowledging of the truth; And that they may recover themselves out of the snare of the devil, who are taken captive by him at his will.

I do not question that the assertion that the Devil does not want anyone to be saved; however, salvation is not a battle between the will of God and the will of Satan. There is a definite tinge of dualism in this argument that a battle between good and evil settles salvation.

Is salvation the result of a victory in which God "conquers Satan, and a victory in which "He conquers puny man as well, to the praise of His irresistible grace"? This strange Calvinist proposition would seem to grant to man the capability to resist God with such a power than God must gain the victory by conquest. Is it not astounding that Calvinism will grant that ability of will to man, but insists that man has no such corresponding ability to repent?

Completely contrary to this proposition, however, the apostle Paul clearly recorded by the inspiration of the Holy Ghost in 2 Timothy 2:14–16 that man *could repent and could acknowledge the truth.* Nevertheless, Calvinism, consistently following the writings of Augustine and John Calvin, requires man to be regenerated through Irresistible Grace so that he receives the gift of faith, which enables him to repent. Calvin insists that repentance is so conjoined with faith that it cannot be separated.

> Repentance, the inseparable attendant of faith ... Repentance follows faith, and is produced by it ... Repentance just a renewal of the divine image in us. Not completed in a moment, but extends to the last moment of life.[107]

> Repentance has its origin in the grace of God, as communicated to the elect, whom God is pleased to save from death ... That repentance not only always follows faith, but is produced by it, ought to be without controversy (see Calvin in Joann. 1:13). For since pardon and forgiveness are offered by the preaching of the Gospel, in order that the sinner, delivered from the tyranny of Satan, the yoke of sin, and the miserable bondage of iniquity, may pass into the kingdom of God, it is certain that no man can embrace the grace of the Gospel without retaking himself from the errors of his former life into the right path, and making it his whole study to practice repentance. Those who think that repent-

---

[107]Calvin, *Institutes*, Book Three, chapter 3, 477.

> ance precedes faith instead of flowing from, or being produced by it, as the fruit by the tree, have never understood its nature, and are moved to adopt that view on very insufficient grounds.[108]
>
> Still, when we attribute the origin of repentance to faith, we do not dream of some period of time in which faith is to give birth to it: we only wish to show that a man cannot seriously engage in repentance unless he knows that he is of God.[109]
>
> In one word, then, by repentance I understand regeneration, the only aim of which is to form in us anew the image of God, which was sullied, and all but effaced by the transgression of Adam.[110]

Calvin insisted that no man could have faith and have the ability to be repentant *until* that man is regenerated by the Holy Spirit. The TULIP, therefore, declares that each person who is the recipient of Unconditional Election will be regenerated, *at the appointed time*, through Irresistible Grace and then, *having received the gift of faith*, the elect will be enabled to repent.

Calvinism teaches that while the non-elect, as well as the elect before regeneration, may see himself as a sinner, that unregenerated person even though he is "stung with a sense of his sin, and overwhelmed with fear of the divine anger, remains in that state of perturbation, unable to escape from it." After regeneration, the elect "though grievously downcast in himself, yet looks up and sees in Christ the cure of his wound, the solace of his terror; the haven of rest from his misery."[111]

108Calvin, *Institutes*, Book Three, chapter 3, 478.
109Calvin, *Institutes*, Book Three, chapter 3, 479.
110Calvin, *Institutes*, Book Three, chapter 3, 484.
111Calvin, *Institutes*, Book Three, chapter 3, 480.

Calvin could write of souls that saw themselves under the condemnation of their sins and who realized, with fear and sorrow, that they had offended the Holy God of Heaven and then write, "Their repentance, therefore, was nothing better than a kind of threshold to hell, into which having entered even in the present life, they began to endure the punishment inflicted by the presence of an offended God."[112]

Calvin is describing repenting sinners in the hands of an implacable God who refuses propitiation. Their "fear and sorrow" at having offended God and "their repentance" produces nothing more than a "state of perturbation," which is a disturbed mind, from which they cannot escape and "was nothing better than a kind the threshold to hell." The God of John Calvin ignores the cry for forgiveness and deliverance.

Where within the Scriptures that John Calvin professed himself to teach, can one find such a God as Calvin describes? Only in 1 Kings 18 on Mount Carmel where Baal ignored the pleading and the bleeding of his worshippers does an alleged god appear that is pitiless, merciless, and totally deafened to the cries of his worshippers.

With teaching that is diametrically opposite to that of Calvin under the influence of Augustine, the apostle Paul, under the inspiration of the Holy Spirit, explains salvation as built upon "the foundation of repentance from dead works, and of faith toward God." (Hebrews 6:1)

Paul preached repentance as the responsibility of the individual and as being within the capability of everyone that heard him preach.

> Acts 17:30 And the times of this ignorance God winked at; but now commandeth all

---

[112]Calvin, *Institutes,* Book Three, chapter 3, 480.

men every where to repent: 31 Because he hath appointed a day, in the which he will judge the world in righteousness by *that* man whom he hath ordained; *whereof* he hath given assurance unto all *men*, in that he hath raised him from the dead.

Acts 20:18 And when they were come to him, he said unto them, Ye know, from the first day that I came into Asia, after what manner I have been with you at all seasons, 19 Serving the Lord with all humility of mind, and with many tears, and temptations, which befell me by the lying in wait of the Jews: 20 *And* how I kept back nothing that was profitable *unto you*, but have shewed you, and have taught you publickly, and from house to house, 21 Testifying both to the Jews, and also to the Greeks, repentance toward God, and faith toward our Lord Jesus Christ.

Acts 26:12 Whereupon as I went to Damascus with authority and commission from the chief priests, 13 At midday, O king, I saw in the way a light from heaven, above the brightness of the sun, shining round about me and them which journeyed with me. 14 And when we were all fallen to the earth, I heard a voice speaking unto me, and saying in the Hebrew tongue, Saul, Saul, why persecutest thou me? *it is* hard for thee to kick against the pricks. 15 And I said, Who art thou, Lord? And he said, I am Jesus whom thou persecutest. 16 But rise, and stand upon thy feet: for I have appeared unto thee for this purpose, to make thee a minister and a witness both of these things which thou hast seen, and of those things in the which I will appear unto thee; 17 Delivering thee from the people, and *from* the Gentiles, unto whom now I send thee, 18 To open their eyes, *and* to turn *them* from darkness to light, and *from* the power of Satan unto God, that they may receive

> forgiveness of sins, and inheritance among them which are sanctified by faith that is in me. 19 Whereupon, O king Agrippa, I was not disobedient unto the heavenly vision: 20 But shewed first unto them of Damascus, and at Jerusalem, and throughout all the coasts of Judaea, and *then* to the Gentiles, that they should repent and turn to God, and do works meet for repentance.

Calvinism will not accept the words of Scripture as they are written. The invitations and the promises must be reworded in order that the wording will conform to the TULIP. This altering of the text to make Scripture read so that Calvinism is sustainable is not sporadic or occasional; it is pervasive and inclusive. Even the words of the LORD Jesus must be scrupulously reconfigured or meticulously defined for the purpose of sustaining the TULIP.

> Matthew 11:28 Come unto me, all *ye* that labour and are heavy laden, and I will give you rest. 29 Take my yoke upon you, and learn of me; for I am meek and lowly in heart: and ye shall find rest unto your souls. 30 For my yoke *is* easy, and my burden is light.

To the Calvinist, the *all* that may find rest cannot really mean *all*. These words cannot be an indiscriminate general invitation to *all* men; instead, the word *all* must refer only to the *elect*. John Calvin wrote in his commentary on Matthew 11:28: "*Come to me all that labor* He now kindly invites to himself those whom he acknowledges to be fit for becoming his disciples ... his elect ... ." Calvin defines the word *all* as *those that are fit to become* the disciples of Christ. In following sentences, Calvin identifies those addressed as being *the elect*. The invitation of Christ according to the thinking of Calvin was only open to the all that are the elect.

Regarding this same verse, Matthew Poole wrote in his *Commentary on the Whole Bible*, "Christ will give rest to all those of his people that are any ways weary and heavy laden ....” Calvinism sees this all as restricted to the elect.

Calvinism requires that the Scriptures be read through special lenses that provide the unique meanings for Bible words that enable the TULIP to be palatable. Without those definitions, the TULIP is unsustainable. With or without the invented meanings, Calvinism is distasteful.

Gracious invitations such as Isaiah 55:6–7 cannot be viewed as evangelical or worse as evangelistic under Calvinism. Calvin saw these verses as directed to the Jews as the elect nation. Gill held that it was addressed to the people of God. If those adjustments be true, then the sinner that stumbles across these verses and believes them to be an invitation to salvation would be deceived.

> Isaiah 55:6 Seek ye the LORD while he may be found, call ye upon him while he is near: 7 Let the wicked forsake his way, and the unrighteous man his thoughts: and let him return unto the LORD, and he will have mercy upon him; and to our God, for he will abundantly pardon.

I believe that Isaiah and the LORD Jesus gave the same *whosoever will* invitation. If that is so, then grace is not irresistible.

Paul surely speaks of the grace of God being received in vain and doing so in the context of receiving or rejecting the salvation that is offered in Christ?

> 2 Corinthians 5:17–21 Therefore if any man be in Christ, he is a new creature: old things are passed away; behold, all things are become new. And all things are of God, who hath reconciled us to himself by Jesus Christ, and hath given to us the ministry of reconciliation; To wit, that God was in Christ, reconciling the world unto himself, not imputing their trespasses un-

> to them; and hath committed unto us the word of reconciliation. Now then we are ambassadors for Christ, as though God did beseech you by us: we pray you in Christ's stead, be ye reconciled to God. For he hath made him to be sin for us, who knew no sin; that we might be made the righteousness of God in him.

> 2 Corinthians 6:1–2 We then, as workers together with him, beseech you also that ye receive not the grace of God in vain. (For he saith, I have heard thee in a time accepted, and in the day of salvation have I succoured thee: behold, now is the accepted time; behold, now is the day of salvation.)

The loving Heavenly Father *extends* His grace; He does not *exert* His grace. Grace is not forced compliance.

The LORD Jesus settles the issue of whether grace is resistible or irresistible in one verse and destroys an election that is unconditional at the same time.

> Matthew 23:37 O Jerusalem, Jerusalem, *thou* that killest the prophets, and stonest them which are sent unto thee, how often would I have gathered thy children together, even as a hen gathereth her chickens under *her* wings, and ye would not!

The LORD Jesus states that Jerusalem would not respond to His attempt "to gather thy children together"; but rebuked the citizens because while "I would," "ye would not." Their will was able to withstand the will of Christ. Jesus of Nazareth was God manifested in the flesh; His will was the will of God. His will was for them to be gathered to Him; however their will was not to be gathered. He did not compel them to gather. Grace was extended; grace was not exerted.

The LORD Jesus specifically addressed His will and the will of God: "For I came down from heaven, not to do mine own will, but the will of him that sent me." (John 6:38) There can be no question of a difference of will between the Father and the Son.

Three verses that are found in the Gospel of John and that bracket this just cited verse in chapter 6 provide a detailed explanation of the will of God in relationship to the provision of salvation. These three verses read in sequence reveal that the will of God is that all who believe on the LORD Jesus will have everlasting life. Take notice of the phrase "the will of him that sent me."

> John 4:34 Jesus saith unto them, My meat is to do the will of him that sent me, and to finish his work.
>
> John 6:38 For I came down from heaven, not to do mine own will, but the will of him that sent me.
>
> John 6:40 And this is the will of him that sent me, that every one which seeth the Son, and believeth on him, may have everlasting life: and I will raise him up at the last day.

Salvation is offered and that offer is accepted or it is rejected: the offer is not imposed. Grace does not force salvation upon any individual. Grace is not a power or an ability; grace is unmerited favor.

> John 1:11 He came unto his own, and his own received him not. 12 But as many as received him, to them gave he power to become the sons of God, *even* to them that believe on his name: 13 Which were born, not of blood, nor of the will of the flesh, nor of the will of man, but of God.
>
> John 5:39 Search the scriptures; for in them ye think ye have eternal life: and they are they which testify of me. 40 And ye will not come to me, that ye might have life.

CHAPTER 12

PERSEVERANCE

Only the doctrine of the Perseverance of the Saints remains for examination. The Perseverance of the Saints, as defined by the Calvinist, is not *eternal security*. Many individuals, both Calvinists and non-Calvinists attempt to present the Perseverance of the Saints in such a manner as to equate the two. However, this doctrine as defined by Calvinism does not deal with the security of those that trust in Christ, but with the perseverance of the saints. The *Security* of the believers is not the same as the doctrine of the *Perseverance* of the Saints.

Even though the *M-WD* defines perseverance with the word *steadfastness*, the Calvinist does not define the doctrine that way nor does he use the word in that manner.

There is no better example of a Calvinist speaking of his laboring for his personal perseverance than that of Dr. R. C. Sproul to whom I have already referred. His comments are so relevant to this discussion that I will repeat them. It is a law of education that repetition is a great aid to learning.

Sproul is recognized as a gifted expositor of Calvinist doctrine. That which follows is his personal testimony. This material was not transcribed by someone that might have misunderstood and then misrepresented his intent; these are his words. I concur with the presumption that anyone may misspeak, and that even recorded comments may not be accurate as to the actual intent, since facial expressions cannot be observed; however, when a work is (1) written to be placed in print, (2) reprinted, and (3) allowed to stand uncorrected on a website for twenty-two years as of this writing, then the presumption must be accepted that the words are accurate and in proper context.

This statement should be read carefully, because it was written carefully. As you read, you should take notice that Sproul was unable to express any confidence that he is one of the elect or that he has any sense of assurance that he will be in Heaven when he dies.

> There are people in this world who are not saved, but who are convinced that they are. The presence of such people causes genuine Christians to doubt their salvation. After all, we wonder, suppose I am in that category? Suppose I am mistaken about my salvation and am really going to hell? How can I know that I am a real Christian?
>
> A while back I had one of those moments of acute self-awareness that we have from time to time, and suddenly the question hit me: "R. C., what if you are not one of the redeemed? What if your destiny is not heaven after all, but hell?" Let me tell you that I was flooded in my body with a chill that went from my head to the bottom of my spine. I was terrified.
>
> I tried to grab hold of myself. I thought, "Well, it's a good sign that I'm worried about this. Only true Christians really

> care about salvation." But then I began to take stock of my life, and I looked at my performance. My sins came pouring into my mind, and the more I looked at myself, the worse I felt. I thought, "Maybe it's really true. Maybe I'm not saved after all."
>
> I went to my room and began to read the Bible. On my knees I said, "Well, here I am. I can't point to my obedience. There's nothing I can offer. I can only rely on Your atonement for my sins. I can only throw myself on Your mercy." Even then I knew that some people only flee to the Cross to escape hell, not out of a real turning to God. I could not be sure about my own heart and motivation. Then I remembered John 6:68. Jesus had been giving out hard teaching, and many of His former followers had left Him. When He asked Peter if he was also going to leave, Peter said, "Where else can I go? Only You have the words of eternal life." In other words, Peter was also uncomfortable, but he realized that being uncomfortable with Jesus was better than any other option![113]

Sproul is no novice at understanding his doctrinal beliefs nor is he a neophyte at expressing his thoughts in words. He is fully capable to convey, in either the verbal expression or the written presentation, exactly what he intends to be understood. His ministry extends over a number of decades and reaches throughout the world. His beliefs are well documented in his multiple books, his continuing broadcasts, his weekly sermons, and his extended travels. I need not read anything into what he has written; I simply need to let him speak through his own chosen words.

---

[113]R. C. Sproul, *Assurance of Salvation*, Tabletalk, Ligionier Ministries, Inc., November 1989.

The simple fact that Sproul is moved to question whether he himself is actually among the elect dramatically reveals the precept that, while every Calvinist believes doctrinally that the elect will persevere and that all of the elect have been predestined for heaven, no Calvinist knows with absolute certitude that he is himself numbered among the elect.

The Calvinist, like the Arminian, has no more than a *hope-so* salvation. The Calvinist Baptist, whether he be called Particular, Primitive, Hardshell, or Reformed, and the Arminian Baptist, whether he be called General or Free Will Baptist, believes *that "he that endureth to the end shall be saved."*

For *the Calvinist,* salvation *was* determined before the foundation of the world, but only the perseverance of the individual to the end *proves* that he was one of the elect, unless, of course, all of his efforts were performed in and of the flesh and were thereby only works of the flesh.

For *the Arminian,* salvation *is* determined by the perseverance of the believer and his effort to hold out faithfully unto the end.

Intriguingly, both the Calvinist and the Arminian often cite the same verses, such as those that follow, but each affirms that these verses support his doctrines in opposition against the doctrines of the other.

> Mark 13:13 And ye shall be hated of all men for my name's sake: but he that shall endure unto the end, the same shall be saved.
>
> Hebrews 3:6 But Christ as a son over his own house; whose house are we, if we hold fast the confidence and the rejoicing of the hope firm unto the end.
>
> Hebrews 3:14 For we are made partakers of Christ, if we hold the beginning of our confidence stedfast unto the end;

> Revelation 2:26 And he that overcometh, and keepeth my works unto the end, to him will I give power over the nations:

Quoting from the 1689 London Confession of Faith,[114] which is the standard for Reformed Baptists, Seaton writes:

> 'Those whom God has accepted in the Beloved,' it says, 'effectually called and sanctified by His Spirit, and given the precious faith of His elect unto, can neither totally nor finally fall from the state of grace, but shall certainly persevere therein to the end, and be eternally saved, seeing the gifts and callings of God are without repentance.[115]
>
> If man cannot save himself, then God must save him. If all are not saved, then God has not saved all. If Christ has made satisfaction for sins, then it is for the sins of those who are saved. If God intends to reveal this salvation in Christ to the hearts of those whom He chooses to save, then, God will provide the means of effectually doing so. If, therefore, having *ordained* to save, *died* to save, and *called* to salvation those who could never save themselves, He will also *preserve* those saved ones unto eternity to the glory of His name.[116]

By now, it may be boring (but it should be informative and revealing) to see the repetitive *if-then* argument brashly flung forward again. Yet, the *if-then* arguments are the justification of Calvinism.

---

[114]Overtly Calvinist Baptist churches are found in growing numbers under the names of Reformed Baptist, Covenant Baptist, or Grace (Graceway) Baptist, or without any indication in the name. Calvinism appears to have entered a new period of acceptability and of accommodation within many Baptist churches and institutions that were formerly opposed to Calvinism. The London Confession of 1689 is generally used by these churches.

[115]Seaton, *The Five Points of Calvinism*, 20.

[116]Seaton, *The Five Points of Calvinism*, 21.

An assumption will be presented as a fact; that assumption will be followed by an assertion that is entirely predicated upon that assumption. *However, the assertion is worthless if the assumption is flawed.*

Calvinism's *if-then* system is flawed beyond reclamation. When the foundation of the TULIP system, Total Inability, is accepted, the natural sequence of the proposed logic requires each link of the chain exactly as they are presented in TULIP, ending with, the capstone, the Perseverance of the Saints.

To the Calvinist, perseverance is "the believer's hallmark that he belongs to Christ; that he is persevering in the things of Christ; that he is 'giving all diligence to make his calling and election sure.'" The Calvinist is quick and firm to assert that the elect will never fall "totally nor finally." However, no Five-Point Calvinist is ever positive that he is one of the elect. He is never certain that he will continue faithfully "unto the end" without falling at the last moment. He fears that he may fall into sin but not repent or that he might recant his testimony on his deathbed, thereby proving that he is not one of the elect.

The *M-WD* defines perseverance with the word steadfastness ("the action or condition or an instance of persevering: STEADFASTNESS"). Steadfastness is defined in the same dictionary as "firmly fixed in place: IMMOVABLE ... not subject to change ... firm in belief, determination, or adherence: LOYAL" and importantly provides the synonym "FAITHFUL."[117]

The Calvinist transforms this word perseverance to mean continual faithfulness, which is defined by Calvinism to mean persistent obedience to the will of God demonstrated by the performance of good works that continues indefinitely in time without

[117]The capitalizations are in the original.

interruption. Those that might appear to fall away never were real believers or else they would return to faithfulness. Apostasy is unimpeachable proof that the individual is not one of the elect.

While this doctrine is covered in some detail earlier in this material, it is reintroduced here for the reason that it is a battlefield issue today, because of the ability of a Calvinist to infiltrate a Baptist church that uses the time-honored wording of the *New Hampshire Confession of Faith* in its statement on the Perseverance of the Saints. It is the record of history that the Baptist churches of the north largely followed the Philadelphia Confession of Faith, which was strongly Calvinist, and steadily progressed into cold formalism and dead liberalism, while the Baptist churches of the south more often adopted the *New Hampshire Confession of Faith* for their doctrinal position. Those Baptist churches in the southern states, both convention and independent, retained their fervor and their faith long after the preponderance of northern Baptist churches was gravitating into apostasy.

It is also a matter of record that the majority of those Baptist churches located in the southern portion of the United States that adopted the *New Hampshire Confession of Faith* did not believe or preach the Calvinist definitions for the doctrine of the Perseverance of the Saints.

However, men with a Calvinist mindset are able today to use that statement from the *New Hampshire Confession* as the *backdoorway*[118] to steal the labors of good people and, by subversion, to produce a Calvinist church, most often without the vote of the congregation to do so. These men simply ignore the written documents governing the church and

---

[118]*Backdoorway* is not a dictionary word. It is formed by my combining of backdoor and doorway. I define it as a stealth entrance through an unguarded opening.

openly disregard the historical stand of the church. This hijacking of churches is an increasing event.

Every Baptist church should recognize this potential *backdoorway* as an open and unprotected avenue that allows infiltration and each church should take serious measures to close that portal securely.

The *New Hampshire Confession of Faith* has the following statement concerning the Perseverance of the Saints.

> We believe that such only are real believers as endure unto the end;[1] that their persevering attachment to Christ is the grand mark which distinguishes them from superficial professors;[2] that a special providence watches over their welfare;[3] and that they are kept by the power of God through faith unto salvation.[4]
>
> [1]John 8:31; First John 2:27, 28; First John 3:9; First John 5:18.
> [2]First John 2:19; John 13:18; Matthew 13:20, 21; John 6:66–69; Job 17:9.
> [3]Romans 8:28; Matthew 6:30–33; Jeremiah 32:40; Psalm 121:3; Psalm 91:11, 12.
> [4]Philippians 1:6; First Peter 1:5; Philippians 2:12, 13; Jude 24, 25; Hebrews 1:14; Second Kings 6:16; Hebrews 13:5; First John 4:4.

Though I have a profound respect for the *New Hampshire Confession of Faith,*[119] I do not ascribe inspiration or infallibility to the document. Even so, I do not lightly propose changing the wording that those godly men chose. The length of their labors testifies to their deliberation in the selection of the construction of the statements. Traditions, whether

---

[119]*The New Hampshire Confession of Faith* was framed by John Newton Brown, Barton Stow, Jonathan Going, and I. Person laboring together from June 1830 to January 1833 at the direction of the New Hampshire Baptist Convention. It gained a wide publication through its inclusion in the *Baptist Church Manual,* written by James M. Pendleton.

in practice or wording, are assuredly not binding as are the Scriptures; however, what godly men have left for us ought not to be revised or altered without due consideration and without just and righteous cause.

This statement, as written, has been used as a means of the entrance of Calvinism into churches and institutions because of the various ways in which the individual phrases may be interpreted. It has become an avenue for those who wish to promote Calvinism within a non-Calvinistic church.

As for me, I read this statement today precisely as I read it over fifty years ago in my grandfather's copy of the *Baptist Church Manual* when I first entered the ministry. Perseverance meant *steadfastness* to me then, as it has in the English tongue since the fourteenth century; and it means the same today. However, every church using the statement needs to consider seriously the possibility of rewriting this statement to remove the potential of a different interpretation by some future pastor, staff member, officer, or member that uses the wording as the opportunity to introduce the doctrine of either traditional or contemporary Calvinism.

This is an increasingly real possibility, because of the growing resurgence of *traditional* Calvinism and Reformationists ***and*** the arrival of the *New Calvinists* within seminaries and Bible colleges where Baptist pastors and staff members are trained, and the infiltration appearing within Baptist pulpits of the *new Calvinists*, also identified as Neo-Reformationists and Neo-Calvinists (which are not to be confused with neocalvinists).[120]

---

[120]New Calvinists (neo-Calvinists) are **missional**, *going into culture and embracing it*, **libertarian**, *holding that whatever is not specifically forbidden in the Bible is permitted*, **continuationists**, *advocating that all of the gifts of the Spirit are available and active*, and **contextualists**, *believing that Christianity must be made relevant to the culture and time.*

Since I first read the statement from the *New Hampshire Confession*, I have not changed my understanding of the wording; but some of those using the name Baptist have, and they are not to be extended any possible opening for a foothold in any church that I pastor. The shepherd is responsible to protect the sheep committed to his care.

To develop an understanding of how this statement is used wrongly to introduce Calvinism, I suggest the careful consideration of the first two verses and the last two verses of the Book of Jude.

> Jude 1–2, the servant of Jesus Christ, and brother of James, to them that are sanctified by God the Father, and preserved in Jesus Christ, *and* called: Mercy unto you, and peace, and love, be multiplied.
>
> 24–25 Now unto him that is able to keep you from falling, and to present *you* faultless before the presence of his glory with exceeding joy, To the only wise God our Saviour, *be* glory and majesty, dominion and power, both now and ever. Amen.

Jude, under the inspiration of the Holy Spirit, is moved to record the phrase, "preserved in Jesus Christ." Those are not words used to fill space or to convey a nebulous concept. Every word of Scripture is a God-breathed word, and no word of Scripture is to be considered of lesser importance. That word

---

Prominent New Calvinists are Mark Driscoll, Tim Keller, Matt Chandler, Mark Dever, Al Mohler and Joshua Harris.
Neocalvinist: "The term refers to a Dutch Calvinist movement associated with the theologian ... Abraham Kuyper. The defining credo of neocalvinism is often summarized by Kuyper's claim that, 'There is not a square inch in the whole domain of human existence over which Christ, who is sovereign over all, does not cry: Mine!' ... While New Calvinists tend to focus on renewal of the local church and use terms associated with traditional Calvinism, the Kuyperians generally aim at cultural renewal and use jargon whose connotations are specific to the movement (e.g., sphere sovereignty)." http://thegospelcoalition.org/blogs/tgc/2012/01/30/whats-the-difference-neo-calvinist-vs-neocalvinist/

preserved is a key word for this small Book. Consider the words in bold font in the verses that follow.

> 1 Jude, the servant of Jesus Christ, and brother of James, to them that are sanctified by God the Father, and **preserved** in Jesus Christ, *and* called:
>
> 6 And the angels which **kept** not their first estate, but left their own habitation, he hath **reserved** in everlasting chains under darkness unto the judgment of the great day.
>
> 13 Raging waves of the sea, foaming out their own shame; wandering stars, to whom is **reserved** the blackness of darkness for ever.
>
> 21 **Keep** yourselves in the love of God, looking for the mercy of our Lord Jesus Christ unto eternal life.

While both my vocabulary and my audience is English speaking, it is worth calling attention to the intriguing fact that the words that I emphasized in those four verses are all translated from the same Greek word according to *Strong's Exhaustive Concordance* [*Strong's*]. The original Greek words underlying the translated English of our Authorized Version [AV], the King James Version [KJV], are not a secret language reserved only for preachers and theologians.

Every believer ought to have access to two books for his ready use. These are (1) the *M-WD*[121] for the understanding of the English words of the text of Scripture, and (2) a *Strong's* for the information of the Greek word that lies behind the English choice. In printed form, *Strong's* lists the English words in

[121]The use of the word Webster in the title of dictionary signifies nothing. It is a generic term. The best choice, in my opinion, for a dictionary is one in the lineage of Noah Webster's *1828 Dictionary of the American Language*. The only contemporary currently published dictionary meeting that qualification is the *M-WD*.

their alphabetical order and assigns a number to the Hebrew or Greek word that was translated as that English word. Those numbers are then listed in two sections: Hebrew words for the Old Testament and Greek words for the New Testament. In addition to the traditional hardback book format, *Strong's* is available as a component of many Bible software programs[122] or as a standalone program. There are multiple opportunities for every believer to avail himself of both of these essential resources for personal Bible study.

In this particular instance, the *Strong's* word number is 5083 **τηρεω**. The English words given to us by the translators for this word are *preserved, kept, reserved,* and *to keep,* all of which reflect this same Greek word. *Strong's* defines this Greek word as meaning:

> to attend to carefully, take care of; "to guard;" metaphorically "to keep, one in the state in which he is;" "to observe"; "to reserve: to undergo something"

We discover from the information provided by *Strong's* that the AV translators gave us this particular Greek word in our English translation as *keep* a total of 57 times, *reserve* 8 times, *observe* 4 times, *watch* twice, *preserve* twice, *keeper* once, and *hold fast* once; for a total of 75 times. It is evident that the translators understood the meaning and accurately reflected the shades of the original for the context of the use of the word.

Very interestingly, there is *another* Greek word translated *keep* in verse 24 in this same passage. *Strong's* number for this different word is 5442 **φυλασσω**.

---

[122]SwordSearcher is my choice for Bible study software: King James Version orientated, with an amazing assortment of helps, and available for a modest cost. I have no direct or indirect connection, involvement, or financial interest in SwordSearcher. The program is available for purchase and download at http://www.swordsearcher.com.

> 24 Now unto him that is able to **keep** you from falling, and to present you faultless before the presence of his glory with exceeding joy. [Emphasis is added.]

The translators bring this word into English as *keep* 23 times, *observe* twice, *beware* twice, *keep* (one's) *self* once, *save* once, and *beware* once; totaling 30 times. *Strong's* defines **φυλασσω** as meaning:

- 1) to guard
  - 1a) to watch, keep watch
  - 1b) to guard or watch, have an eye upon: lest he escape
  - 1c) to guard a person (or thing) that he may remain safe
    - 1c1) lest he suffer violence, be despoiled, etc. to protect
    - 1c2) to protect one from a person or thing
    - 1c3) to keep from being snatched away, preserve safe and unimpaired
    - 1c4) to guard from being lost or perishing
    - 1c5) to guard one's self from a thing
  - 1d) to guard i.e. care for, take care not to violate
    - 1d1) to observe
- 2) to observe for one's self something to escape
  - 2a) to avoid, shun flee from
  - 2b) to guard for one's self (i.e. for one's safety's sake) so as not to violate, i.e. to keep, observe (the precepts of the Mosaic law)

Very helpfully, *Strong's* additionally informs us that "The first word **τηρεω** expresses watchful care and is suggestive of present possession; the second word, **φυλασσω** indicates safe custody and often implies assault from without." *Strong's* continues to provide the intriguing comment that **τηρεω** "may mark the result of which **φυλασσω** is the means."

What a wonderful truth unfolds from this almost effortless excursion into the original Greek words underlying our English words. We may now understand that the keeping of the child of God is the result of the *watchful care* of God. We are preserved, and we are kept by the ability of the God of Heaven exactly as verse 24 declares. Assuredly, this truth is revealed in the English words of the AV; however, we do not need to fear the consideration of the original Greek text, because those Greek words, honestly presented, always and without exception, will confirm the accuracy of the translation found in the AV and the integrity of the translators in reflecting the nuances of the Greek.

Beware of anyone or any publication that seeks to use the Greek to alter or to refute the rendering of the AV translation. If a meaning was in the original Greek, it will be found in the English of the AV. If a meaning is in the English text of the AV, it was found in the original Greek. Every flavor of a word may be found by either the *M-WD* or *Strong's*. Those who seek changes in the English text do so because they have already altered the Greek text.

The Scriptures found in Jude, whether read in English or in the original Greek, are abundantly clear to all who will take the words as they stand. The true worshipper (believer)[123] is preserved because he is kept by the power of God—in the words of 1 Peter, as given by the Holy Spirit:

> 1:3–5 Blessed be the God and Father of our Lord Jesus Christ, which according to his abundant mercy hath begotten us again unto a lively hope by the resurrec-

[123]John 4:23 But the hour cometh, and now is, when the true worshippers shall worship the Father in spirit and in truth: for the Father seeketh such to worship him.

> tion of Jesus Christ from the dead, To an inheritance incorruptible, and undefiled, and that fadeth not away, reserved in heaven for you, Who are kept by the power of God through faith unto salvation ready to be revealed in the last time.

The words that the Holy Spirit moved Paul to record emphasize the same truth:

> 2 Timothy 1:12 For the which cause I also suffer these things: nevertheless I am not ashamed: for I know whom I have believed, and am persuaded that he is able to keep that which I have committed unto him against that day.

The preservation of the saints is a blessed truth of Scripture that moves the believer to keep himself faithful in his life and to maintain fidelity to the faith. *It is not the perseverance of the saints that preserves the saints. It is the preservation of the saint that causes the saint to persevere in the faith.*

That statement, however, requires some discussion. The perseverance of the saints is also presented in Scripture, but not under the definition imposed by the Calvinist. As with all of their doctrines, the Calvinist must substitute the private and special definitions of Calvinism in order to prove this Point.

The Calvinist never knows with assurance or certainty that he is a true believer this side of eternity, because he never knows with assurance and certainty that he is in truth an elect saint. The reason is that Calvinism teaches that the evidence of actually being one of the elect is that of maintaining good works and of remaining in the faith until the very end of earthly life.

The Calvinist will never budge from affirming that the elect will persevere and that the elect are eternally saved. Yet for himself, the Calvinist can never say with absolute certainty that he knows he is one of the elect. The proof of election to the Calvinist is perseverance, and he will never be able to say that he has persevered until he finally enters Heaven.

In effect, the Calvinist makes the witness of salvation something entirely different than does the Scripture. Calvinism affirms perseverance as the test. Scripture pronounces, “His Spirit beareth witness with our Spirit, that we are the children of God.” (Romans 8:16)

Simply stated, the Calvinist changes the meaning of the word perseverance from that of the *M-WD*.

> the action or condition or an instance of persevering: STEADFASTNESS
>
> 1 a: firmly fixed in place: IMMOVABLE b: not subject to change
> 2: firm in belief, determination, or adherence: LOYAL
>
> Synonyms: FAITHFUL, LOYAL, CONSTANT, STAUNCH, STEADFAST, RESOLUTE firm in adherence to whatever one owes allegiance.
>
> FAITHFUL implies unswerving adherence to a person or thing or to the oath or promise by which a tie was contracted “faithful to her promise.”
>
> LOYAL implies a firm resistance to any temptation to desert or betray “remained loyal to the czar.”
>
> CONSTANT stresses continuing firmness of emotional attachment without necessarily implying strict obedience to promises or vows “constant friends.”
>
> STAUNCH suggests fortitude and resolution in adherence and imperviousness to influences that would weaken it “a staunch defender of free speech.”
>
> STEADFAST implies a steady and unwavering course in love, allegiance, or conviction “steadfast in their support.”

> RESOLUTE implies firm determination to adhere to a cause or purpose "a resolute ally."

I believe that the statement from the *New Hampshire Confession of Faith* entitled *This We Believe of the Perseverance of Saints* was written so that it could be understood with the non-Calvinist definitions provided above.

> 1 Corinthians 15:58 Therefore, my beloved brethren, be ye stedfast, unmoveable, always abounding in the work of the Lord, forasmuch as ye know that your labour is not in vain in the Lord.

May I suggest that the Scriptures provide an excellent example of the use of the word immovable or unmovable (AV: unmoveable).

> Acts 27:41 And falling into a place where two seas met, they ran the ship aground; and the forepart stuck fast, and remained unmoveable, but the hinder part was broken with the violence of the waves.

That is an excellent picture of perseverance of the saints—the saints being all those who have received the LORD Jesus as personal Saviour.

Because of the recent resurgence of Calvinism, a church using a doctrinal statement that is based on the *New Hampshire Confession of Faith* may be compelled to consider changing the words to protect that church from the introduction of that false teaching.

While the Arminians deny eternal security and require persevering as the condition of continued salvation, the Calvinist affirms the eternal security of **the saints**, but in addition, Calvinism **also requires persevering**—except to the Calvinist, perseverance is not the condition of salvation, it is the evidence. Both place an extra-Biblical emphasis upon the persevering (the outward works and inward faithfulness) of professing believers.

In effect, both Calvinists and Arminians connect *human works* with the eventual attainment of salvation. While proponents of each system deny that works obtain salvation, the practical application of the teaching of both is that works are required as the evidence.

In spite of what followers of these systems of theology declare that they believe about how they are kept saved or how they prove their salvation, there will be those in heaven who were Arminians or Calvinists on earth. They will be there by the grace of God in spite of what they claimed to believe and not because of their works to keep their salvation or to prove their salvation.

If the individual is trusting entirely in the finished work of the LORD Jesus Christ in His death and resurrection for his salvation, that person will be in heaven regardless of, even in spite of, how he identified himself on earth.

As to the keeping of a believer, the LORD Jesus Christ affirmed His personal involvement in the preservation, the security, of the believer.

> John 10 27–29 My sheep hear my voice, and I know them, and they follow me: And I give unto them eternal life; and they shall never perish, neither shall any *man* pluck them out of my hand. My Father, which gave *them* me, is greater than all; and no *man* is able to pluck *them* out of my Father's hand.

It is important to understand that this security in Christ is not a license for the Christian to live as he pleases. While the person who has been saved will always be saved, the term *Once Saved Always Saved* is often used by the proponent of Calvinism, and by the advocate of Arminianism, to discredit the teaching of assurance and the teaching of the security of the believer. Both the Calvinist and the Arminian define the phrase *Once Saved Always*

Saved to mean the teaching that anyone who has ever made a profession of faith will be kept saved *regardless of lifestyle, unrepentant and habitual sin, or even apostasy.*

That connotation is a fabricated straw man constructed solely for the benefit of a destructive blow by the Calvinist or the Arminian. Neither the doctrine of Assurance nor the doctrine of the Security of the Believer is connected with a concept of living as one pleases or with the ability to apostatize.[124] The Calvinist and the Arminian attribute their special distorted definitions of eternal security to their particular understanding of salvation; however, both of these systems discredit Biblical truth. Both theologies make two serious errors, which are: (1) The fact that faith produces works is ignored. (2) The teaching of the chastening of the hand of the LORD upon His children is not recognized.

While few have actually sincerely preached this concocted straw man, to many individuals the concept that the phrase *Once Saved Always Saved* conveys is one of easy believism, cheap grace, and a means to enlist numbers; therefore, the phrase must be used only with a careful explanation.

In one sense, *Once Saved Always Saved* is biblically true in that when a person is born into the family of God, that person receives eternal life and not some sort of temporary life. This cannot be given a clearer affirmation than the direct confirmation "He that hath the Son hath life; *and* he that hath not the Son of God hath not life." One does not need a set of special definitions to understand those words.

---

[124] 1 John 2:19 They went out from us, but they were not of us; for if they had been of us, they would *no doubt* have continued with us: but *they went out*, that they might be made manifest that they were not all of us.

> 1 John 5:11 And this is the record, that God hath given to us eternal life, and this life is in his Son. 12 He that hath the Son hath life; *and* he that hath not the Son of God hath not life. 13 These things have I written unto you that believe on the name of the Son of God; that ye may know that ye have eternal life, and that ye may believe on the name of the Son of God.

Once he has been born again, the person cannot be unborn. That concept is absurd to consider.

> John 1:12–13 But as many as received him, to them gave he power to become the sons of God, *even* to them that believe on his name: Which were born, not of blood, nor of the will of the flesh, nor of the will of man, but of God.

> John 3:14–21 And as Moses lifted up the serpent in the wilderness, even so must the Son of man be lifted up: That whosoever believeth in him should not perish, but have eternal life. For God so loved the world, that he gave his only begotten Son, that whosoever believeth in him should not perish, but have everlasting life. For God sent not his Son into the world to condemn the world; but that the world through him might be saved. He that believeth on him is not condemned: but he that believeth not is condemned already, because he hath not believed in the name of the only begotten Son of God. And this is the condemnation, that light is come into the world, and men loved darkness rather than light, because their deeds were evil. For every one that doeth evil hateth the light, neither cometh to the light, lest his deeds should be reproved. But he that doeth truth cometh to the light, that his deeds may be made manifest, that they are wrought in God.

However, *the security of the believer* does not mean that repeating certain words, praying a particular prayer, or identifying with Christianity will make a person a Christian.

Additionally, *the security of the believer* does not mean that a person can claim to be a child of God and live as if he were a child of the devil. Moreover, *the security of the believer* is not a license for a genuine believer to sin. Furthermore, no Christian can sin and get away with that sin.

The somber words of Hebrews 12:6–11 are not to be taken lightly. The sinning believer is chastened for his sin.

> For whom the Lord loveth he chasteneth, and scourgeth every son whom he receiveth. If ye endure chastening, God dealeth with you as with sons; for what son is he whom the father chasteneth not? But if ye be without chastisement, whereof all are partakers, then are ye bastards, and not sons. Furthermore we have had fathers of our flesh which corrected us, and we gave them reverence: shall we not much rather be in subjection unto the Father of spirits, and live? For they verily for a few days chastened us after their own pleasure; but he for our profit, that we might be partakers of his holiness. Now no chastening for the present seemeth to be joyous, but grievous: nevertheless afterward it yieldeth the peaceable fruit of righteousness unto them which are exercised thereby.

In His exercise of mercy, the LORD offers to His children the way of restoration through confession. The Christian may confess his sin and be forgiven and restored to fellowship.

> 1 John 1:6–2:6 If we say that we have fellowship with him, and walk in darkness, we lie, and do not the truth: But if we walk in the light, as he is in the light, we have fellowship one with another, and the blood of Jesus Christ his Son cleanseth us

> from all sin. If we say that we have no sin, we deceive ourselves, and the truth is not in us. If we confess our sins, he is faithful and just to forgive us *our* sins, and to cleanse us from all unrighteousness. If we say that we have not sinned, we make him a liar, and his word is not in us. My little children, these things write I unto you, that ye sin not. And if any man sin, we have an advocate with the Father, Jesus Christ the righteous: And he is the propitiation for our sins: and not for ours only, but also for *the sins of* the whole world. And hereby we do know that we know him, if we keep his commandments. He that saith, I know him, and keepeth not his commandments, is a liar, and the truth is not in him. But whoso keepeth his word, in him verily is the love of God perfected: hereby know we that we are in him. He that saith he abideth in him ought himself also so to walk, even as he walked.

If the Christian stubbornly will not confess and repent, he will be chastened for that sin.

> Psalm 89:30–34 If his children forsake my law, and walk not in my judgments; If they break my statutes, and keep not my commandments; Then will I visit their transgression with the rod, and their iniquity with stripes. Nevertheless my lovingkindness will I not utterly take from him, nor suffer my faithfulness to fail. My covenant will I not break, nor alter the thing that is gone out of my lips.

> Revelation 3:19 As many as I love, I rebuke and chasten: be zealous therefore, and repent.

I sadly recall the response of a deacon, long years ago, that I had to confront for his attempted affair with the church pianist. He had imbibed the intoxicating elixir of the unbiblical, even anti-Biblical concepts of *Once Saved Always Saved.* With a haughty attitude, he bluntly told me, "I am saved and I going to Heaven and there is nothing God or you or anybody else can do about it. I will do as I please." That is not the attitude of a child of God; at least, not a child of God that is in fellowship with his Heavenly Father. The only hope that I have of that man's salvation is that he was shortly afterward stricken with a crippling disease and spent the remaining years of his life with serious physical challenges. I trust that his infirmity was from the chastening hand of God upon His rebellious and foolish child. The expression that the man made is itself a wicked perversion of truth. No one with any Bible understanding would ever make such a statement or anything close to it.

The apostle John (1 John 1:1–2 John 6) presents a very strong statement concerning this warped thinking that "since I am saved I will live as I please."

> That which was from the beginning, which we have heard, which we have seen with our eyes, which we have looked upon, and our hands have handled, of the Word of life; (For the life was manifested, and we have seen *it*, and bear witness, and shew unto you that eternal life, which was with the Father, and was manifested unto us;) That which we have seen and heard declare we unto you, that ye also may have fellowship with us: and truly our fellowship *is* with the Father, and with his Son Jesus Christ. And these things write we unto you, that your joy may be full. This then is the message which we have heard of him, and declare unto you, that God is light, and in him is no darkness at all. **If we say** that we have fellowship with him, and walk in darkness, we lie, and do not the truth: But **if we walk** in the light, as he is in the light, we have fellowship one with another, and the blood of Jesus

> Christ his Son cleanseth us from all sin. **If we say** that we have no sin, we deceive ourselves, and the truth is not in us. **If we confess** our sins, he is faithful and just to forgive us *our* sins, and to cleanse us from all unrighteousness. **If we say** that we have not sinned, we make him a liar, and his word is not in us. My little children, these things write I unto you, that ye sin not. And **if any man sin**, we have an advocate with the Father, Jesus Christ the righteous: And he is the propitiation for our sins: and not for ours only, but also for *the sins of* the whole world. **And hereby we do know that we know him, if we keep his commandments. He that saith, I know him, and keepeth not his commandments, is a liar, and the truth is not in him. But whoso keepeth his word, in him verily is the love of God perfected: hereby know we that we are in him.** [Emphasis is added.]

Those words are as clear as it is possible to place words into print. The child of God has assurance of salvation, and his knowledge of this relationship with his Heavenly Father and His Saviour leads naturally to the next verse.

> He that saith he abideth in him ought himself also so to walk, even as he walked.

That is perseverance because of preservation.

The Book of Jude, in agreement with the rest of the word of God, declares the assurance of the security of the believer, which is *the perseverance of the saints because of the preservation of the saints*. The child of God preserves not because of some ability the child of God possess or of any effort that the child of God expends, but entirely because of the power of God.

Over the course of recent years, I have read with profit and appreciation the works of several men who have labored with this statement from the *New*

Hampshire Confession of Faith. I have sought to determine their thinking on perseverance.

Beginning about twenty years before his death, I consulted at some length with Dr. Art Wilson[125] as to how best to handle explaining the statement of the *New Hampshire Confession of Faith.* He rejected the use of the term *Perseverance of the Saints* entirely because of the misuse of Calvinism. Others continue to use the phrase, but acknowledge that they must devote continuing efforts to explain why what the Calvinist has made the accepted definition of the term must be rejected. The issue will not go away; I believe that it must be met straightforwardly, effectively, and finally.

I desired to construct something that retained the steadfastness element of the believer but focused on the preservation of the believer and was anchored to the preserving work of God. To that end, I offer the following attempt.

A Proposal for Rewording the Statement on Perseverance as found in the *New Hampshire Confession of Faith*

This We Believe of the Security of the Believer

We believe that true believers[1] are those that repent from dead works[2] and turn toward God,[3] and that, by faith,[4] believe that Jesus of Nazareth is the Christ, the Son of the living God,[5] Who is the Savior of all men, specially of those that believe,[6] Whom God hath set forth to be a propitiation for our sins through faith in His blood[7] and not for ours only but also for the sins of the whole world,[8] and that believe that God hath raised Him from the dead for our justification.[9] We further believe

[125]Dr. Wilson was a pastor, church planter, evangelist, author, and a leader among independent Baptists for over seventy years and was my mentor and friend for over forty years.

that these are given eternal life by the Son and that no man can pluck them out of the hand of the Son[10] or out of the Father's hand,[11] but that they are sealed with the Holy Spirit of promise[12] and are kept by the power of God through faith unto salvation,[13] and that a special providence watches over their welfare,[14] for the Lord Himself shall preserve their whole spirit and soul and body blameless unto His heavenly kingdom.[15] We further believe that the believers have assurance because of the witness of the Spirit of God with their spirits,[16] and that they give testimony to others of their salvation by their obedience to good works,[17] and that their love for Christ distinguishes them from superficial professors.[18]

[1]John 4:23; Matthew 15:7–9; First John 2:19.

[2]Hebrews 6:1.

[3]Acts 26:20.

[4]Habakkuk 2:4; Acts 15:9; Acts 26:18; Romans 1:17; Romans 3:22; Romans 3:28, 30; Romans 5:1–2; Galatians 3:11; Galatians 3:22, 24, 26; Philippians 3:9; Hebrews 10:38.

[5]Matthew 16:16; John 6:69.

[6]First Timothy 4:10; Galatians 2:22.

[7]Romans 3:25.

[8]First John 2:2.

[9]Romans 10:9.

[10]John 10:28.

[11]John 10:29.

[12]Second Corinthians 1:22; Second Corinthians 5:5; Ephesians 1:13, 4:30.

[13]Philippians 1:6; First Peter 1:5; Philippians 2:12, 13; Jude 24, 25; Hebrews 1:14; Second Kings 6:16; Hebrews 13:5; First John 4:4.

[14]Romans 8:28; Matthew 6:30–33; Psalm 121:3.

[15]First Thessalonians 5:23; Second Timothy 4:18; Jude 1:1.
[16]Romans 8:16; First John 4:13.
[17]John 14:15, 21–24; 8:42; 15:14; James 2:14–26; First Peter 1:8; First John 2:3–5.
[18]John 8:31; First John 2:19, 27–28; Luke 6:46–49.

The doctrines commonly defined as Calvinism will not disappear from churches and institutions while those entities choose to ignore them. The best possible method of preventing the acceptance of Calvinism within a church or institution is by the exposure of the congregation or students to the dangers of those individual doctrines prior to their arrival at the backdoorway. However, should they appear, they must be confronted and challenged straightforwardly and prevented from finding any lodging. The potential conflict must not be avoided in the hopes that the Calvinist will not spread his doctrine. The Calvinist is more zealous in spreading the seeds of the TULIP than he is (*or we are*) of sowing the seed of the Gospel. To the Calvinist, the beloved TULIP *is* the Gospel.

Understand that the Calvinist is convinced that (1) he has the truth and (2) he must spread that truth. Doing so, is a vital part of his persevering. Not to do so, is to him inexcusable, unforgiveable failure. The commitment of Calvinists to convert professing Christians into adherents of the TULIP is unswerving; it is a *mission from God*. His faithfulness in extending Calvinism is the mark of his perseverance. He must proselytize.

I commend their zeal. I admire their devotion. I do not question that they believe that they are following in the footsteps of Calvin and are seeking to insure that God receives all glory for the salvation of the elect. I believe they wrongly interpret the Scriptures.

Benjamin B. Warfield,[126] one of the leaders in the Modernist-Fundamentalist Controversy and also noted for his passionate defense of Calvinism,[127] wrote the following tribute for John Calvin.

> His zeal in asserting the doctrine of two-fold predestination is grounded in the clearness with which he perceived—as was indeed perceived with him by all the Reformers—that only so can the evil leaven of "synergism" be eliminated and the free grace of God be preserved in its purity in the saving process. The roots of his zeal are planted, in a word, in his consciousness of absolute dependence as a sinner on the free mercy of a saving God. The sovereignty of God in grace was an essential constituent of his deepest religious consciousness. Like his great master, Augustine—like Luther, Zwingli and Butzer (Bucer), and all the rest of those high spirits who brought about that great revival of religion which we call the Reformation—he

---

[126]"Benjamin Breckenridge Warfield (1851–1921) Graduated with highest honors, 1871, at nineteen years of age, from the College of New Jersey, later to be named Princeton University. In 1872, while in Heidelberg, Germany, he decided to enter the ministry. He entered Princeton Theological Seminary and graduated with the class of 1876. In 1878 he took a position at Western Theological Seminary as instructor in New Testament language and literature, becoming a professor in 1879. He left the seminary after nine years to take the chair of Systematic Theology at Princeton University that had once been occupied by Charles Hodge, who had been Warfield's teacher." http://www.theopedia.com/B._B._Warfield

[127]"It is very odd how difficult it seems for some persons to understand just what Calvinism is. And yet the matter itself presents no difficulty whatever. It is capable of being put into a single sentence; and that, on level to every religious man's comprehension. For Calvinism is just religion in its purity. We have only, therefore, to conceive of religion in its purity, and that is Calvinism ... In proportion as we are religious, in that proportion, then, are we Calvinistic; and when religion comes fully to its rights in our thinking, and feeling, and doing, then shall we be truly Calvinistic. This is why those who have caught a glimpse of these things, love with passion what men call 'Calvinism,' sometimes with an air of contempt; and why they cling to it with enthusiasm. It is not merely the hope of true religion in the world: it is true religion in the world—as far as true religion is in the world at all." http://www.reformed.org.ua/1/153/Warfield

> could not endure that the grace of God should not receive all the glory of the rescue of sinners from the destruction in which they are involved, and from which, just because they are involved in it, they are unable to do anything towards their own recovery ... .
>
> Here then is probably Calvin's greatest contribution to theological development. In his hands, for the first time in the history of the Church, the doctrine of the Holy Spirit comes to its rights. Into the heart of none more than into his did the vision of the glory of God shine, and no one has been more determined than he not to give the glory of God to another. Who has been more devoted than he to the Saviour, by whose blood he has been bought? But, above everything else, it is the sense of the sovereign working of salvation by the almighty power of the Holy Spirit which characterizes all Calvin's thought of God. And above everything else he deserves, therefore, the great name of the theologian of the Holy Spirit.[128]

While the tribute nearly seems to pass hyperbole, elevating Calvin above even the apostles in his perception of the Holy Spirit or his devotion to the Saviour and approaches very closely to worship, even if it is conceded that Calvin had a vision of the glory of God, *the philosophy or theology that bears his name does not bring glory to God.* His two-fold predestination portrays God as a king that is more despotic and tyrannical than any earthly king.

For no other reason than the exercise of His determinate will to achieve glory to Himself, God is alleged to have created man so that a chosen predetermined number, the elect, should have eternal life

---

[128]http://www.thirdmill.org/newfiles/bb_warfield/Warfield.Calvin.pdf

and that all other humanity, another predetermined number, should have an eternal existence in the Lake of Fire. I shudder to write those words.

I find it difficult to believe that anyone could read *only* the Scriptures and believe that the Bible teaches such a conception of the Triune God as creating souls for the purpose of eternal damnation. I have read nothing in the descriptions of the vilest of the heathen deities of antiquity that suggests that any proponent of those devil-derived religions ever attributed such villainy to his god. John Calvin may have been motivated to devise a theology that would bring glory to God, but the TULIP attributed to him does the exact opposite.

CHAPTER 13

PERPLEXITIES

One of the perplexities in dealing with a Calvinist is that every theological, doctrinal, or scriptural word in any discussion must be understood as having a meaning that is *particular,* and, in most instances, *peculiar* to Calvinism. It is simply not possible to take a given statement as having the commonly understood meaning or even the English dictionary definition, because Calvinism requires its own language with its own vocabulary. The words of that unknown tongue have meanings that those same words do not have in any other language, therefore, requiring the intervention of the Calvinist interpreter's wisdom. It is not always that deception is intended; it is that Calvinism is only provable when those special definitions conceived by Calvinists are used.

Every Point of the TULIP is based upon the assertion of a certain proposition that is presented as a presumed absolute and from which a subsequent conclusion is declared to be an unimpeachable doctrine. Central to each of the five declarations is the special definition that has been determined by Calvinism for the words that are used in that proposition and that are required for that proposition to be true. However, when those contrived definitions are examined and properly rejected, the validity of each of those propositions, with all of its assertion and presumption becomes patently obviously false. Stated plainly, the *if* propositions of Calvinism do not justify the *then* conclusions of the system. The definitions are essential for the TULIP to be acceptable.

From the First Point, the Second grows; and the development continues through the Fifth and final petal of the TULIP. As with the petals of the literal flower, when one petal is broken from the flower, that petal dies, and the remaining parts of the tulip wilt. The TULIP lives or dies as a unified system. Refute any one of the Five Points of the TULIP or rebut any definition used in the five points of the TULIP and the entire TULIP must wither and wilt. The argument of this book is that the TULIP is wilted.

When we discuss the perplexities connected with Calvinism, one that cannot be avoided is the powerful enigma of Charles Haddon Spurgeon.

Seaton quotes Spurgeon (1834–1892) as endorsing Calvinism, "The old truth that Calvin preached, that Augustine preached, that Paul preached, is the truth that I must preach today, or else be false to my conscience and my God."[129] Indeed, it cannot be denied that Spurgeon, repeatedly and clearly, did describe himself as a Calvinist.

> We only use the term 'Calvinism' for shortness. That doctrine which is called 'Calvinism' did not spring from Calvin; we believe that it sprang from the great founder *[sic]* of all truth. Perhaps Calvin himself derived it mainly from the writings of Augustine. Augustine obtained his views,

[129]Seaton, *The Five Points of Calvinism*, 24.

> without doubt, through the Spirit of God, from the diligent study of the writings of Paul, and Paul received them of the Holy Ghost, from Jesus Christ, the great founder *[sic]* of the Christian dispensation. We use the term then, not because we impute any extraordinary importance to Calvin's having taught these doctrines. We would be just as willing to call them by any other name, if we could find one which would be better understood, and which on the whole would be as consistent with fact.
>
> The old truth that Calvin preached, that Augustine preached, that Paul preached, is the truth that I must preach today, or else be false to my conscience and my God. I cannot shape truth; I know of no such thing as paring off the rough edges of a doctrine. John Knox's gospel is my gospel, that which thundered through Scotland must thunder through England again.[130]

Spurgeon is without question one of my favorite writers. I am fortunate to have printed copies of almost everything that he wrote, except for those articles that appeared in the periodical *The Sword and The Trowel.* More than possessing his writings, I have read nearly all of his works that I own. Additionally, I have multiple volumes accessible on CDs for ease of access.

Spurgeon is traditionally given the title *Prince of Preachers*, which is a proper recognition of his ability to use words that are very precise, highly descriptive, and easily understood. Spurgeon is among the most influential of men upon my personal ministry and biblical understanding. With that for background, I add this observation.

---

[130]Charles Haddon Spurgeon, *A Defence [sic] of Calvinism*, The Banner of Truth Trust, 2008, forward.

Reading the rich inheritance that Spurgeon left us in his writings reveals the portrait of a man and his preaching that appears to present a great paradox. To me, he is the epitome of an example for the perplexity caused by the doctrines of Calvinist. He declared his unswerving acceptance of every Point of the TULIP; moreover, Spurgeon consistently defended each Point of the TULIP throughout his ministry. These are undeniable facts easily verified from the voluminous writings that he left us as a rich inheritance.

However, the evidence that Spurgeon preached the *Gospel of whosoever will* from his youth to his death is also both undeniable and unimpeachable. Attempting to reconcile the conflict between these incompatible messages has strained greater abilities than those possessed by this writer. Selective plucking of comments from the years of his printed sermons and articles and disassociating those statements from the context of that particular sermon or article and even more so from the setting of the whole of his ministry does not solve the conflict; it only demonstrates it. The preaching of Charles Haddon Spurgeon has been used to endorse and to bolster the positions of both the TULIP and the *Gospel of whosoever will.* That is why Spurgeon becomes, or at least his preaching becomes, an enigma.

Spurgeon identifies himself with Augustine, Calvin, and Knox. This is strange on several levels. While Calvin and Knox followed Augustine in his belief in baptismal regeneration in some measure, Spurgeon did not believe in infant baptism either to remove original sin or to bring the child into the covenant. Spurgeon did believe in the necessity of baptism for adult salvation.

The teachings of Augustine have been explored previously in this paper and Spurgeon most assuredly did *not* believe all, or even most, of that which Augustine advanced. In addition to the necessity of baptism for salvation, Augustine held to many other doctrines that Spurgeon strongly opposed in his preaching. Among these are: (1) the perpetual virginity of Mary; (2) the creation as described in Genesis being allegorical; (3) the intercession of the saints; (4) "the view that the Biblical text should not be interpreted as properly literal, but rather as metaphorical, if it contradicts what we know from science and our God-given reason"; (5) in the "real presence of Christ in the Eucharist"; (6) in purgatory and prayers for the dead; (7) in papal succession, and also a host of other doctrines, all of which, Spurgeon rejected.

Therefore, for Spurgeon to credit Augustine with having received his views "without doubt, through the Spirit of God" is very strange, if not absurd. *The teachings mentioned above did not come from the influence of the Spirit of Truth.* Spurgeon is saying far more than he intended to say in his affirmation of his own association with Augustine, Calvin, and Knox. Even if he is selectively associating himself only with a common agreement on the doctrines of Calvinism, Spurgeon is compelled to overlook the additional blatantly false and damning teachings to which they also held and which identified their ministries more strongly than even those identified in the TULIP. We are left to marvel at his desire to identify himself in particular with those false doctrines of Augustine without a specific disclaimer of the errors that they entail.

This perplexing question of how it was possible that Spurgeon could, or would, continue to preach the *Gospel of whosoever will* and, yet simultaneously affirm that he believed in the TULIP appears to be answered by Spurgeon in two separate and yet complementary, while not contradictory, statements. The extensive record of his sermons proves that Spurgeon did preach *whosoever will may come while professing a belief in Calvinism* throughout his public ministry.

First, as his normal practice, Spurgeon did not preach the TULIP when he was addressing those who were not already professing believers. Read his words on the issue and draw your own conclusions.

> Be it known unto you, therefore, men and brethren, that through this man is preached unto you the forgiveness of sins and by him all that believe are justified from all things from which they could not be justified by the law of Moses.—Acts 13:38, 39.
>
> APOSTOLICAL preaching was widely different from the common sermonizing of this age. Doubtless, when the Apostles addressed assemblies of believers, they took distinct subjects, and kept to them, opening up and expounding the particular truths they had in view. But when speaking to the outside world, and making their appeals to unbelievers, they do not usually appear to have selected any one doctrine as their topic. The manner in which they preached did not so much consist in inculcating a specific doctrine, and showing the inferences that would naturally arise from it, as it did in declaring certain facts of which they had been actual witnesses themselves, and had been chosen to bear witness to others. Turn to Peter's sermon at Pentecost, or the same Apostle's sermon to Cornelius, or to the record of Paul's preaching at Perga or at Antioch. You will find these discourses were an argument from the Scriptures that as God had of old promised to send a Savior, so Jesus Christ had come into the world, had lived a holy life, had been put to death, being falsely accused, had been laid in the grave, after three days had risen again, that afterwards the had ascended, according to the testimony of the Prophets. Of him they spoke, that whosoever believed in this man, who was very God, should

> certainly be saved by him. This was the declaration which they made.

I interrupt the long paragraph to isolate and to emphasize the last sentence and the next sentence so that what their message will not be missed.

> I do not find them, as a rule, expounding the doctrine of election in promiscuous assemblies of unbelievers; arguing the subtle questions of free agency and predestination, or striving about words to no profit, to the subverting of the hearers.
>
> Their resolute purpose it was to declare those things that pertain directly to the salvation of the soul, this being the all important matter which they would have all men to heed. Thus they charged every one *[sic]* who heard them, at the peril of his soul, to accept the revelation and embrace the faith of the gospel. Listen to the Apostle Paul in that famous fifteenth chapter in the first Epistle to the Corinthians which is usually read at funerals. He says there: "Moreover, brethren, I declare unto you the gospel which I delivered unto you." Now you expect him to begin a long list of doctrines; but instead of that he says, "How that Christ died for our sins according to the Scriptures; and that he was buried, and that on the third day he rose again according to the Scriptures." This it is that he emphatically describes as the gospel. To assert these facts, to exhort men to believe them, and to put their trust in the Man who thus lived, and died, and rose again, was the preaching of the gospel which of old shook the hoary systems of superstition, fastened though they seemed to be upon their thrones most securely; which enlightened the darkness of heathendom, and made, in those first ages of Christianity, the whole world to be

> astonished with the light and the glory of Christ.[131]

Additionally, Spurgeon always preached the Gospel as an invitation that must be accepted by faith and insisted that the Gospel must be preached to all men without any restriction and without any reservation. His consistent pattern of preaching would seem to contradict his avowed doctrinal position.

The examples of such preaching are far too vast and much too easily accessed to be included in this size book. A few samples scattered through his ministry will serve adequately to validate the assertion that Spurgeon preached, the *Gospel of whosoever will may come.*

EXAMPLE 1:

> But sirs, ye must die. Since last we met together, probably some have gone to their long last home; and ere we meet again in this sanctuary, some here will be amongst the glorified above, or amongst the damned below. Which will it be? Let your soul answer. If to-night *[sic]* you fell down dead in your pews, or where you are standing in the gallery, where would you be? in *heaven* or in *hell*? Ah! deceive not yourselves; let conscience have its perfect work; and if, in the sight of God, you are obliged to say, "I tremble and fear lest my portion should be with unbelievers," listen one moment, and then I have done with thee. "He that believeth and is baptized shall be saved, and he that believeth not shall be damned." Weary sinner, hellish sinner, thou who art the devil's castaway, reprobate, profligate, harlot, robber, thief, adulterer, fornicator, drunkard, swearer, Sabbath-breaker-list! I speak to thee as

---

[131]Charles H. Spurgeon, *Metropolitan Tabernacle Pulpit*, Volume 63, 31. The sermon was published twenty-five years after his death in 1917; however, the date that the sermon was delivered is unknown.

well as the rest. I exempt no man. God hath said there is no exemption here. "*Whosoever* believeth in the name of Jesus Christ shall be saved." Sin is no barrier: thy guilt is no obstacle. Whosoever—though he were as black as Satan, though he were filthy as a fiend—whosoever this night believes, shall have every sin forgiven, shall have every crime effaced, shall have every iniquity blotted out; shall be saved in the Lord Jesus Christ, and shall stand in heaven safe and secure. That is the glorious gospel. God apply it home to your hearts, and give you faith in Jesus![132]

EXAMPLE 2:

But to the poor trembling sinner, whose pride is gone, I repeat the comforting assurance. Wouldst thou shun sin? Wouldst thou avoid the curse? My Master tells me to say this morning,—" Come unto me all ye that are weary and heavy laden, and I will give you rest." I remember the saying of a good old saint. Some one *[sic]* was talking about the mercy and love of Jesus, and concluded by saying, "Ah, is it not astonishing?" She said, "No, not at all." But they said it was. "Why," she said, "it is just like him: it is just like him!" You say, can you believe such a thing of a person? "Oh yes!" it may be said, "that is just his nature." So you, perhaps, cannot believe that Christ would save you, guilty creature as you are. I tell you it is just like him. He saved Saul—he saved me—he may save you. Yea, what is more, he *will* save you. For whosoever cometh unto him, he will in no wise cast out.[133]

---

[132]Spurgeon, *Metropolitan Tabernacle Pulpit*, Volume 1, 82. The sermon was delivered January 21, 1855.

[133]Spurgeon, *Metropolitan Tabernacle Pulpit*, Volume 1, 159. The sermon was delivered February 25, 1855.

EXAMPLE 3:

On the back of that sweet title came this question, "Why stand ye here gazing into heaven?" They might have said, "We stay here because we do not know where to go. Our Master is gone." But oh, it is the same Jesus, and he is coming again, so go down to Jerusalem and get to work directly. Do not worry yourselves; no grave accident has occurred; it is not a disaster that Christ has gone, but an advance in his work. Despisers tell us nowadays, "Your cause is done for! Christianity is spun out! Your divine Christ is gone; we have not seen a trace of his miracle-working hand, nor of that voice which no man could rival." Here is our answer: We are not standing gazing up into heaven, we are not paralyzed because Jesus is away. He lives, the great Redeemer lives; and though it is our delight to lift up our eyes because we expect his coming, it is equally our delight to turn our heavenly gazing into an earthward watching, and to go down into the city, and there to tell that Jesus is risen, that men are to be saved by faith in him, and that whosoever believeth in him shall have everlasting life. We are not defeated, far from it: his ascension is not a retreat, but an advance. His tarrying is not for want of power, but because of the abundance of his long-suffering. *[sic]* The victory is not questionable. All things work for it; all the hosts of God are mustering for the final charge. This same Jesus is mounting his white horse to lead forth the armies of heaven, conquering and to conquer.[134]

---

[134]Spurgeon, *Metropolitan Tabernacle Pulpit*, Volume 31, 13. The sermon was delivered December 28, 1884.

EXAMPLE 4:

> First, a man can realize all this *when he knows that he is reconciled to God.* What is God's way of effecting reconciliation between a sinner and himself? Every sinner is under the curse of the broken law; for it is written, "Cursed is every one that continueth not in all things which are written in the book of the law to do them." No one of us has continued in the perfect observance of the whole law, and therefore God's righteous verdict is against us. The only way of escape from the curse is through the glorious Son of God, who took our nature, and was made a curse for us, as it is written, "Cursed is every one that hangeth on a tree." He stood in our room and stead, bore the punishment due to our guilt, and thus became a curse on our behalf. All the sacrifices of the Jews were types of this: they were fingers of light pointing to the one all-sufficient sacrifice. That sacrifice the Lord has accepted for men, and he has set forth the Lord Jesus to be the propitiation for our sins, and not for ours only, but for the sins of the whole world; so that whosoever believeth in Jesus Christ, God's appointed sacrifice, is set free from sin, and being set free from sin he can then delight in the Almighty, and lift up his face unto God.[135]

Spurgeon's preaching to the unsaved is simply not in keeping with the doctrines of Calvinism. His Calvinism is reserved for teaching believers.

EXAMPLE 5:

> "Hath God forgotten to be gracious?" Then why are all the old arrangements for grace still standing? There is the mercy-seat;

---

[135]Spurgeon, *Metropolitan Tabernacle Pulpit,* Volume 31, 339. The sermon date was May 3, 1885.

surely that would have been taken away if God had forgotten to be gracious. The gospel is preached to you, and this is its assurance, "Whosoever believeth in him is not condemned." If the Lord had forgotten to be gracious he would not have mocked you with empty words.

Our Lord Jesus Christ himself is still living, and still stands as a priest to make intercession for transgressors. Would that be the case if God had forgotten to be gracious? The Holy Spirit is still at work convincing and converting; would that be so if God had forgotten to be gracious? Oh brothers, while Calvary is still a fact, and the Christ has gone into the glory bearing his wounds with him, there is a fountain still filled with blood wherein the guilty may wash. While there is an atoning sacrifice there must be grace for sinners. I cannot enlarge on these points, for time flies so rapidly; but the continuance of the divine arrangements, the continuance of the Son of God as living and pleading, and the mission of the Holy Spirit as striving, regenerating, comforting—all this proves that God hath not forgotten to be gracious.[136]

EXAMPLE 6:

For God so loved the world, that he gave his only begotten Son, that whosoever believeth in him should not perish, but have everlasting life.—John 3:16.

I was very greatly surprised the other day, in looking over the list of texts from which I have preached, to find that I have no record of ever having spoken from this verse. This is all the more singular, because I can truly say that it might be put

[136]Spurgeon, *Metropolitan Tabernacle Pulpit*, Volume 31, 401. The sermon date was May 31, 1885.

in the forefront of all my volumes of discourses as the sole topic of my life's ministry. It has been my one and only business to set forth the love of God to men in Christ Jesus. I heard lately of an aged minister of whom it was said, "Whatever his text, he never failed to set forth God as love, and Christ as the atonement for sin." I wish that much the same may be said of me. My heart's desire has been to sound forth as with a trumpet the good news that "God so loved the world, that he gave his only begotten Son, that whosoever believeth in him should not perish, but have everlasting life."[137]

EXAMPLE 7:

This also is a necessary part of the doctrine: that whosoever believeth in him is justified from all sin; that whosoever trusts in the Lord Jesus Christ is in that moment forgiven, justified, and accepted in the Beloved. "As Moses lifted up the serpent in the wilderness, even so must the Son of man be lifted up; that whosoever believeth in him should not perish, but have eternal life." Paul's doctrine was, "It is not of him that willeth, nor of him that runneth, but of God that showeth mercy"; and it was his constant teaching that salvation is not of doings, nor of ceremonies, but simply and alone by believing in Jesus. We are to accept by an act of trust that righteousness which is already finished and completed by the death of our blessed Lord upon the cross. He who does not preach atonement by the blood of Jesus does not preach the cross; and he who does not declare justification by faith in Christ Jesus has missed the mark altogether. This is the very bowels of the

---

[137]Spurgeon, *Metropolitan Tabernacle Pulpit*, Volume 31, 497. The sermon was preached June 7, 1885.

> Christian system. If our ministry shall be without blood it is without life, for "the blood is the life thereof." He that preacheth not justification by faith knows not the doctrine of grace; for the Scripture saith, "Therefore it is of faith that it might be by grace; to the end the promise might be sure to all the seed." Paul gloried both in the fact of the cross and in the doctrine of the cross.[138]

EXAMPLE 8:

> God "so loved the world that he gave"—and still gives—"his only begotten Son, that whosoever believeth in him might not perish, but have everlasting, "life." The Lord is giving Christ away to-night. *[sic]* Oh, that thousands of you may gladly accept the gift unspeakable! Will anyone refuse? This good gift, this perfect gift,—can you decline it? Oh, that you may have faith to lay hold on Jesus, for thus he will be yours. He is God's free gift to all free receivers; a full Christ for empty sinners. If you can but hold out your empty willing hand, the Lord will give Christ to you at this moment. Nothing is freer than a gift. Nothing is more worth having than a gift which comes fresh from the hand of God, as full of effectual power as ever it was. The fountain is eternal, but the stream from it is as fresh as when first the fountain was opened. There is no exhausting this gift.[139]

This next excerpt is extensive; however, that length only serves to reveal how deeply and how completely Spurgeon was devoted to the "whosoever Gospel."

---

[138]Spurgeon, *Metropolitan Tabernacle Pulpit,* Volume 31, 639. The date of the sermon was September 13, 1885.

[139]Spurgeon, *Metropolitan Tabernacle Pulpit,* Volume 31, 503. The sermon date was June 7, 1885.

EXAMPLE 9:

Now notice secondly, and, I think I may say, with equal admiration, the love of God in THE PLAN OF SALVATION. He has put it thus: "that whosoever believeth on him should not perish but have everlasting life." The way of salvation is extremely simple to understand, and exceedingly easy to practice, when once the heart is made willing and obedient. The method of the covenant of grace differs as much from that of the covenant of works as light from darkness. It is not said that God has given his Son to all who will keep his law, for that we could not do, and therefore the gift would have been available to none of us. Nor is it said that he has given his Son to all that experience terrible despair and bitter remorse, for that is not felt by many who nevertheless are the Lord's own people. Rut the great God has given his own Son, that "whosoever believeth in him" should not perish. Faith, however slender, saves the soul. Trust in Christ is the certainty of eternal happiness.

Now, what is it to believe in Jesus? It is just this: it is to trust yourself with him. If your hearts are ready, though you have never believed in Jesus before, I trust you will believe in him now. O Holy Spirit graciously make it so.

What is it to believe in Jesus?

It is, first, to give your firm and cordial assent to the truth, that God did send his Son, born of a woman, to stand in the room and stead of guilty men, and that God did cause to meet on him the iniquities of us all; so that he bore the punishment due to our transgressions, being made a curse for us. We must heartily believe the Scripture which saith,—"the chastisement of our peace was upon him; and with his stripes we are healed." I ask for your assent to the grand doctrine of substitution, which is the marrow of the gospel. Oh, may God the Holy Spirit lead you to give a cordial assent to it at once; for wonderful as it is, it is a fact that God was in Christ reconciling the world unto himself, not imputing their trespasses unto them. Oh that you may rejoice that this is true, and be thankful that such a blessed fact is revealed by God himself. Believe that the substitution of the Son of God is certain; cavil not at the plan, nor question its validity, or efficacy, as many do. Alas! they nick at God's great sacrifice, and count it a sorry invention. As for me, since God has ordained to save man by a substitutionary sacrifice, I joyfully agree to his method, and see no reason to do anything else but admire it and adore the Author of it. I joy and rejoice that such a plan should have been thought of, whereby the justice of God is vindicated, and his mercy is set free to do all that he desires. Sin is punished in the person of the Christ, yet mercy is extended to the guilty. In Christ mercy is sustained by justice, and justice satisfied by an act of mercy. The worldly wise say hard things about this device of infinite wisdom; but as for me, I love the very name of the cross, and count it to be the center of wisdom, the focus of love, the heart of righteousness. This is a main point of faith—to give a hearty assent to the giving of Jesus to suffer in our place and stead, to agree with all our soul and mind to this way of salvation.

The second thing is that you do accept this for yourself. In Adam's sin, you did not sin personally, for you were not then in existence; yet you fell; neither can you now complain thereof, for you have willingly endorsed and adopted Adam's sin by committing personal transgressions. You have laid your hand, as it were, upon Adam's sin, and made it your own, by committing personal and actual sin. Thus you perished by the sin of another, which you adopted and endorsed; and in like manner must you be saved by the righteousness of another, which you are to accept and appropriate. Jesus has offered an atonement, and that atonement becomes yours when you accept it by putting your trust in him. I want you now to say,

My faith doth lay her hand
On that dear head of thine,
While, like a penitent, I stand
And here confess my sin.

Surely this is no very difficult matter. To say that Christ who hung upon the cross shall be my Christ, my surety, needs neither stretch of intellect, nor splendor of character; and yet it is the act which brings salvation to the soul.

One thing more is needful; and that is personable trust. First comes assent to the truth, then acceptance of that truth for yourself, and then a simple trusting of yourself wholly to Christ, as a substitute. The essence of faith is trust, reliance, dependence. Fling away every other confidence of every sort, save confidence in Jesus. Do not allow a ghost of a shade of a shadow of a confidence in anything that you can do, or in anything that you can be; but look alone to him who God has set forth to be the propitiation for sin. This I do at this very moment; will you not do the same? Oh, may the sweet Spirit of God lead you now to trust in Jesus! See, then, the love of God in putting it in so plain, so easy a way. Oh, thou broken, crushed and despairing sinner, thou canst not work, but canst thou not believe that which is true? Thou canst not sigh; thou canst not cry; thou canst not melt thy stony heart; but canst thou not believe that Jesus died for thee, and that he can change that heart of thine and make thee a new creature? If thou canst believe this, then trust in Jesus to do so, and thou art saved; for he that believes in him is justified. “He that believeth in him hath everlasting life.” He is a saved man. His sins are forgiven him. Let him go his way in peace, and sin no more.

Thirdly, the love of God shines forth with transcendent brightness in a third point, namely, in THE PERSONS FOR WHOM THIS PLAN IS AVAILABLE, and for whom this gift is given. They are described in these words—"Whosoever believeth in him." There is in the text a word which has no limit—"God so loved the world"; but then comes in the descriptive limit, which I beg you to notice with care: “He gave his Only Begotten Son that whosoever believeth in him might not perish. God did not so love the world that any man who does not believe in Christ shall be saved; neither did God so give his Son that any man shall be saved who refuses to believe in him. See how it is put—"God so loved the world, that he gave his only begotten Son, that whosoever believeth in him should not perish.” Here is the compass of the love: while every unbeliever is excluded, every believer is included. “Whosoever believeth in him.” Suppose there be a man who has been guilty of all the lusts of the flesh to an infamous degree, suppose that he is so detestable that he is only fit to be treated like a moral leper, and shut up in a separate house for fear he should contaminate those who hear or see him; yet if that man shall believe in Jesus Christ, he shall at once be made clean from his defilement, and shall not perish because of his sin. And suppose there be another man who, in the pursuit of his selfish motives, has ground down the poor, has robbed his fellow-traders, and has even gone so far as to commit actual crime of which the law has taken cognisance *[sic]*, yet if he believes in the Lord Jesus Christ he shall be led to make restitution, and his sins shall be forgiven him. I once heard of a preacher addressing a company of men in chains, condemned to die for murder and other crimes. They were such a drove of beasts to all outward appearances that it seemed hopeless to preach to them; yet were I set to be chaplain to such a wretched company I should not hesitate to tell them that "God so loved the world, that he gave his Only Begotten Son, that whosoever believeth in him should not perish, but have everlasting life." O man, if thou wilt believe in Jesus as the Christ, however horrible thy past sins have been they shall be blotted out; thou shalt be saved from the power of thine evil habits; and thou shaft begin again like a child newborn, with a new and true life, which God shall give thee. "Whosoever believeth in him,"—that takes you in, my aged friend, now lingering within a few tottering steps of the grave. O grey-headed sinner, if you believe in him, you shall not perish. The text also includes you, dear boy, who have scarcely entered your teens as yet: if you believe in him, You shall not perish. That takes you in, fair maiden, and gives you hope and joy while yet young. That comprehends all of us, provided we believe in the Lord Jesus Christ. Neither can all the devils in hell find out any reason why the man that believes in Christ shall be lost, for it is written, "Him that cometh to me I will in no wise cast out." Do they say, "Lord, he has been so long in coming"? The Lord replies,—"Has he come? Then I will not cast him out for all his delays." But, Lord, he went back after making a profession. "Has he at length come? Then I will not cast him out for all his backslidings." But, Lord, he was a foul-mouthed blasphemer.

> "Has he come to me? Then I will not cast him out for all his blasphemies." But, says one, "I take exception to the salvation of this wicked wretch. He has behaved so abominably that in all justice he ought to be sent to hell." Just so. But if he repents of his sin and believes in the Lord Jesus Christ, whoever he may be, he shall not be sent there. He shall be changed in character, so that he shall never perish, but have eternal life.
>
> Now, observe, that this "whosoever" makes a grand sweep; for it encircles all degrees of faith. "Whosoever believeth in him." It may be that he has no full assurance; it may be that he has no assurance at all; but if he has faith, true and childlike, by it he shall be saved. Though his faith be so little that I must needs put on my spectacles to see it, yet Christ will see it and reward it. His faith is such a tiny grain of mustard seed that I look and look again but hardly discern it, and yet it brings him eternal life, and it is itself a living thing. The Lord can see within that mustard seed a tree among whose branches the birds of the air shall make their nests.[140]

After reading the evidence of the above statements from the sermons of Spurgeon, any individual that denies Spurgeon preached the *Gospel of whosoever will* is simply being dishonest. I make no effort to raise any doubt whether Spurgeon believed the TULIP. He said that he did; I accept his word. At the same time, I must insist that his preaching does not strictly conform to the TULIP.

I believe that Spurgeon never allowed his mind to override his heart.

---

[140]Spurgeon, *Metropolitan Tabernacle Pulpit,* Volume 31, 503–507. The sermon was preached June 7, 1885.

The confliction, it seems to me, between what Spurgeon believed in his mind and what he preached from his heart is clearly revealed in the following paragraphs from his booklet *A Defence [sic] of Calvinism*, written to explain his beliefs.

> I know there are some who think it necessary to their system of theology to limit the merit of the blood of Jesus: if my theological system needed such a limitation, I would cast it to the winds. I cannot, I dare not allow the fault to find a lodging in my mind, it seemed so near akin to blasphemy. In Christ's finished work I see an ocean of merit; my plummet finds no bottom, my eye discovers no sure. There must be sufficient efficacy in the blood of Christ, if God had so willed it, to have saved not only all in this world, but all in ten thousand worlds, had they transgressed their Makers law. Once admit infinity into the matter, and the limit is out of the question. Having a Divine Person for an offering, it is not consistent to conceive of limited value; bound and made sure our terms and applicable to the Divine sacrifice.[141]

> The system of truth revealed in the Scriptures is not simply one straight line, but two; and no man will ever get a right view of the Gospel until he knows how to look at the two lines at once. For instance, I read in one Book of the Bible, 'The Spirit and the bride say, Come. And let him that hears say, Come. And let him that is athirst come. And whosoever will, let him take the water of life freely.' Yet I am told, in another part of the same inspired Word, that, 'it is not of him that willeth, nor of him that runneth, but of God that show with mercy.' I see, in one place, God in

---

[141]Spurgeon, *A Defence [sic] of Calvinism*, 20.

providence presiding over all, and yet I see, and I cannot help saying, that man acts as he pleases, and that God has left his actions, in a great measure, to his own free-will. Now, if I were to declare that man was so free to act that there was no control of God over his actions, I should be driven very near to atheism; and if, on the other hand, I should declare that God so over rules all things that man is not free enough to be responsible, I should be driven at once into Antinomianism or fatalism.[142]

That God predestines,[143] and yet that man is responsible, are two facts that few can see clearly. They are believed to be inconsistent and contradictory to each other. If, then, I find in one part of the Bible that everything is foreordained, that is true; and if I find, in another Scripture, that man is responsible for all his actions, that is true; and it is only my folic that leads me to imagine that these two truths can ever contradict each other. I do not believe they can ever be welded into one upon any earthly anvil, but they certainly shall be one in eternity. They are two lines that are so nearly parallel, that the human mind which pursues them farthest will never discover that they converge, but they do converge, and they will meet somewhere in eternity, closed the throne of God, whence all truth doth spring.[144]

---

[142]Spurgeon, *A Defence [sic] of Calvinism*, 25, 26.

[143]Were Spurgeon to have used the words: "That God is sovereign" in place of "That God predestinates," his statement would have resolved his problems in reconciling the two concepts of sovereignty and responsibility. I believe that the Scriptures clearly state that in the exercise of His sovereignty, God has willed, elected, determined, chosen, established, decided, designated, etc., that man shall have free will and is, therefore, entirely responsible for his personal eternal destiny.

[144]Spurgeon, *A Defence [sic] of Calvinism*, 26.

Some persons love the doctrine of universal atonement because they say, 'It is so beautiful. It is a lovely idea that Christ should have died for all men; it commends itself,' they say, 'to the instincts of humanity; there is something in it full of joy and beauty.' I admit there is, but beauty may be often associated with falsehood. There is much which I might admire in the theory of universal redemption, but I will just show what the supposition necessarily involves. If Christ on his cross intended to save every man, then he intended to save those who were lost before he died. If the doctrine be true, that he died for all men, then he died for some who were in hell before he came into this world, for doubtless there were even then myriads there who had been cast away because of their sins. Once again, if it was Christ's intention to save all men, how deplorably has he been disappointed, for we have his own testimony that there is a lake which burneth with fire and brimstone, and into that pit of woe have been cast some of the very persons who, according to the theory of universal redemption, were bought with his blood. That seems to me a conception 1000 times more repulsive than any of those consequences which are said to be associated with the Calvinistic and Christian doctrine of special and particular redemption. To think that my Savior died for men who were or are in hell, seems a supposition to horrible for me to entertain.

To imagine for a moment that he was the Substitute for all the sons of men, and that God, having first punished the Substitute, afterwards punished the sinners themselves, seems to conflict with all my ideas of Divine justice. That Christ should offer an atonement and satisfaction for the sins of all men, and then afterwards some of those very men should be punished for the sins for which Christ had already

> atonement, appears to me to be the most monstrous iniquity that could ever have been imputed to Saturn, to Janus, to the goddess of the Thugs, or to the most diabolical heathen deities. God forbid that we should ever think the loss of Jehovah, the just and wise and good![145]

Spurgeon acknowledges that he cannot reconcile the dual truths of Scripture that God is sovereign and that man has the freewill to choose or to reject. Spurgeon expressed the sovereignty of God as "God predestines." By the choice to use that word *predestines,* he acknowledges all of the Five Points of Calvinism. Yet, he continues to be unable to reconcile the Total Inability, the Unconditional Election, the Limited Atonement, the Irresistible Grace, and the Perseverance of the Saints with the *whosoever will may come* of the Gospel. It appears that his problem was that he accepted the terminology and the definitions of Calvinism, but found that they produced contradictions and tension with Scripture that he could not explain.

The struggle that I believe existed between his heart and his mind and that I have shown was unquestionably present in the preaching of Spurgeon finds careful expression in the following passage.

> Furthermore, we would remind you that faith in Jesus is a sign of life. If in your heart you can trust yourself to Christ, and believe in him that he can save you, you have eternal life already. "He that believeth on the Son hath everlasting life." If thou canst now, though it be for the first time, trust thyself alone on Christ, faith is the surest evidence of the work of the Holy Ghost. Thou "hast passed from death unto life" already. Thou canst not see the Spirit any more than thou canst see the wind;

---

[145]Spurgeon, *A Defence [sic] of Calvinism,* 22, 23.

but, if thou hast faith, that is a blessed vane that turns in the way the Spirit of God blows. "Whosoever believeth that Jesus is the Christ, is born of God." If thou believest, this is true of thee, and if thou dost cast thyself wholly upon Christ, remember that it is written, "He that believeth on him is not condemned;" wherefore be of good cheer.

We beg you not to be led aside to the discussion of difficulties. There are a great many difficulties. To tell dry bones to live, is a very unreasonable sort of thing when tried by rules of logic; and for me to tell you, a dead sinner, to believe in Christ, may seem perfectly unjustifiable by the same rule. But I do not need to justify it. If I find it in God's Word, that is quite enough for me; and if the preacher does not feel any difficulty in the matter, why should you? There is a difficulty, but you have nothing to do with it. There are difficulties everywhere. There is a difficulty in explaining how it is that bread sustains your body; and how that bread, sustaining your body, can be the means of prolonging your life. We cannot understand how the material can impinge upon the spiritual; and there are difficulties in almost everything connected with life. If a man will not do anything till he has solved every difficulty, we had better dig his grave. And you will be in hell if you will not go to heaven without having every difficulty solved for you. Leave the difficulties; there will be time enough to settle them when we get to heaven; meanwhile, if life comes through Jesus Christ, let us have it, and have done with nursing our doubts.[146]

---

[146]Spurgeon, *Metropolitan Tabernacle Pulpit,* Volume 38,146–147. The sermon was delivered May 15, 1890.

I call attention to two particular statements in these comments from Spurgeon that demonstrate how strong that confliction was.

The first is, "There is a difficulty, but you have nothing to do with it." That statement would seem to be understood as meaning that the individual has no part in salvation and to emphasize that salvation is entirely the work of God. The statement would fit within the TULIP.

The second is, "And you will be in hell if you will not go to heaven without having every difficulty solved for you. Leave the difficulties; there will be time enough to settle them when we get to heaven; meanwhile, if life comes through Jesus Christ, let us have it, and have done with nursing our doubts."

This last statement places unequivocally all of the responsibility on the individual. "You will be in hell ... if you will not go to heaven ... resolved for you ... if life comes through Jesus Christ, let us have it." Those declarations by Spurgeon place the full responsibility upon the person to exercise faith to receive the salvation offered in Christ. Those statements will not find comfort or rest within the doctrines of the TULIP.

The confliction within the heart of Charles Haddon Spurgeon was evident in his private conversations with his fellowmen and *even* in his conversations with his God. Speaking of the love of Spurgeon for the lost, a biographer records the following comments:

> He thundered out the message of the wrath of God, but in an intimate moment he ventured to say, "While I believe in eternal punishment, and must, or throw away my Bible, I also believe that God will give to the lost every consideration, consistent with His love. There is nothing vindictive in Him, nor can there be in His punishment of the ungodly." In fact, though he contended earnestly for the

> truth in Jesus, he was no bigot, nor did he ever imagine that any finite mind could comprehend, much less systematise, *[sic]* the whole of divine truth. But he knew what he knew, and would not be moved from it. He gloried in the Cross, and in the sacrifice of Christ as a substitute for guilty men, but he recognised *[sic]* the mystery of redemption that lies beyond man's understanding … .
>
> This breadth of heart was revealed on another occasion when in his prayer at a Thursday evening service **he dared to go far beyond his creed**, and in his passion for the souls of men cried, "Lord, hasten to bring in all Thine elect—and then elect some more."[147] [Emphasis is added.]

Spurgeon was, by his own description, a TULIP Calvinist; however, I must repeat that what he believed in his mind never seems to have found lodging in his heart.

While I have already expressed my admiration for the *preaching* of Spurgeon, I am not willing to follow *the practice* of Spurgeon of preaching personal responsibility, while also believing that no such personal responsibility is possible. It seems to me that this requires too much in the way of mental gymnastics for me to attempt.

While I reject that *practice* of his, I have chosen with my freewill that both my mind and my heart will follow his *advice; even when* it seems to be advice that he unfortunately did not follow himself. I believe that it is folly to attempt to confine the revelation found in the word of the living God within the boundaries of a humanly developed system based upon the reasoning of fallen humanity.

---

[147]http://www.spurgeon.org./misc/bio8.htm

No TULIP will grow in the soil of the following cited Scriptures until they are wrested and forcibly altered by being redefined with Calvinistic definitions.

> 1 Timothy 2:3–6 For this *is* good and acceptable in the sight of God our Saviour; Who will have all men to be saved, and to come unto the knowledge of the truth. For *there is* one God, and one mediator between God and men, the man Christ Jesus; Who gave himself a ransom for all, to be testified in due time.

> John 5:1–47 After this there was a feast of the Jews; and Jesus went up to Jerusalem. Now there is at Jerusalem by the sheep *market* a pool, which is called in the Hebrew tongue Bethesda, having five porches. In these lay a great multitude of impotent folk, of blind, halt, withered, waiting for the moving of the water. For an angel went down at a certain season into the pool, and troubled the water: whosoever then first after the troubling of the water stepped in was made whole of whatsoever disease he had. And a certain man was there, which had an infirmity thirty and eight years. When Jesus saw him lie, and knew that he had been now a long time *in that case*, he saith unto him, Wilt thou be made whole? The impotent man answered him, Sir, I have no man, when the water is troubled, to put me into the pool: but while I am coming, another steppeth down before me. Jesus saith unto him, Rise, take up thy bed, and walk. And immediately the man was made whole, and took up his bed, and walked: and on the same day was the sabbath. The Jews therefore said unto him that was cured, It is the sabbath day: it is not lawful for thee to carry *thy* bed. He answered them, He that made me whole, the same said unto me, Take up thy bed, and walk. Then asked they him, What man is that

which said unto thee, Take up thy bed, and walk? And he that was healed wist not who it was: for Jesus had conveyed himself away, a multitude being in *that* place. Afterward Jesus findeth him in the temple, and said unto him, Behold, thou art made whole: sin no more, lest a worse thing come unto thee. The man departed, and told the Jews that it was Jesus, which had made him whole. And therefore did the Jews persecute Jesus, and sought to slay him, because he had done these things on the sabbath day. But Jesus answered them, My Father worketh hitherto, and I work. Therefore the Jews sought the more to kill him, because he not only had broken the sabbath, but said also that God was his Father, making himself equal with God. Then answered Jesus and said unto them, Verily, verily, I say unto you, The Son can do nothing of himself, but what he seeth the Father do: for what things soever he doeth, these also doeth the Son likewise. For the Father loveth the Son, and sheweth him all things that himself doeth: and he will shew him greater works than these, that ye may marvel. For as the Father raiseth up the dead, and quickeneth *them*; even so the Son quickeneth whom he will. For the Father judgeth no man, but hath committed all judgment unto the Son: That all *men* should honour the Son, even as they honour the Father. He that honoureth not the Son honoureth not the Father which hath sent him. Verily, verily, I say unto you, He that heareth my word, and believeth on him that sent me, hath everlasting life, and shall not come into condemnation; but is passed from death unto life. Verily, verily, I say unto you, The hour is coming, and now is, when the dead shall hear the voice of the Son of God: and they that hear shall live. For as the Father hath life in himself; so hath he given to the Son to have life in himself; And hath given him authority to execute judgment also, because he is the Son of man. Marvel not at this: for the hour is coming, in the which all that are in the graves shall hear his voice, And shall come forth; they that have done good, unto the resurrection of life; and they that have done evil, unto the resurrection of damnation. I can of mine own self do nothing: as I hear, I judge: and my judgment is just; because I seek not mine own will, but the will of the Father which hath sent me. If I bear witness of myself, my witness is not true. There is another that beareth witness of me; and I know that the witness which he witnesseth of me is true. Ye sent unto John, and he bare witness unto the truth. But I receive not testimony from man: but these things I say, that ye might be saved. He was a burning and a shining light: and ye were willing for a season to rejoice in his light. But I have greater witness than *that* of John: for the works which the Father hath given me to finish, the same works that I do, bear witness of me, that the Father hath sent me. And the Father himself, which hath sent me, hath borne witness of me. Ye have neither heard his voice at any time, nor seen his shape. And ye have not his word abiding in you: for whom he hath sent, him ye believe not. Search the scriptures; for in them ye think ye have eternal life: and they are they which testify of me. And ye will not come to me, that ye might have life. I receive not honour from men. But I know you, that ye have not the love of God in you. I am come in my Father's name, and ye receive me not: if another shall come in his own name, him ye will receive. How can ye believe, which receive honour one of another, and seek not the honour that *cometh* from God only? Do not think that I will accuse you to the Father: there is *one* that accuseth you, *even* Moses, in whom ye trust. For had ye believed Moses, ye would have believed me: for he wrote of me. But if ye believe not his writings, how shall ye believe my words?

John 8:24 I said therefore unto you, that ye shall die in your sins: for if ye believe not that I am *he*, ye shall die in your sins.

John 12:44–50 Jesus cried and said, He that believeth on me, believeth not on me, but on him that sent me. And he that seeth me seeth him that sent me. I am come a light into the world, that whosoever believeth on me should not abide in darkness. And if any man hear my words, and believe not, I judge him not: for I came not to judge the world, but to save the world. He that rejecteth me, and receiveth not my words, hath one that judgeth him: the word that I have spoken, the same shall judge him in the last day. For I have not spoken of myself; but the Father which sent me, he gave me a commandment, what I should say, and what I should speak. And I know that his commandment is life everlasting: whatsoever I speak therefore, even as the Father said unto me, so I speak.

Romans 10:1–17 Brethren, my heart's desire and prayer to God for Israel is, that they might be saved. For I bear them record that they have a zeal of God, but not according to knowledge. For they being ignorant of God's righteousness, and going about to establish their own righteousness, have not submitted themselves unto the righteousness of God. For Christ *is* the end of the law for righteousness to every one that believeth. For Moses describeth the righteousness which is of the law, That the man which doeth those things shall live by them. But the righteousness which is of faith speaketh on this wise, Say not in thine heart, Who shall ascend

> into heaven? (that is, to bring Christ down *from above*:) Or, Who shall descend into the deep? (that is, to bring up Christ again from the dead.) But what saith it? The word is nigh thee, *even* in thy mouth, and in thy heart: that is, the word of faith, which we preach; That if thou shalt confess with thy mouth the Lord Jesus, and shalt believe in thine heart that God hath raised him from the dead, thou shalt be saved. For with the heart man believeth unto righteousness; and with the mouth confession is made unto salvation. For the scripture saith, Whosoever believeth on him shall not be ashamed. For there is no difference between the Jew and the Greek: for the same Lord over all is rich unto all that call upon him. For whosoever shall call upon the name of the Lord shall be saved. How then shall they call on him in whom they have not believed? and how shall they believe in him of whom they have not heard? and how shall they hear without a preacher? And how shall they preach, except they be sent? as it is written, How beautiful are the feet of them that preach the gospel of peace, and bring glad tidings of good things! But they have not all obeyed the gospel. For Esaias saith, Lord, who hath believed our report? So then faith *cometh* by hearing, and hearing by the word of God.

Therefore, I reject all of the teachings that are associated with Calvinism.

Lest I be misunderstood, I reject both the system of Jacob Arminius *and* the system of John Calvin equally and unequivocally. I do not believe that either Arminianism *or* Calvinism rightly divides the word of God. I reject each of the individual Five Points of both systems.

In place of their human systematization of Biblical revelation, I state again that I am content to follow the advice of Spurgeon.

> If I find it in God's Word, that is quite enough for me; and if the preacher does not feel any difficulty in the matter, why should you? There is a difficulty, but you have nothing to do with it. ... Leave the difficulties; there will be time enough to settle them when we get to heaven; meanwhile, if life comes through Jesus Christ, let us have it, and have done with nursing our doubts.

The sovereign God of Heaven has decreed that man shall be responsible for accepting or rejecting the gift of eternal life; that is the clear and repeated revelation of Scripture. I cannot explain the obvious apparent difficulties nor do I attempt to solve the multiple problems alleged by various objectors; I do not need to try to do so. Preaching the Gospel is not a logical dissertation; it is a simple proclamation.[148]

The apostle Peter preached the Gospel of *whosoever will may come.*

> Acts 10:34–43 Then Peter opened *his* mouth, and said, Of a truth I perceive that God is no respecter of persons: But in every nation he that feareth him, and worketh righteousness, is accepted with him. The word which *God* sent unto the children of Israel, preaching peace by Jesus Christ: (he is Lord of all:) That word, *I say*, ye know, which was published throughout all Judaea, and began from Galilee, after the baptism which John preached; How God anointed Jesus of Nazareth with the Holy Ghost and with power: who went about doing good, and healing all that were oppressed of the devil; for God was with him. And we are witnesses of all things which he did both in

[148]Isaiah 45:22 Look unto me, and be ye saved, all the ends of the earth: for I am God, and there is none else. Romans 1:16 For I am not ashamed of the gospel of Christ: for it is the power of God unto salvation to every one *[sic]* that believeth; to the Jew first, and also to the Greek.

> the land of the Jews, and in Jerusalem; whom they slew and hanged on a tree: Him God raised up the third day, and shewed him openly; Not to all the people, but unto witnesses chosen before of God, *even* to us, who did eat and drink with him after he rose from the dead. And he commanded us to preach unto the people, and to testify that it is he which was ordained of God *to be* the Judge of quick and dead. To him give all the prophets witness, that through his name whosoever believeth in him shall receive remission of sins.

The apostle Paul preached the Gospel of *whosoever will may come.*

> Romans 9:33–10:17 As it is written, Behold, I lay in Sion a stumblingstone and rock of offence: and whosoever believeth on him shall not be ashamed. Brethren, my heart's desire and prayer to God for Israel is, that they might be saved. For I bear them record that they have a zeal of God, but not according to knowledge. For they being ignorant of God's righteousness, and going about to establish their own righteousness, have not submitted themselves unto the righteousness of God. For Christ *is* the end of the law for righteousness to every one that believeth. For Moses describeth the righteousness which is of the law, That the man which doeth those things shall live by them. But the righteousness which is of faith speaketh on this wise, Say not in thine heart, Who shall ascend into heaven? (that is, to bring Christ down *from above*:) Or, Who shall descend into the deep? (that is, to bring up Christ again from the dead.) But what saith it? The word is nigh thee, *even* in thy mouth, and in thy heart: that is, the word of faith, which we preach; That if thou shalt confess with thy mouth the Lord Jesus, and shalt believe in thine heart that

> God hath raised him from the dead, thou shalt be saved. For with the heart man believeth unto righteousness; and with the mouth confession is made unto salvation. For the scripture saith, Whosoever believeth on him shall not be ashamed. For there is no difference between the Jew and the Greek: for the same Lord over all is rich unto all that call upon him. For whosoever shall call upon the name of the Lord shall be saved. How then shall they call on him in whom they have not believed? and how shall they believe in him of whom they have not heard? and how shall they hear without a preacher? And how shall they preach, except they be sent? as it is written, How beautiful are the feet of them that preach the gospel of peace, and bring glad tidings of good things! But they have not all obeyed the gospel. For Esaias saith, Lord, who hath believed our report? So then faith *cometh* by hearing, and hearing by the word of God.

The LORD Jesus Christ preached the Gospel of *whosoever will may come.*

> John 3:10–21 Jesus answered and said unto him, Art thou a master of Israel, and knowest not these things? Verily, verily, I say unto thee, We speak that we do know, and testify that we have seen; and ye receive not our witness. If I have told you earthly things, and ye believe not, how shall ye believe, if I tell you of heavenly things? And no man hath ascended up to heaven, but he that came down from heaven, even the Son of man which is in heaven. And as Moses lifted up the serpent in the wilderness, even so must the Son of man be lifted up: That whosoever believeth in him should not perish, but have eternal life. For God so loved the world, that he gave his only begotten Son, that whosoever believeth in him should

> not perish, but have everlasting life. For God sent not his Son into the world to condemn the world; but that the world through him might be saved. He that believeth on him is not condemned: but he that believeth not is condemned already, because he hath not believed in the name of the only begotten Son of God. And this is the condemnation, that light is come into the world, and men loved darkness rather than light, because their deeds were evil. For every one that doeth evil hateth the light, neither cometh to the light, lest his deeds should be reproved. But he that doeth truth cometh to the light, that his deeds may be made manifest, that they are wrought in God.

The Son of God did not commission a group of theologians to proclaim the Gospel. To the contrary, his disciples were dismissed as "ignorant and unlearned"[149] by the theologians and academicians of their day. However, those men had been with Jesus; they had been taught His message; they were trained in His methods, and they turned the world upside down.[150]

The *Gospel of whosoever will* was their *message.* The *Gospel of whosoever will* was also their *method.* That message with that method turned the world upside down. Without the printing press, radio, television, or the internet, those men and the other first generation believers seem to have carried the Gospel into every nook and cranny of the world.

If the traditions and historical records are to be trusted, then that first generation conveyed the

---

[149]Acts 4:13 Now when they saw the boldness of Peter and John, and perceived that they were unlearned and ignorant men, they marvelled; and they took knowledge of them, that they had been with Jesus.

[150]Acts 17:6 And when they found them not, they drew Jason and certain brethren unto the rulers of the city, crying, These that have turned the world upside down are come hither also;

Gospel *with their feet* and *by their mouth* westward through the breadth of North Africa and across southern Europe to Spain, as far north as the British Isles, and eastward into India, if not to China. Wherever the trade routes stretched its tentacles, there that first generation faithfully extended their witness.

Their faithfulness with so little in the way of means ought to shame us, who have so much in the way of means. Today, twenty centuries later, the *Gospel of whosoever will* must be faithfully published. We have multiple times more tools, but it might be that we have multiple times less faithfulness.

While we hesitate to witness for fear of offending someone or of being rebuked for our zeal, severe persecution to the first generation of believers was received as a motivation and was not accepted as a deterrent. When facing death and exile for *believing* the Gospel, "they that were scattered abroad went every where *[sic]* preaching the word." (Acts 8:4)

While preachers and commentators have a general tendency to add qualifiers to the extent of the spread of the testimony of the Gospel in Romans 1:8, it may well be that the apostle Paul was moved by the Holy Spirit to convey a far greater distance than that which stretched between Rome and Jerusalem.

> Romans 1:8 First, I thank my God through Jesus Christ for you all, that your faith is spoken of throughout the whole world.

Smilin' Ed McConnell was a radio personality of my childhood. Among the multiple programs that he conducted was the *Buster Brown Show*, with Froggy the Gremlin, which was popular with children and was enjoyed by adults. He was a Christian entertainer, a Baptist in his church membership, who included Biblical truths and Gospel music in his life and in his broadcasts. I imagine that my readers might have a difficult time imagining a contemporary television personality having a believable fervent Christian testimony. My childhood was lived in a better age with better heroes.

Most believers have sung the chorus from one of the Gospel songs that he wrote, but very few believers have known that the composer was my childhood friend, Smilin' Ed McConnell of the *Buster Brown Show*, (and multiple other broadcasts) that wrote it.

> I am happy today, and the sun shines bright,
> The clouds have been rolled away;
> For the Savior said, whosoever will
> May come with Him to stay (to stay).
>
> All my hopes have been raised, O His name be praised,
> His glory has filled my soul;
> I've been lifted up, and from sin set free,
> His blood has made me whole (me whole).
>
> O what wonderful love, O what grace divine,
> That Jesus should die for me;
> I was lost in sin, for the world I pined,
> But now I am set free (set free).
>
> Refrain:
>
> Whosoever surely meaneth me,
> Surely meaneth me, O surely meaneth me;
> Whosoever surely meaneth me,
> Whosoever meaneth me.[151].

As a personal matter, if whosoever does not mean me, then whosoever means nothing to me. As a practical matter, if whosoever means my neighbor, then I need to be using my feet and my mouth to tell them so.

---

[151]In Public Domain.

CHAPTER 14

QUE SERA, SERA

The deeper that I study the theological philosophy of what is commonly termed Calvinism, the more I am convinced that the driving force of Calvinism is not, as is often proclaimed, the desire to give all glory to God, *Soli Deo Gloria!* I am increasingly compelled to believe that the attraction of Calvinism and the motivation to follow Calvinism is the desire to find a simplistic solution to the problems of life and to do so by completely removing man from the equation through shifting all responsibility to God. I have concluded that Calvinism is devoted wholly to the exaltation of the sovereignty of God.

Calvinism is indeed Christianized fatalism. By that, I mean that Calvinism is fatalism defined and expressed with the use of Christian or even Biblical terminology. Calvinists recoil from the use of the word *fatalism* as a description of Calvinism by insisting that fatalism is driven by an impersonal fate, but that God is personally involved in predestination and makes His choices based on His glory and on His love for the elect.[152]

In spite of the protestations and the attempts at redefinitions of terminology by the Calvinists, the word *fatalism* is the perfect word to describe the philosophy of Calvinism. The *M-WD* defines the word *fatalism* as "a doctrine that events are fixed in advance so that human beings are powerless to change them; also: a belief in or attitude determined by this doctrine."

"Events that are fixed in advance so that human beings are powerless to change them"—what sentence could better describe the proclamation of the Calvinist regarding the trail of the raindrops, the swirl of the dust motes, and the eternal destiny of every individual soul?

While protesting that the two are not the same, the following paragraphs[153] actually demonstrate the discernible unity of fatalism and Calvinism.

> What is the difference between Calvinism and fatalism? Is Calvinism just 'a hair shy' of fatalism? By postulating a God who is absolutely sovereign over all, does this make God the "gasp" *[sic]* author of sin, or render us robots?
>
> First of all, let us define our terms. Calvinism broadly speaking is that system of theology whereby God who is sovereign works out ALL *[sic]* things for His own good purpose, which is hereby especially emphasized in the realm of salvation or soteriology. This is done through the use

---

[152]"Contrary to what many non-Calvinists think and say: Calvinism is not fatalism. Fatalism is belief in an impersonal determinism. It does not include God or any other personal power guiding or governing the course of human affairs." http://www.patheos.com/blogs/rogereolson/2011/06/arminians-and-others-who-misrepresentcalvinism-should-also-be-ashamed-of-themselves/

[153]http://www.angelfire.com/falcon/ddd_chc82/theology/fatalism.html

> of primary and secondary, and active and passive causes. By primary, we mean that God did it directly. By secondary, we mean that God did it through intermediaries, who may not by themselves be fully obedient to God's commands. Active causes refer to God doing such an action by an *[sic]* positive extension of His will, while passive causes refer to God doing such an action by NOT *[sic]* interfering and thus causing the event to be aborted.

According to this argument, God is sovereign and "works out all things for His own good purposes." However, He also uses intermediaries to work out "all things for His own good purposes"; however, the intermediaries "may not by themselves be fully obedient to God's commands." Somehow, it is considered logical to assert that God "works all things out" even when the intermediaries that He chooses to use *are not fully obedient.* Apparently, he is alleging that though God does not interfere with the intermediaries, the lack of full obedience by the intermediaries is used by God to work out *"His own good will."* He moves to explain this unusual reasoning.

> Now, all these terms are not found in the Bible per se, but they are used so as to give the issues we face clarity, much as how the term Trinity expresses a vital Truth of the Godhead. From this categorization *[sic]*, we can obtain the following chart:

CAUSES	PRIMARY	SECONDARY
Active	God personally does this action by a positive extension of His will	God does this action through intermediaries by a positive extension of His will
Passive	God personally does this action by not doing something in order to accomplish His will	God does this action through intermediaries by not doing something in order to accomplish His will

His chart plainly asserts that "God personally *does*" something "by not doing something." For those Calvinists who exercise themselves in the attempt to make palatable the odious doctrine of Double Predestination, it is crucial to establish this precise complex and extremely convoluted distinction. The incongruity of the statement is lost on the Calvinist.

He then endeavors to establish a narrow distinction between fatalism and Calvinism.

> Fatalism teaches that everything has been predetermined, thus regardless of what we do, everything has already been decided, and thus whatever has been decreed to happen will happen, and nothing anyone can do will thwart this event from happening. The conclusion drawn from this is that we might as well do nothing, since whatever we do will not matter; all has been predetermined anyway.
>
> As a cursory look between Christianity and Fatalism would show, Christianity has nothing whatsoever to do with Fatalism. Christianity has God working through intermediary causes, which includes us humans by the way, while fatalism denies the presence of intermediaries. In fatalism, God cannot work His will through using a person to implement it, which God often does as shown in the biblical narratives.

The writer uses Christianity as a synonym for Christianity. Certainly, Christianity has nothing to do with fatalism; however, the concern regarding fatalism is with the relationship between Calvinism and fatalism and that of not Christianity with fatalism. Fatalism is patently not a Bible concept. The writer gives diligent labor to the effort, but he reasons in a circle as he insists that whatever God has decreed will unalterably be accomplished. He clearly defines Calvinism as determinism.

> Nevertheless, doesn't Calvinism approach fatalism in a certain way? After all, if God is absolutely sovereign, doesn't that mean that nothing we do will ever change the will and actions of God?
>
> To this question, we answer: Yes and No. Yes, if by that it is meant that we cannot alter God's wills *[sic]* and foil or determine God's actions. No, if by that is meant that we cannot seem to alter God's wills *[sic]* and redirect God's plans. The key word here is 'seem'. God's will is something that will be done, but as He does work through intermediaries to implement it, and no one except God Himself know *[sic]* what His will is, sometimes God may not appear to get His way, but rest assured that whatever we do, the outcome is exactly as *[sic]* what God has planned and desired, even when it seemed otherwise and go *[sic]* against what we think we know about what God desires.

The use of the plural for God's will is not a misprint. The Calvinist speaks of God having two wills: the revealed *will* and the secret *will*. The first, the revealed will of God, is knowable at the present; the second *will*, the secret *will* of God, may become known in eternity. In any situation where the revealed will of God does not appear to be being accomplished, the Calvinist is assured that this development is because God is working His unknowable secret will. This secret will may even appear to conflict with the revealed will. The secret will is somewhat of an escape clause for the Calvinist.

> It is because of this reason that Calvinists are not fatalists. We acknowledge that God works through secondary causes (intermediaries) which include us. Whatever we do, we do so boldly, knowing that regardless of what we do, God's plans will still be accomplished. In fact, if anyone behaves like a fatalist, their *[sic]* idea of God is too

> small as compared to the true biblical God. To the fatalist, what their *[sic]* beliefs basically amount to is that God could possibly be thwarted by their actions, or the other extreme that God does not have use of me *[sic]*, of which both are refuted by Scripture. For the latter, God desires to use us in His endeavors *[sic]*, as the men of God throughout the Bible have known. For the former, they have a very small view of God, to think that their actions could in any way change God's plans.

His wording is somewhat confusing to me; he refers to the *former* and the *latter*. He mentions Calvinists first in the paragraph and follows that introduction with the pronoun *we*. However, his closing comments appear to be reversed, because he condemns the "very small view of God" by which he must surely have reference to the fatalists.

He strangely describes the fatalist as believing that "God could possibly be thwarted by their actions" and believing that it is possible "their actions could in any way change God's plans." He also ascribes to the fatalists a belief that God has no need of their actions. It seems that he does not understand that the fatalist believes instead that his actions cannot be anything more than the fulfillment of the plan of God.

At the same time, he describes himself and his fellow Calvinists as believing that "Whatever we do, we do so boldly, knowing that regardless of what we do, God's plans will still be accomplished." That last statement meets the *M-WD* definition of fatalism: "a doctrine that events are fixed in advance so that human beings are powerless to change them." To declare that whatever is done by anyone, the plan of God's will "will still be accomplished" is to profess a belief that is determinism, which is fatalism.

> In the area of Evangelism, for example, Evangelism is ultimately of God. Yet the reason why we do Evangelism is that God

> has commanded us to do so, and that He has made it such that we are the intermediaries of His will through the proclaimation *[sic]* of the Gospel. Evangelism is thus implemented by God through primary active and secondary active causes; the former through the Spirit's regeneration and the latter through us in priviledge *[sic]* of the Gospel proclaimation *[sic]*. And lest anyone should think that the idea of God including us in His plans means that the job might be botched, let them mediate on the words of Scripture which says that God is able from the stones to raise up children for Abraham (Mt. 3:9, Lk. 3:8). If any person thinks that his/her disobedience would foil the plans of God, let them think twice, for their disobedience has already been planned by God and would be punished by Him, and others will have taken up the duty which was not attended to by him/her.

The sentence structure requires attention as you read. However, the somewhat confusing structure does not obscure two declarative statements.

The first statement declares that the assigned job cannot be "botched," because it is God's plan.

> "And lest anyone should think that the idea of God including us in His plans means that the job might be botched, let them mediate on the words of Scripture which says that God is able from the stones to raise up children for Abraham."
>
> If any person thinks that his/her disobedience would foil the plans of God, let them think twice, for their disobedience has already been planned by God and would be punished by Him, and others will have taken up the duty which was not attended to by him/her.

He continues in that second paragraph to assert that the disobedience of the person does not "foil the plans of God," because that disobedience was *planned* by God. I repeat for emphasis: the person disobeys, because the disobedience was planned by God. Moreover, though God planned the disobedience, God will still punish that disobedience.

It is tempting to argue (for the sake of arguing) that since the disobedience was planned by God and the person is fulfilling the plan of God that the person is being obedient by being disobedient. That is as logical as charging God will punishing someone for fulfilling His will.

Those assertions in these quoted paragraphs surely read as if they were made by a fatalist. As he continues his argument, the absolute inescapable determinative decisions of God are stressed as the justification for his belief in Calvinism.

> Others might then ask, what about the Fall? Was the Fall of Adam predetermined by God? Well, since God is absolutely sovereign, the Fall must be something which He has ordained to happen. Furthermore, if election in Christ was done before the foundation of the world, that means that God has already known beforehand that men would fall and thus needed to be elected in Christ in order to be saved. In fact, since before the foundation of the world, and thus before the Fall, God has already elected some to salvation, the Fall must be seen as unavoidable and thus in a sense decreed in the eyes of God, otherwise God's election makes no sense, as it would be foiled if Adam did not sin.
>
> Nonetheless, God is not responsible for the Fall. The Fall was wholely *[sic]* due to Man's disobedience towards God. Since God did not cause Adam and Eve to fall, yet that event was inevitable, the implementation of the Fall was through secondary, passive causes. God did not cause Adam to sin, but let him do so, thus it was passive, and He was not the one primarily

> involved in the entire episode also, with Satan being the chief instigator and God only allowing it to happen.

With amazing linguistic legerdemain, he argues that the fall was "ordained," "known beforehand," "unavoidable," "decreed," and "inevitable." Nonetheless, though God *ordained* the Fall, *decreed* it, and *knew it beforehand*, God is not responsible for that *unavoidable* and *inevitable* Fall, which He *ordained* and *decreed*. Moreover, he writes that were Adam not to have sinned, the election that God made "before the foundation of the world" would have been "foiled." However, he also writes that "God did not cause Adam to sin."

That reasoning is very difficult for the non-Calvinist to follow because it is circuitous and tortuous logic. It will only resonate as logical or reasonable with a Calvinist.

Satan is identified as the "chief instigator" and assigned the legal responsibility, because "God only allowed it to happen." In this approach, Satan is the intermediary assigned to fulfill the will of God. How that removes the God that *ordained* it, *decreed* it, and *allowed* it to *happen* from bearing the responsibility for His will being accomplished is left unanswered.

The use of that word *happen* by a Calvinist to defend predestination and to describe the Fall is strange, because the word *happen* means, according to the *M-WD*, "to occur by chance." The entire paragraph alleged that the Fall did not occur as a *happening*, but as a planned event. That is the essence of the argument: "God did not cause Adam to sin, but let him do so ... God only allowing it to happen."

While the word *happen* is very often used with less precision than the definition would require, this argument would seem to use the word in accordance with the dictionary definition. The explanation offered is intended to prove that the will of God will always be accomplished, while also saying that God is not to be held responsible for what He only allowed to happen—that which just occurred, when nothing is supposed to just occur. For the Calvinist, the Fall did not happen, but it happened.

It is obvious that the advocate of this complicated tortuous analysis does not grasp that ***if*** God allowed the Adam to sin without being compelled to do so ***then*** Adam was permitted to act with freewill. The attempt to avoid making God responsible for what the Calvinist insist that God has decreed effectively dismantles Calvinism.

> What then of the decree of election and reprobation? Election is something whereby God does so personally and actively (Eph. 1:1–11), thus it is a primary active action. Reprobation, however was never said to be something God did actively, as God does not cause anyone to go to hell, but Scripture does say that God is personally involved in the process of reprobation (Rom. 9:17–22; Prov. 16:4; Jude 1:4; 1 Peter 2:8), therefore the process of reprobation is of a primary, passive nature.
>
> With this settled, it is hoped that it can be seen that Calvnism *[sic]* is NOT fatalism. Those who choose to continue to think it is show their ignorance of Calvinism, Scripture, and even philosophy, from which their objection is supposedly grounded in *[sic]* (since fatalism is not a biblical word or concept).

Before responding to the comments in these paragraphs, may I suggest that his final parenthetical comment is to be answered with *neither is Calvinism*? The weakness of the argument in support of separating Calvinism from fatalism is revealed by such frivolous evidence.

If the reader has managed to read the above paragraphs defending Calvinism from the charge of teaching fatalism, then the verbal contortions required to avoid affirming what is being affirmed must surely have been observed. Read once more the following statements from the article. While these are not the only examples of strange logic in the article, they will serve to show the necessity of some Calvinists to deny the reality of what they have declared as fact.

> God's will is something that will be done, but as He does work through intermediaries to implement it, and no one except God Himself know *[sic]* what His will is, sometimes God may not appear to get His way, but rest assured that whatever we do, the outcome is exactly as *[sic]* what God has planned and desired, even when it seemed otherwise and go *[sic]* against what we think we know about what God desires ... .
>
> If any person thinks that his/her disobedience would foil the plans of God, let them think twice, for their disobedience has already been planned by God and would be punished by Him, and others will have taken up the duty which was not attended to by him/her ... .
>
> Was the Fall of Adam predetermined by God? Well, since God is absolutely sovereign, the Fall must be something which He has ordained to happen. Furthermore, if election in Christ was done before the foundation of the world, that means that God has already known beforehand that men would fall and thus needed to be elected in Christ in order to be saved. In fact, since before the foundation of the world, and thus before the Fall, God has already elected some to salvation, the Fall must be seen as unavoidable and thus in a sense decreed in the eyes of God, otherwise God's election makes no sense, as it would be foiled if Adam did not sin.

> Nonetheless, God is not responsible for the Fall. The Fall was wholely *[sic]* due to Man's disobedience towards God. Since God did not cause Adam and Eve to fall, yet that event was inevitable … .

Though the author of the comments just cited declares that for me or anyone else to continue to suggest that Calvinism is fatalism is to "show their ignorance of Calvinism, Scripture, and even philosophy," the reality is that when he denies that Calvinism is fatalism he shows a lack of familiarity with the dictionary.

I have made the assertion that if Calvinism is to be accepted, the terms used by the Calvinist must be understood to have special meanings in particular settings; however, one word never fluctuates in meaning or in use by the true Calvinist. That word is sovereign.

Everything in the previous cited article, as in all of the teachings of Calvinism, is anchored in the one phrase: "since God is absolutely sovereign." The sovereignty of God in Calvinism is of ultimate importance; it is the identifiable foundation of Augustinianism and Calvinism. Using the metaphor of the TULIP, the sovereignty of God is the stem of the tulip and that stem may be accurately labeled "*Que, sera, sera.*"

That phrase became an American proverb when it was set to music in 1956. Doris Day sang *Que sera, sera* in a film directed by Alfred Hitchcock, *The Man Who Knew Too Much.* Written by Jay Livingston and Ray Evans, the song won an Academy Award and soon became the identifying song for Miss Day.

Through the song, Miss Day, in her storyline character, is relating an event from her childhood to her son. She says that one day she asked her mother what she would be when she grew up. She asked if she would be pretty or if she might be rich. Her mother responded with the motto "*Que sera, sera, whatever will be, will be."* The mother's reasoning is that since we are not permitted to look into the future, our thinking is to be that *whatever will be, will be.* In her words, "*Que sera, sera.*"

Unintentionally—*or is it*—the song summarizes Calvinism as if it were made for it—perhaps it was! To say that *Que sera, sera* is the Calvinist Anthem has been used as a comedic line. However, the story of that phrase is actually historically anchored in Calvinism. That history is well worth sharing.

The origin of the Spanish phrase "*Que sera, sera*" is very revealing. The co-writers of the song left a record of how they arrived at the use of the phrase.[154] They traced it to an Italian phrase, which was moved into Spanish for convenience. The Oxford English Dictionary[155] makes the same connection, but traces the phrase *specifically to a theological discussion* in the work of playwright, Christopher Marlowe. He wrote *The Tragical History of Doctor Faustus,*[156] which was written in the late 1500s.

> Faustus is alone with a volume in his hands:
>
> Such is the subject of the institute,
> And universal body of the law:
> This study fits a mercenary drudge,
> Who aims at nothing but external trash;
> Too servile and illiberal for me.
> When all is done, divinity is best:
> Jerome's Bible, Faustus: view it well.

---

[154]http://www.artdaily.com/section/anecdotes/idex.asp?int_sec=114

[155]The *Oxford English Dictionary* has an article headed que sera sera. The first quotation that the OED gives is "(a)1593 MARLOWE Faustus (1604) sig. A3, What doctrine call you this, Che sera, sera, What will be, shall be?"

http://forum.wordreference.com/showthread.php?t=1289478

[156]The citation is taken from "The Quarto of 1616" and has been ref ormatted. http://www.classicliterature.co.uk/Britishauthors/16th-centu ry/christopher-marlowe/the-tragical-history-of-doctor-faustus/ebook-p age-02.asp

He then reads:
Stripendium peccati mors est.

And then speaks:
Ha! Stipendium peccati mors est!
The reward of sin is death: that's hard.

He continues reading:
Si peccasse negamus, fallimur,
et nulla est in nobis veritas;
If we say that we have no sin,
we deceive ourselves,
and there is no truth in us.
Why, then, belike we must sin,
and so consequently die:
Ay, we must die an everlasting death.
What doctrine call you this,
Che sera, sera,
What will be, shall be?
Divinity, adieu!

Marlowe, in the person of Faustus, misuses and abuses the Scriptures (1) by presenting the Scriptures (the Latin Vulgate of Jerome) as stating that it is impossible for men not to sin, and (2) by presenting the Scriptures as not containing any provision for a means for those who have sinned to obtain forgiveness. These terrible misconceptions lead Faustus to the conclusion that both the act of sinning and the resulting consequent everlasting death are inevitable and unavoidable.

Therefore, he decides, "*Che sera, sera. What will be, shall be.*" Faustus reads the passage from Jerome's Latin translation and reaches the conclusion that since such a God as he perceives is revealed, there is no God that he will choose to worship; therefore, he says, "What will be, shall be! Divinity Adieu!"

The unavoidable inevitability of "What will be, shall be" is precisely what the TULIP of Calvinism teaches—whether eternal life or everlasting death, the teaching of Calvinism is "What will be, shall be." Far worse, Calvinism actually teaches that for the non-elect the God of Faustus exists. The non-elect is incapable of not sinning and the God of Calvinism provides no method whereby the non-elect is ever able to find forgiveness for his sins. In exalting the sovereignty of God, Calvinism brings disrepute to the character of God.

The application of this devotion by the Calvinist to *Que sera, sera* is demonstrated in a sermon by an affirmed Calvinist on John 3:16. This sermon reinforces the testimony given by Pastor J. C. Stevens.[157] The Calvinist does not believe that God loves every individual; the Calvinist believes that even to say that God loves every individual is "to oppose and combat God's sovereign, elective grace." Pastor L. R. Shelton wrote an article entitled, *God's Sovereign Love*[158] from which the following is taken.

> I want to bring you a series of Bible studies on one of the strangest and most misunderstood texts, I believe, of the entire Bible. You will find it in John 3:16, "FOR GOD SO LOVED THE WORLD, THAT HE GAVE HIS ONLY BEGOTTEN SON, THAT WHOSOEVER BELIEVETH IN HIM SHOULD NOT PERISH, BUT HAVE EVERLASTING LIFE." [Emphasis is in the original.]
>
> This is one of the greatest texts of the entire Bible, and yet one of the most misunderstood texts, as well as one of the most misemphasized texts. The average individual's mind runs in a certain groove when he reads it or quotes it, and therefore he emphasizes the text incorrectly and destroys its great meaning.
>
> It has been so used by the average Arminian, or freewiller, to try to oppose and combat God's sovereign, elective grace un-

---

[157]Pastor Stevens's testimony is found on page 138.

[158]L. R. Shelton, Sr. was the pastor of First Baptist Church, Algiers, Louisiana. http://www.the-highway.com/election_Shelton1.html

til the deep meaning of the text has literally been destroyed and in thousands of instances the minds of people have been prejudiced against it. So today IN THE AVERAGE RELIGIOUS CIRCLE THIS GREAT, GRACIOUS, MAGNIFICENT TEXT HAS LITERALLY BEEN BURIED UNDER THE RUBBISH OF FALSE DOCTRINE. [Emphasis is in the original.]

There is a popular belief abroad in the land today, and that is, THAT GOD LOVES EVERYBODY. There is no such doctrine taught in God's Word. This teaching is so popular among all classes that it ought to arouse the suspicion of everyone who loves the eternal truth of God's Word. This doctrine that God loves everybody is a modern belief. You will not find such a doctrine taught in God's Word or among the old church fathers, the Reformers, or the Puritans. [Emphasis is in the original.]

Many will modify the above statement by saying that God loves the sinner but hates his sins. This states nothing at all, because the sinner is sin himself. The above false statement is born in the heart and mind of an individual that knows nothing of the total depravity of the human heart. Everyone quoting the above statement will call your attention to Rom. 5:8, which reads thus,

"But God commendeth his love toward us, in that, while we were yet sinners, Christ died for us."

I want you to notice that word, "US, *[sic]* " in this Scripture does not refer to all sinners, but only to those who have come to know Christ as their Lord and Saviour, those who are God's elect. Nowhere in the Scripture is it taught that God loves everybody.

According to the doctrines of Calvinism, God does not love the world; He loves only the elect. The pastor mentioned above was not a fringe Calvinist, a hyper-Calvinist; he was an honest Calvinist that openly and accurately stated Calvinism. He is to be commended for his integrity.

I began my preaching ministry in 1958. Since then, the LORD of the Harvest has been gracious in providing me the privilege of telling the Gospel story to thousands of individuals. My father gave me some instructive counsel when I left home to preach. He said for me to remember that sheep ate off the ground and not from the trees. The apostle Paul was moved to record much the same philosophy:

> 1 Corinthians 14:8–9 For if the trumpet give an uncertain sound, who shall prepare himself to the battle? So likewise ye, except ye utter by the tongue words easy to be understood, how shall it be known what is spoken? for ye shall speak into the air.

The preacher is to use "words easy to be understood." The complexity of the contrived dictionary of Calvinism disqualifies that system for consideration for any preacher that desires to "utter by the tongue words easy to be understood." As Pastor Shelton so dramatically illustrates by his sermon, Calvinism requires its own interpreter. Even to understand John 3:16 necessitates the intervention of a Calvinist to explain *what God intended to say.*

This trumpet has never given an uncertain sound in regards to salvation because I have never found the *maybe* that the Calvinist system requires. I cannot preach, "It may be that Christ died for you; perhaps you will be saved." To proclaim *may be* is introducing a *maybe*, which is defined by the *M-WD* as meaning "perhaps" when used as an adverb and "uncertainty" when used as a noun. There is an uncertain sound in the gospel of "*maybe* Christ died for you; and *perhaps* He did, but only if you are one of the elect." *Que sera, sera* offers no comfort to the sinner.

The LORD Jesus chose to call our attention to a particular *type* in the Old Testament so that we might understand what we must do in order to be saved. There is no *Que sera, sera* in the *type,* the prophetic picture, or in the *antitype,* the fulfillment.

> Numbers 21:4–9 And they journeyed from mount Hor by the way of the Red sea, to compass the land of Edom: and the soul of the people was much discouraged because of the way. And the people spake against God, and against Moses, Wherefore have ye brought us up out of Egypt to die in the wilderness? for *there is* no bread, neither *is there any* water; and our soul loatheth this light bread. And the LORD sent fiery serpents among the people, and they bit the people; and much people of Israel died. Therefore the people came to Moses, and said, We have sinned, for we have spoken against the LORD, and against thee; pray unto the LORD, that he take away the serpents from us. And Moses prayed for the people. And the LORD said unto Moses, Make thee a fiery serpent, and set it upon a pole: and it shall come to pass, that every one that is bitten, when he looketh upon it, shall live. And Moses made a serpent of brass, and put it upon a pole, and it came to pass, that if a serpent had bitten any man, when he beheld the serpent of brass, he lived.

> John 3:14–18 And as Moses lifted up the serpent in the wilderness, even so must the Son of man be lifted up: That whosoever believeth in him should not perish, but have eternal life. For God so loved the world, that he gave his only begotten Son, that whosoever believeth in him should not perish, but have everlasting life. For God sent not his Son into the world to condemn the world; but that the world

> through him might be saved. He that believeth on him is not condemned: but he that believeth not is condemned already, because he hath not believed in the name of the only begotten Son of God.

Since the Old Testament uses the terms "every one" *[sic]* and "any man" for the *type,* and since the LORD Jesus, the *antitype,* twice uses the term whosoever, dare we change the words to mean *only the elect* and add the uncertainty of a nebulous *perhaps*? "God forbid: yea, let God be true, but every man a liar; as it is written, That thou mightest be justified in thy sayings, and mightest overcome when thou art judged" (Romans 3:4).

That third chapter of Romans continues emphatically to state that the offer of salvation is freely extended to all.

> Romans 3:22–26 Even the righteousness of God *which is* by faith of Jesus Christ unto all and upon all them that believe: for there is no difference: For all have sinned, and come short of the glory of God; Being justified freely by his grace through the redemption that is in Christ Jesus: Whom God hath set forth *to be* a propitiation through faith in his blood, to declare his righteousness for the remission of sins that are past, through the forbearance of God; To declare, *I say,* at this time his righteousness: that he might be just, and the justifier of him which believeth in Jesus.

The testimony of Charles Haddon Spurgeon as to his own path to salvation exemplifies the consistency of both Testaments in the presentation of salvation.

> While under concern of soul, I resolved that I would attend all the places of worship in the town where I lived, in order that I might find out the way of salvation. I was willing to do anything, and be any-

thing, if God would only forgive my sin. I set off, determined to go round to all the chapels, and I did go to every place of worship; but for a long time I went in vain. I do not, however, blame the ministers. One man preached Divine Sovereignty; I could hear him with pleasure, but what was that sublime truth to a poor sinner who wished to know what he must do to be saved? There was another admirable man who always preached about the law; but what was the use of ploughing *[sic]* up ground that needed to be sown? Another was a practical preacher. I heard him, but it was very much like a commanding officer teaching the manoeuvres *[sic]* of war to a set of men without feet. What could I do? All his exhortations were lost on me. I knew it was said, "Believe on the Lord Jesus Christ, and thou shalt be saved;" but I did not know what it was to believe on Christ. These good men all preached truths suited to many in their congregations who were spiritually-minded people; but what I wanted to know was,—"How can I get my sins forgiven?"—and they never told me that. I desired to hear how a poor sinner, under a sense of sin, might find peace with God; and when I went, I heard a sermon on "Be not deceived, God is not mocked," which cut me up still worse; but did not bring me into rest. I went again, another day, and the text was something about the glories of the righteous; nothing for poor me! I was like a dog under the table, not allowed to eat of the children's food. I went time after time, and I can honestly say that I do not know that I ever went without prayer to God, and I am sure there was not a more attentive hearer than myself in all the place, for I panted and longed to understand how I might be saved.

I sometimes think I might have been in darkness and despair until now had it not been for the goodness of God in sending a snowstorm, one Sunday morning, while I was going to a certain place of worship. When I could go no further, I turned down a side street, and came to a little Primitive Methodist Chapel. In that chapel there may have been a dozen or fifteen people. I had heard of the Primitive Methodists, how they sang so loudly that they made people's heads ache; but that did not matter to me. I wanted to know how I might be saved, and if they could tell me that, I did not care how much they made my head ache. The minister did not come that morning; he was snowed up, I suppose. At last, a very thin-looking man, a shoemaker, or tailor, or something of that sort, went up into the pulpit to preach. Now, it is well that preachers should be instructed; but this man was really stupid. He was obliged to stick to his text, for the simple reason that he had little else to say. The text was,—"LOOK UNTO ME, AND BE YE SAVED, ALL THE ENDS OF THE EARTH." [Emphasis is in the original.]

He did not even pronounce the words rightly, but that did not matter. There was, I thought, a glimpse of hope for me in that text. The preacher began thus—"My dear friends, this is a very simple text indeed. It says, 'Look.' Now lookin' don't take a deal of pains. It ain't liftin' your foot or your finger; it is just, 'Look.' Well, a man needn't go to College to learn to look. You may be the biggest fool, and yet you can look. A man needn't be worth a thousand a year to be able to look. Anyone can look; even a child can look. But then the text says, 'Look unto *Me.*' Ay!" said he, in broad Essex, "many on ye are lookin' to yourselves, but it's no use lookin' there. You'll never find any comfort in yourselves. Some look to God the Father. No, look to Him by-and-by. Jesus Christ says, 'Look unto *Me.*' Some on ye say, 'We must wait for the Spirit's workin'.' You have no business with that just now. Look to *Christ*. The text says, 'Look unto *Me*.'"

Then the good man followed up his text in this way:—"Look unto Me; I am sweatin' great drops of blood. Look unto Me; I am hangin' on the cross. Look unto Me; I am dead and buried. Look unto Me; I rise again. Look unto Me; I ascend to Heaven. Look unto Me; I am sittin' at the Father's right hand. O poor sinner, look unto Me! look unto Me!

When he had gone to about that length, and managed to spin out ten minutes or so, he was at the end of his tether. Then he looked at me under the gallery, and I daresay, with so few present, he knew me to be a stranger. Just fixing his eyes on me, as if he knew all my heart, he said, "Young man, you look very miserable." Well, I did; but I had not been accustomed to have remarks made from the pulpit on my personal appearance before. However, it was a good blow, struck right home. He continued, "and you always will be miserable—miserable in life, and miserable in death,—if you don't obey my text; but if you obey now, this moment, you will be saved." Then, lifting up his hands, he shouted, as only a Primitive Methodist could do, "Young man, look to Jesus Christ. Look! Look! Look! You have nothin' to do but to look and live." I saw at once the way of salvation. I know not what else he said,—I did not take much notice of it,—I was so possessed with that one thought. Like as when the brazen serpent was lifted up, the people only looked and were healed, so it was with me. I had been waiting to do fifty things, but when I heard that word, "Look!" what a charming word it seemed to me! Oh! I looked until I could almost have looked my eyes away. There and then the cloud was gone, the dark-

> ness had rolled away, and that moment I saw the sun; and I could have risen that instant, and sung with the most enthusiastic of them, of the precious blood of Christ, and the simple faith which looks alone to Him. Oh, that somebody had told me this before, "Trust Christ, and you shall be saved." Yet it was, no doubt, all wisely ordered, and now I can say,—
>
> "Ever since by faith I saw the stream
> Thy flowing wounds supply,
> Redeeming love has been my theme,
> And shall be till I die."[159]

When Spurgeon wrote that testimony for his autobiography, he assuredly did not sound as if he were a Calvinist believing in *Que sera, sera.* Spurgeon testified that he was saved because he believed the Gospel of *whosoever will may come.*

> By faith I understand that the blessed Son of God redeemed my soul with His own heart's blood; and by sweet experience I know that He raised me up from the pit of dark despair, and set my feet on the rock. He died for me. This is the root of every satisfaction I have. He put all my transgressions away. He cleansed me with His precious blood; He covered me with His perfect righteousness; He wrapped me up in His own virtues. He has promised to keep me, while I abide in this world, from its temptations and snares; and when I depart from this world, He has already prepared for me a mansion in the Heaven of unfading bliss, and a crown of everlasting joy that shall never, never fade away. To me, then, the days or years of my mortal sojourn on this earth are of little moment. Nor is the manner of my decease of much consequence. Should foemen sentence me to martyrdom, or physicians de-

---

[159]http://www.spurgeon.org/misc/abio011.htm

clare that I must soon depart this life, it is all alike,—

A few more rolling suns at most
Shall land me on fair Canaan's coast."

When only the Scriptures as they are written are consulted or preached, the Gospel invitation will never be misconstrued for a message of *Que sera, sera!* **until** the *whosoever will* is made to be code for *the elect*. The Bible as it is written knows only the Gospel of Whosoever will may come. Therefore, the message of salvation may be taken wherever men may be found and every man that is found may be told that God loves them individually and that the LORD Jesus died for each one of them personally.

> 1 John 4:14 And we have seen and do testify that the Father sent the Son *to be* the Saviour of the world.

Philip P. Bliss took those simple words of the Gospel invitation, placed them into poetic meter, coupled that with a melody, and gave Christians a song that has challenged the hearts of believers to share the Gospel of Whosoever will may come. The words have also offered hope to multitudes of individuals in need of a Saviour.

"Whosoever heareth," shout, shout the sound!
Spread the blessèd tidings all the world around;
Spread the joyful news wherever man is found;
"Whosoever will may come."

Whosoever cometh need not delay,
Now the door is open, enter while you may;
Jesus is the true, the only Living Way;
"Whosoever will may come."

"Whosoever will," the promise secure,
"Whosoever will," forever must endure;
"Whosoever will," 'tis life forevermore:
"Whosoever will may come."

Refrain:

> "Whosoever will, whosoever will,"
> Send the proclamation over vale and hill;
> 'Tis a loving Father, calls the wanderer home:
> "Whosoever will, may come."[160]

I cannot find the authority within the Scriptures to preach the Gospel of *Que sera, sera.* No verse, no passage suggests, let alone reads, "It may be that Christ died for you; it may be that you can be saved. *Que sera, sera.* "

I will not exchange the certain words of the LORD Jesus for the systems of theologians, even such elevated theologians as Augustine and John Calvin, or the sermons of a great preacher, such as Charles Haddon Spurgeon.

I reject completely all aspects of the philosophical and theological system of Calvinism. I believe that Calvinism manipulates the words and modifies the meaning of John 3:16–18 until those verses are mutated into a misrepresentation of the Gospel.

John Calvinist 3:16–18

> For God so loved the ~~world~~ elect, that he gave his only begotten Son, that ~~whosoever believeth~~ those who were chosen before the foundation of the world will be regenerated so that these will be given the gift of faith so that they will be able to believe in him [and] should not perish, but have everlasting life. For God sent not his Son into the world to condemn the ~~world~~ elect; but that the ~~world~~ elect through him might be saved. He that is regenerated so that he is enabled to receive the gift of faith and thereby he is able to respond and believeth on him is not condemned: but he that believeth not is condemned ~~already~~ from before the foundation of the

[160]In Public Domain.

> world, because he hath not ~~believed~~ been regenerated so that he could be given the gift of faith so that he may believe in the name of the only begotten Son of God.

The Whosever Gospel of John 3:16–18

> For God so loved the world, that he gave his only begotten Son, that whosoever believeth in him should not perish, but have everlasting life. For God sent not his Son into the world to condemn the world; but that the world through him might be saved. He that believeth on him is not condemned: but he that believeth not is condemned already, because he hath not believed in the name of the only begotten Son of God.

As for me and my ministry, the *Gospel of whosoever will* has been and will continue to be the theme, *exactly* as it was that of the LORD Jesus and of His ministry.

CHAPTER 15

UNNUMBERED BUT INSEPARABLE

Understand that not all of those who do identity themselves as Calvinists are willing to concede that the conclusions that I have made are an actual representation of their position. They will assert that these *extreme* views are restricted to those Calvinists that are *hyper-Calvinists.* I believe that this is entirely because they see the flaws in these assumptions of Calvinism and wish to exclude themselves from defending the indefensible.

Some describe themselves as Calvinistic, but are unwilling to identify themselves as Calvinists. Others will claim to be Four-Point, Three-Point, Two-Point, and even One-Point Calvinists.[161] The latter

[161]"There's plenty of room under the umbrella for anyone who is anything from a one- *[sic]* to five-point Calvinist," Patterson said, stipulating that any Southern Baptist would have to agree upon the doctrine known as perseverance of the saints or "once saved, always saved." "There's room for a two- *[sic]* or three-pointer like me, provided he can explain what is meant by two and three," Patterson said. "There's room for four- *[sic]* and five-pointers whom I believe lack scriptural justification for that, but I'm certainly not in favor of running them out." Dr. Paige Patterson: twice President of the Southern Baptist Convention; Past President Criswell Center for Biblical Studies; past President,

would state that they do believe in eternal security; however, eternal security is not one of the Five Points of Calvinism.

In actuality, it is theologically logical for only two kinds of Calvinists to exist: (1) Calvinists who are consistent, and (2) Calvinists who are inconsistent. It is disingenuous to attempt to separate the five cardinal points of Calvinism from each other. For the logic of Calvinism to be sustained, each Point of the TULIP must be accepted in the exact order of the TULIP acrostic.

To reject the first Point is to reject the subsequent Point and each of the others. To reject any single Point of the Five-Points is to reject every other Point that comes before that Point and to invalidate whatever Point follows that discarded Point. By way of example, when Total Inability (Total Depravity) is rejected, Unconditional Election has *no necessity*, Limited Atonement has *no purpose*, Irresistible Calling (Irresistible Grace) has *no possibility*, and the Perseverance of the Saints has *no reality*.

Loraine Boettner recognized this when he described the Five Points as being "so inter-related *[sic]* that they form a simple, harmonious, self-consistent system." He continued:

> "Prove any one of them true and all the others will follow as logical and necessary parts of the system. Prove any one of them false and the whole system must be abandoned ... and not one of them can be taken away without marring and subverting

---

Southeastern Baptist Theological Seminary, Wake Forest, NC; presently on the Board of Trustees, Cedarville University; currently President of Southwestern Baptist Theological Seminary, Forth Worth, TX. http://assets.baptiststandard.com/archived/1999/11_24/pages/calvinism.html

I find it tragic that a recognized leader with the biography of Dr. Paige Patterson *seems* to misunderstand Calvinism so woefully. He *misguides* his followers when he equates *once-saved-always-saved* with Perseverance of the Saints and he *misinforms* them when he speaks of the possibility of any genuine form of Calvinism that is less than the five points.

> the whole Gospel plan of salvation through Christ. We cannot conceive of this agreement arising merely by accident, nor even being possible, unless these doctrines are true."[162]

Seaton also acknowledges this by writing:

> ... our acceptance of total depravity as a true biblical statement of man's condition by nature will largely determine our attitude towards the next point that came under review at the Synod of Dort." ... "The doctrine of unconditional election follows naturally from the doctrine of total depravity.[163]

His reasoning for Unconditional Election is an example that is applicable for all of the Points: "If man is unable to save himself on account of the Fall in Adam being a *total* fall, and if God can alone save, and if all are not saved, then the conclusion must be that God has not chosen to save all." He is compelled to rely on the *if-then* argument.

It is only when that first *if* is accepted as an accurate and truthful doctrine derived from Scripture that the conclusion is allowed to stand as biblically valid. If any part of that first *if* does not present a doctrine from Scripture, then the conclusion does not *naturally* follow.

The Five Points of the TULIP are so interlocked that each requires all of the others. They are not independent or complementary of each other; instead, they are intertwined with each other. Indeed, as stated before, for the logic of Calvinism to be sustained, each Point must be accepted in the exact order of the TULIP acrostic. To disprove any one of the Five Points is to require the rejection of the other

---

[162]Boettner, *The Reformed Doctrine of Predestination*, Grand Rapids, MI, Eerdmans, 1932, Section II, The Five Points of Calvinism.

[163]Seaton, The Five Points of Calvinism, 11.

four. However, the Five Points are not the sum and substance of Calvinism.

Though the five doctrines that are emphasized in the TULIP have become identified in the collective mind of non-Calvinist Christianity and to some extent within Reformed Christianity as the fullness of Calvinism, Reformed Theology requires far more than the five petals of the TULIP.

In part, the limitation to only Five Points has developed simply for convenience of presentation; primarily, the summation of Calvinism into only these five phrases is due to the misunderstanding of the history of what produced those Five Points.

Reducing Calvinism into Five Points was certainly not by design of John Calvin. As has been documented earlier, the TULIP did not originate in the formative days of Calvinism, but it first appeared in print in 1932—three hundred sixty-eight years after the death of John Calvin, May 24, 1564. The TULIP did not appear in the Canons of Dort, which were published by the Synod meeting in 1618–1619, which was just over fifty years after the death of Calvin.

The generating cause of expressing the doctrines of John Calvin into Five Points was not to codify Calvinism or to reduce it to an acrostic for ease of instruction; it was the simple appropriateness of responding to the five remonstrations presented by the followers of Jacobus Arminus. What becomes overlooked is that multiple other issues of doctrine and practice were not in disputation and are not included in the Five Points.

The practice of those who followed Calvin of the baptism of infants was not challenged by followers of Arminius, nor did they challenge the teaching of the sacraments as the means of grace. Arminians were in agreement with the Calvinists on these doctrines and others. That which was not disputed was properly not mentioned by the Synod of Dort because it was not necessary to defend those doctrines. As a result, those areas of their common doctrinal belief do not seem now to be as much Calvinistic as they are deemed Protestant. However, they were then and they remain now an essential part of traditional Calvinism.

The TULIP should be understood as an abridgment of Calvinism, a compendium, and not a comprehensive presentation.

Loraine Boettner, who introduced the TULIP in print, did so because he felt that the doctrines represented "may be more easily remembered if they are associated with the word T-U-L-I-P." He did so with this stern warning attached.

> Let the reader, then, guard against a too close identification of the Five Points and the Calvinistic system. While these are essential elements, the system really includes much more. ... the Westminster Confession is a balanced statement of the Reformed Faith or Calvinism, and it gives due prominence to the other Christian doctrines. The Five Points may be more easily remembered if they are associated with the word T-U-L-I-P; T, Total Inability; U, Unconditional Election; L, Limited Atonement; I, Irresistible (Efficacious) Grace; and P, Perseverance of the Saints.

Because those Five Points do indeed separate Calvinism from other Protestants, I have restricted my critique of Calvinism to those areas delineated by the TULIP. This does not imply an acceptance of the other errors of doctrine comprising Calvinism. These other doctrines that were not disputed are certainly as contrary to the Scriptures as is the TULIP. However, none of these doctrines will find comfortable lodging within Baptist churches until the TULIP has already been allowed entrance.

The Synod of Dort focused the report of the Synod on the five doctrines to which the *Remonstrances;*

however, in addition to the Five Points that became identified as the TULIP in the Twentieth Century, another doctrine is inseparable from Calvinism. This Unnumbered Point is the necessity of the Gospel of Sovereign Grace being introduced into society and implemented so that the world will be subdued under Christianity. This doctrine produced that strange mixture of Calvinism and government that ruled Geneva under John Calvin and it lends itself to the Postmillennial position.

This Christian conquest of the world is presented as the unlisted sixth point of Calvinism in a book, written by Dr. Nigel Lee, with the extensive title of *The Sixth Point Of Calvinism: Eschato-Ethics alias Dordt Decrees Christian Conquest: The Commanded Christian Conquest Of The Cosmos As Enjoined In The Footnotes Of The Dutch States' Bible Commissioned At The International 'T-U-L-I-P' Synod Of Dordt In 1618–19.*

> Dordt drew up the enduring "Five Points of Calvinism" alias the famous "Decrees of Dordt." In those "Five Points of Calvinism"—summarized by the acronym **'T.U.L.I.P.'**
>
> However, the Synod of Dordt decreed not only the "Five Points" of Calvinism. Like Calvin earlier, also Dordt decreed **the Christians' conquest** of the World from the tyranny of **the Antichrist** through what we call the Sixth Point of Calvinism—**S**: Eschato-Ethics. Hence not: 'T.U.L.I.P.'—but: 'T.U.L.I.P.S.'
>
> Rev. Professor Dr. John Calvin (1509–1564), the greatest of all the Protestant Reformers, had committed himself to set about the Christian conquest of the whole World. Under Christ, this is to be achieved especially through Christians' concrete application of Christ's Ten Commandments in every sphere of human endeavour—in their individual and family lives;

> in all ecclesiastical affairs; and also in both commerce and politics.
>
> This virile perspective was again re-emphasized by Calvin's successor Rev. Professor Dr. Theodore Beza. See his great christonomic work *Concerning the Rights of Rulers over their Subjects and the Duty of Subjects towards their Rulers.*[164] [Emphasis is in the original.]

The following material emphasizes that this Unnumbered Point is the theological impetus for the rise of neo-Calvinism. This appeared in a critique by Bojidar Marinov written September 8, 2010, in response to an article in *Christianity Today*, September 22, 2006, titled: *Young, Restless, Reformed* and subtitled: *TULIP Doesn't Mean Reformed—City on a Hill Does.*[165]

> The truth ... is that TULIP is not the essence of the Reformed theology. Of course, the doctrines of Total Depravity, Unconditional Election, Limited Atonement, Irresistible Grace, and Perseverance of the Saints are an important starting step to the immense body of theological truths called "Reformed theology." It follows directly from the greater concept of the Sovereignty of God. It correctly describes the fallen state of man and the work of God in saving the individual. When we look up to God to give thanks for what He has done for us personally, we think "TULIP," even if we never knew the term or never understood it.
>
> To summarize, TULIP is the acronym for the "mechanism" of our personal salvation. And that's it. Nothing more than our personal salvation. But Reformed theology

---

[164]www.historicism.net/readingmaterials/sixthpoint.pdf,introduction
[165]http://americanvision.org/3474/tulip-doesnt-meanreformed-city-on-a-hill-does/

encompasses immeasurably more than just personal salvation. And when a church makes TULIP the summa of its theology, that church is not Reformed. Yes, it has taken the first step to becoming Reformed, but it is still far from the goal.

The Puritans ... would be deeply surprised that someone would focus the whole of God's Sovereignty on the salvation of individual human souls. That would seem rather selfish to them. It would look as if God's Sovereignty is made to serve man's needs, rather than man's salvation serve God's plans. The salvation of individuals has never occupied such a high status in the thinking of the Puritans; the Kingdom of God and its righteousness has. The Puritans did understand that God's plans were top priority over the salvation of individuals; the Pharaoh and his hardened heart were a favorite sermon topic for many a Puritan preachers. They did not see God's sovereignty only in salvation but in damnation also, and in many more things.

The Reformed believers of earlier centuries built a civilization that influenced the world permanently. They changed the world not by the selfishness of the focus on salvation but by the obedience of teaching the nations and building the Kingdom of God.

It was cities on a hill that they left for us as a legacy, and it is the "City on a Hill" motif that best characterizes the Reformed theology today, not TULIP. ... They did believe in God's Sovereignty over salvation, yes, but they believed in much more than that. They knew they were predestined to be God's chosen vessels to manifest God's Sovereignty over the cultures and the societies of men by building a new civilization. "The kingdoms of this world have become a *[sic]* Kingdom of our God" had a

> very specific meaning for the Puritans, and that meaning was what characterized their view of Sovereignty.
>
> And those that today want to be Reformed, cannot limit themselves to the comfortable thought that God gave them personal salvation. Reformed means the Sovereignty of God over everything—all of man's life and thought and action, including man's society and culture.

The essence of Calvinism is that the sovereignty of God cannot be separated from the glory of God. While the contemporary follower of John Calvin might not identify his belief system as such, Calvinism is very much the exaltation of the rule of God and the application of His rulership to every aspect of life—"including man's society and culture." This is the seldom listed, but always present, Unnumbered Point of Calvinism.

This tenet gave Calvinists in Europe in the days of Calvin and afterwards the courage to defy those secular rulers that violated the laws of God. They were the first theologians to provide arguments for the overthrow of monarchies. Calvinism in Europe and in England fomented revolution.

Regarding the Puritan overthrow of Charles I under Cromwell Loraine Boettner wrote in the chapter titled *The History of Calvinism* in *The Reformed Doctrine of Predestination*:

> Cromwell, the great Calvinistic leader and commoner, planted himself upon the solid rock of Calvinism and called to himself soldiers who had planted themselves upon that same rock. The result was an army which for purity and heroism surpassed anything the world had ever seen. "It never found," says Macaulay, "either in the British Isles or on the Continent, an enemy who could stand its onset. In England, Scotland, Ireland, Flanders, the Puritan warriors, often surrounded by difficulties,

> sometimes contending against threefold odds, not only never failed to conquer, but never failed to destroy and break in pieces whatever force was opposed to them. They at length came to regard the day of battle as a day of certain triumph, and marched against the most renowned battalions of Europe with disdainful confidence. Even the banished Cavaliers felt an emotion of national pride when they saw a brigade of their countrymen, outnumbered by foes and abandoned by friends, drive before it in headlong rout the finest infantry of Spain, and force a passage into a counterscarp which had just been pronounced impregnable by the ablest of the marshals of France." And again, "That which chiefly distinguished the army of Cromwell from other armies, was the austere morality and the fear of God which pervaded the ranks. It is acknowledged by the most zealous Royalists that, in that singular camp, no oath was heard, no drunkenness or gambling was seen, and that, during the long dominion of soldiery, the property of the peaceable citizens and the honor of woman were held sacred. No servant girl complained of the rough gallantry of the redcoats. Not an ounce of plate was taken from the shops of the goldsmiths."[Macaulay, History of England, I., p. 119][166]

As historians and commentators have written, the *secular* doctrines of Manifest Destiny and American Exceptionalism, terms that are familiar in American politics, have their roots in the theology of John Calvin. Specifically, they rise from this Unnumbered Point. The Puritans of the New England Colonies came to the New World with a conviction that they were obeying the will of God to establish

---

[166]http://www.apuritansmind.com/arminianism/calvinism-in-history/

residency in a new land that would exist under the hand of God. This is evident in the records that they left.

Those American Calvinists (and the earlier English Calvinists) are evidence that Calvinism was moving *or in their ministries at least* had moved from Calvinism's traditional Amillennialism to Postmillennialism. Calvin himself is generally conceded to favor Amillennialism, though some of his writings seem to countenance Postmillennialism, which encouraged this transition.

In 1650, Edward Johnsonn wrote a work titled *Wonder Working Providence of Zion's Saviour*, in which he declared that in the New World "Jesus Christ had manifested his kingly office toward his churches more fully than ever yet the Sons of men saw." Practically every Puritan tract contained the conviction that the Protestant Reformation reached (or would reach) its culmination here in the American colonies. While the emphasis lay primarily upon the new purity of the church, these Puritans envisaged a new and perfect society. When speaking of New England, Johnson further wrote, "[I] know this is the place where the Lord will create a new Heaven, and a new Earth in, *[sic]* new Churches, and a new Commonwealth together."[167]

From the writings of William Bradford during the days of the Mayflower and John Winthrop a decade later, early Calvinists left the record of their confidence that they were on these shores to build a kingdom for God.

> Glorious Things are spoken of Thee, O thou City of God, whose Street be in thee, O New England; The interpretation of it, be unto you, O American Colonies. ... There are many Arguments to persuade us

---

[167]http://www.questia.com/read/1350523/johnson-s-wonder-working-providence-1628–1651

> That our Glorious Lord will have an Holy City in America; a City, the street whereof shall be Pure Gold. ... There have been Martyrs of Christ in America. The Blood of the Martyrs here, is an Omen that the truths for which they Suffered are to Rise, and Live and carry all before them, in the Land that hath been so marked for the Lord. ... But our Glorious Lord, will order that the Good Seed ere long, to be cast, upon the Fertile regions of America, and it shall be here find a Good Ground, where it shall bring forth fruit unto astonishments; and unto perpetuity.[168]

Cotton Mather, 1710

As did other American Calvinists, Jonathan Edwards, who was a leader in the Second Great Awakening believed that this nation was destined to be involved in the *renewal* of humanity—"the restitution of all things," (Acts 3:21), the return of Jesus Christ.

> The latter-day glory is probably to begin in America. ... It is not unlikely that this work of God's Spirit, so extraordinary and wonderful, is the dawning, or, at least, a prelude of that glorious work of God, so often foretold in Scripture, which, in the progress and issue of it, shall renew the world of mankind. If we consider how long since the things foretold as what should precede this great event, have been accomplished; and how long this event has been expected by the church of God, and thought to be nigh by the most eminent men of God in the church; and withal consider what the state of things now is, and has for a considerable time been, in the church of God, and the world of mankind; we cannot reasonably think other-

---

[168]http://digitalcommons.unl.edu/cgi/viewcontent.cgi?article=1029&context=etas

> wise, than that the beginning of this great work of God must be near. And there are many things that make it probable that this work will begin in America ... And if we may suppose that this glorious work of God shall begin in any part of America, I think, if we consider the circumstances of the settlement of New England, it must needs appear the most likely, of all American colonies, to be the place whence this work shall principally take its rise. And, if these things be so, it gives us more abundant reason to hope that what is now seen in America, and especially in New England, may prove the dawn of that glorious day; and the very uncommon and wonderful circumstances and events of this work, seem to me strongly to argue that God intends it as the beginning or forerunner of something vastly great.[169]

This merger of ethics and the eschaton was the foundation for the development of the Dominion Theologians, which is also titled as the Christian Reconstruction Movement, Kingdom Now theology, and Theonomy. Rousas John (R. J.) Rushdoony is generally considered the modern founder of this resurgent advocacy of the neglected Unnumbered Point from the Canons of Dort. Gary North, David Chilton, Gary Demar, Andrew Sandlin, George Grant, and multiple others have written extensively and their influence on the *Religious Right* is well documented.

Dominion theology advocates that Christians are commanded by Scripture to insure that the Law of God, as set forth by Moses in the moral and civil stipulations of the Levitical Law and by the LORD Jesus in the Sermon n the Mount and elsewhere in the Gospels, is effective worldwide. Christianity is to have dominion in all of society—its culture, its laws,

---

[169]http://www.ccel.org/ccel/edwards/works1.ix.iii.ii.html

its social interactions, its economical activities, its political engagements, and its religious expressions. Christians, therefore, are obliged to conquer the social, economic, and political world through whatever means are necessary.

Christianity is to rule in a worldwide kingdom. It is not a government that is controlled by a church, but it is to be a government that is ruled by the Law of God. The foundational doctrine of Theonomy is that Christ will not return *until* the Christianizing of the world is accomplished. In eschatological position, Theonomy is postmillennial covenantatism.

Reformed theologians have traditionally followed an Amillennial understanding of eschatology; however, Postmillennialism was certainly implied in this Unnumbered Point and was broadly hinted in some of the comments of John Calvin as by well as his governance of Geneva. Presently, New Calvinism has a strong affinity for Postmillennialism. The Calvinists that promote Dominion Theology are all Postmillennialists. Dominion Theology is logically the reasonable development and prosecution of the Unnumbered Point of Calvinism.

The following verses should prove to be sufficient to refute the entirety of Dominion Theology.

> John 18:36 Jesus answered, My kingdom is not of this world: if my kingdom were of this world, then would my servants fight, that I should not be delivered to the Jews: but now is my kingdom not from hence.
>
> 1 Peter 2:13 Submit yourselves to every ordinance of man for the Lord's sake: whether it be to the king, as supreme; 14 Or unto governors, as unto them that are sent by him for the punishment of evildoers, and for the praise of them that do well. 15 For so is the will of God, that with well doing ye may put to silence the ignorance of foolish men: 16 As free, and not using *your* liberty for a cloke of malicious-

> ness, but as the servants of God. 17 Honour all *men*. Love the brotherhood. Fear God. Honour the king.
>
> Romans 13:1 Let every soul be subject unto the higher powers. For there is no power but of God: the powers that be are ordained of God. 2 Whosoever therefore resisteth the power, resisteth the ordinance of God: and they that resist shall receive to themselves damnation. 3 For rulers are not a terror to good works, but to the evil. Wilt thou then not be afraid of the power? do that which is good, and thou shalt have praise of the same: 4 For he is the minister of God to thee for good. But if thou do that which is evil, be afraid; for he beareth not the sword in vain: for he is the minister of God, a revenger to *execute* wrath upon him that doeth evil. 5 Wherefore *ye* must needs be subject, not only for wrath, but also for conscience sake. 6 For for this cause pay ye tribute also: for they are God's ministers, attending continually upon this very thing. 7 Render therefore to all their dues: tribute to whom tribute *is due*; custom to whom custom; fear to whom fear; honour to whom honour.

Postmillennialism would seem to teach that God is entirely dependent upon the faithfulness of believers to transform the world into a place that is prepared for the LORD Jesus to return. It ought to be difficult to convince the Calvinist that Postmillennialism can be reconciled with sovereignty. However, Dominionist David Chilton has a possible solution: time.

> But the Christian does not have to be afraid of the passage of time, because *time is on our side*. History is working toward our objectives. Every day brings us closer to the realization of the knowledge of God covering the entire world. The nations will worship and obey the one true God, and

> will cease to make war; the earth will be changed, restored to Edenic conditions; and people will be blessed with long and happy lives—so long, in fact, that it will be unusual for someone to die at the young age of 100 (Isa. 65:20)!
>
> Consider this promise in the law: "Know therefore that the LORD your God, He is God, the faithful God, who keeps His covenant and His lovingkindness *to a thousandth generation* with those who love Him and keep His commandments" (Deut. 7:9). The God of the Covenant told His people that He would bless them to the thousandth generation of their descendants. That promise was made (in round figures) about 3,400 years ago. If we figure the Biblical generation at about 40 years, a thousand generations is *forty thousand years.* We've got 36,600 years to go before this promise is fulfilled![170]

Dominion Theology is irredeemably wrong in its eschatology and the mentality of the Crusaders that Christianity can be imposed on unregenerate humanity that fuels Theonomy only serves to discredit Christianity. The Religious Right is largely a somewhat modified expression of Dominion Theology.

The Unnumbered Point is as false an understanding of Scripture as are the Five Points that are numbered in the TULIP.

---

[170]http://www.garynorth.com/freebooks/docs/pdf/paradise_restored.pdf

CHAPTER 16

CONCLUSION

It would be a bold venture to attempt to refute an entire theological system in one small book and a bolder writer to assert that he has actually done so.

I certainly make no such presumption. I have given a broad overview of the serious defects in the fundamentals of the foundation of the system, known as Calvinism. I have not attempted a full theological rebuttal.

While my effort will not suffice to challenge the intellectual confidence of the committed Calvinist, I hope that it might cause a person who is tempted with the propositions of Calvinism to rethink giving a commitment to the cloudiness of human reasonings. To follow Augustine, Calvin, *et al* is to reject the clarity of divine revelation.

> 1 Timothy 6:20–21 O Timothy, keep that which is committed to thy trust, avoiding profane and vain babblings, and oppositions of science falsely so called: Which some professing have erred concerning the faith. Grace be with thee. Amen

Calvinism claims to be science, meaning knowledge, but it is falsely so-called, teaching for doctrines the commandments of men. Calvinism is, indeed, more of a human philosophy than it is a Biblically derived theology.

I believe that the TULIP of Calvinism is indeed wilted.

APPENDICES

The inclusion of material in these appendices does not imply my endorsement of all that a particular selection might contain. I have provided certain articles to allow the reader to see the comments of those particular Calvinist that I have quoted in the wider and fuller context in which those statements were written. There is a two-fold reason for doing this.

First, I have no desire to misrepresent the belief of any individual and I know well that a statement can be distorted when removed from its context.

Second, I seek through these APPENDICES to disprove that accusation before it is leveled.

I disagree with Calvinism, but I do not seek to disrespect the Calvinist. I have not written to attack any individual; I have written to warn of what I believe is an erroneous understanding of my Heavenly Father.

APPENDIX 1

TWO GOSPELS

In my view, the difficulty in any discussion of Calvinism is that there are two distinctly different GOSPELS in view. The gospel of Calvinism is *The Gospel of Declaration* and the Gospel of Biblical Christianity is *The Gospel of Invitation.* The first gospel is rather complicated in its explanation; the second is explained with simplicity.

The Gospel of Declaration

In the Gospel of Declaration, the *good news* is that the God of Heaven determined before creation that you are one of the elect, those who were chosen to eternal life, or that you are one of the reprobate, those that were chosen to eternal damnation. Though some Calvinists do not wish to consider the reality of this double-choosing, Double Predestination, preferring to have the elect chosen but to describe the reprobate as simply *not chosen,* those who were *not chosen* were *chosen* not to be chosen. No amount of brilliant rhetoric or glistening verbal sugarcoating can change that fact: *Those excluded from grace are, by that act of exclusion, chosen to perdition.*

Under Calvinism, you are preordained, predestined, predetermined by the pleasure of God to your eternal destiny. If you are one of those elected, then you will rejoice for eternity that you were chosen to glorify God by being a recipient of His grace. If you are not one of the heavenly elect, then God will receive His glory by your eternal damnation.

Calvinism holds that if you are one of the heavenly elect, then, as a vessel of mercy, God loves you; if you are not, then you are a vessel of wrath that was "fitted for destruction" (Romans 9:22).

If you think, as does the Calvinist, that you are or that you might be one of the elect, then you need continuously to persevere faithfully until you depart this life. That perseverance is the evidence of your election; however, it is possible that you might be deceived and that you are only working in human or even deceptive satanic energy. The true saint, nevertheless, will persevere and will depart this world to arrive in the presence of God. Moreover, according to Calvinism, God Himself settled where you would spend eternity before the foundation of the world.

The Calvinist is forced by his theology to rewrite the familiar chorus so that it matches his TULIP.

> One door and only one
> And yet its sides are two.
> God alone decided
> On which side are you!

Calvinism proclaims that your destiny was designed to bring glory to God and it will be accomplished according to His good pleasure. You do not choose Him, He chose you. He will be glorified by your eternal life or by your eternal death.

The Calvinist, it seems to me, is so obsessed with insuring that God receives glory that he cannot be open to any methodology of God receiving that glory except by absolute determinism. No one claiming to believe the Bible can question that God is to receive the glory and that He will receive all glory. The dividing issue is that of how God is to receive ultimate glory.

> Revelation 4:11 Thou art worthy, O Lord, to receive glory and honour and power: for thou hast created all things, and for thy pleasure they are and were created. ... 5:13 And every creature which is in heaven, and on the earth, and under the earth, and such as are in the sea, and all that are in them, heard I saying, Blessing, and honour, and glory, and power, *be* unto him that sitteth upon the throne, and unto the Lamb for ever and ever.

There is no Biblical or logical warrant for ascribing that the only method by which God may receive glory is through the avenue of absolute determinism. God is sovereign, of that there should be no question. Moreover, in the exercise of that sovereignty, God has decreed.

The *logical* question indeed becomes, "What has God decreed?" Calvinism declares that God has decreed absolute determinism. Yet, in order to validate that contention, the Calvinist must redefine Biblical terminology, by assigning the words special meanings. The Calvinist will not, *for he cannot*, allow the text of Scripture to stand as it is written, because his doctrines are not findable in the written text without the special definitions. The Gospel of Declaration does not rise from within the scriptures; it is imposed upon the Scriptures.

The Gospel of Invitation

The Gospel of Invitation, in contrast to the Gospel of Declaration, is simply stated.

> John 3:15–16 That **whosoever believeth** in him should not perish, but have eternal life. For God so loved the world, that he gave his only begotten Son, that **whosoever believeth** in him should not perish, but have everlasting life. ...11:26 And **whosoever** liveth and **believeth** in me

> shall never die. Believest thou this? ... 12:46 I am come a light into the world, that **whosoever believeth** on me should not abide in darkness. Acts 10:43 To him give all the prophets witness, that through his name **whosoever believeth** in him shall receive remission of sins. Romans 9:33 As it is written, Behold, I lay in Sion a stumblingstone and rock of offence: and **whosoever believeth** on him shall not be ashamed. Romans 10:11 For the scripture saith, **Whosoever believeth** on him shall not be ashamed. 1 John 5:1 **Whosoever believeth** that Jesus is the Christ is born of God: and every one that loveth him that begat loveth him also that is begotten of him. [Emphasis is added.]

As Scripture closes, the final invitation is extended in the Book of the Revelation: "And whosoever will, let him take of the water of life freely."

> Revelation 22:16–21 I Jesus have sent mine angel to testify unto you these things in the churches. I am the root and the offspring of David, *and* the bright and morning star. And the Spirit and the bride say, Come. And let him that heareth say, Come. And let him that is athirst come. **And whosoever will, let him take the water of life freely.** For I testify unto every man that heareth the words of the prophecy of this book, If any man shall add unto these things, God shall add unto him the plagues that are written in this book: And if any man shall take away from the words of the book of this prophecy, God shall take away his part out of the book of life, and out of the holy city, and *from* the things which are written in this book. He which testifieth these things saith, Surely I come quickly. Amen. Even so, come, Lord Jesus. The grace of our Lord Jesus Christ *be* with you all. Amen.

For those that allow the words of Scripture to have their normally acceptable meanings, no verse is stronger for the Gospel of Invitation than is found in John 3:36.

> **He that believeth** on the Son hath everlasting life: and **he that believeth not** the Son shall not see life; but the wrath of God abideth on him. [Emphasis is added.]

While the Calvinist delights in citing the apostle Paul, the words that the Holy Spirit gave Paul to record do not lend themselves unchanged to Calvinism.

> Romans 5:6–21 For when we were yet without strength, in due time Christ died for the ungodly. For scarcely for a righteous man will one die: yet peradventure for a good man some would even dare to die. But God commendeth his love toward us, in that, while we were yet sinners, Christ died for us. Much more then, being now justified by his blood, we shall be saved from wrath through him. For if, when we were enemies, we were reconciled to God by the death of his Son, much more, being reconciled, we shall be saved by his life. And not only *so*, but we also joy in God through our Lord Jesus Christ, by whom we have now received the atonement. Wherefore, as by one man sin entered into the world, and death by sin; and so death passed upon all men, for that all have sinned: (For until the law sin was in the world: but sin is not imputed when there is no law. Nevertheless death reigned from Adam to Moses, even over them that had not sinned after the similitude of Adam's transgression, who is the figure of him that was to come. But not as the offence, so also *is* the free gift. For if through the offence of one many be dead, much more the grace of God, and the gift by grace, *which is* by one man, Jesus Christ, hath abounded unto many. And

> not as *it was* by one that sinned, *so is* the gift: for the judgment *was* by one to condemnation, but the free gift *is* of many offences unto justification. For if by one man's offence death reigned by one; much more they which receive abundance of grace and of the gift of righteousness shall reign in life by one, Jesus Christ.) Therefore as by the offence of one *judgment came* upon all men to condemnation; even so by the righteousness of one *the free gift came* upon all men unto justification of life. For as by one man's disobedience many were made sinners, so by the obedience of one shall many be made righteous. Moreover the law entered, that the offence might abound. But where sin abounded, grace did much more abound: That as sin hath reigned unto death, even so might grace reign through righteousness unto eternal life by Jesus Christ our Lord.
>
> Romans 10:9 That if thou shalt confess with thy mouth the Lord Jesus, and shalt believe in thine heart that God hath raised him from the dead, thou shalt be saved. 10 For with the heart man believeth unto righteousness; and with the mouth confession is made unto salvation. 11 For the scripture saith, Whosoever believeth on him shall not be ashamed. 12 For there is no difference between the Jew and the Greek: for the same Lord over all is rich unto all that call upon him. 13 For whosoever shall call upon the name of the Lord shall be saved.

When the Gospel of Declaration with its special interpretation of words is rejected and the Scriptures are read as they were written, the Gospel of Invitation is unmistakably presented.

When only the Bible *as it is written* is followed, the simple little chorus to which I referred earlier needs no revision.

One door and only one
And yet its sides are two.
I'm on the inside
On which side are you?

APPENDIX 2

GRACE

Dr. John MacArthur,[171] recognized Calvinist pastor and author, carefully defined grace[172] thusly:

> Grace is a terribly misunderstood word. Defining it succinctly is notoriously difficult. Some of the most detailed theology textbooks do not offer any concise definition of the term. Someone has proposed an acronym: GRACE is God's Riches At Christ's Expense. That's not a bad way to characterize grace, but it is not a sufficient theological definition.
>
> One of the best-known definitions of grace is only three words: God's unmerited favor. A. W. Tozer expanded on that: "Grace is the good pleasure of God that inclines him to bestow benefits on the undeserving." Berkhof is more to the point: grace is

[171]"Dr. John MacArthur is pastor-teacher of Grace Community Church ... president of the Master's College and Seminary." http://www.gty.org/connect/biography

[172]http://www.oneplace.com/ministries/grace-to-you/read/articles/what-is-grace-10339.html

> "the unmerited operation of God in the heart of man, effected through the agency of the Holy Spirit."
>
> Grace is not merely unmerited favor; it is favor bestowed on sinners who deserve wrath. Showing kindness to a stranger is "unmerited favor"; doing good to one's enemies is more the spirit of grace (Luke 6:27–36).
>
> Grace is not a dormant or abstract quality, but a dynamic, active, working principle: "The grace of God has appeared, bringing salvation...and instructing us" (Titus 2:11–12). It is not some kind of ethereal blessing that lies idle until we appropriate it. Grace is God's sovereign initiative to sinners (Ephesians 1:5–6).

Grace, according to MacArthur, "is favor bestowed on sinners who deserve wrath," "a dynamic, active, working principle." "Grace is God's sovereign initiative to sinners"—"the unmerited operation of God" "effected through the agency of the Holy Spirit." Read the following paragraphs from MacArthur giving careful attention his definitions and to his applications of the word grace.

> God's grace is not a static attribute whereby He passively accepts hardened, unrepentant sinners. Grace does not change a person's standing before God yet leave His character untouched. Real grace does not include, as Chafer claimed, "the Christian's liberty to do precisely as he chooses." True grace, according to Scripture, teaches us "to deny ungodliness and worldly desires and to live sensibly, righteously and godly in the present age" (Titus 2:12). Grace is the power of God to fulfill our New Covenant duties (cf. 1 Cor. 7:19), however inconsistently we obey at times. Clearly, grace does not grant permission to live in the flesh; it supplies power to live in the Spirit (cf. Rom. 6:1–2).

> Faith, like grace, is not static. Saving faith is more than just understanding the facts and mentally acquiescing. It is inseparable from repentance, surrender, and a supernatural longing to obey. None of those responses can be classified exclusively as a human work, *[sic]* any more than believing itself is solely a human effort.
>
> Misunderstanding on that key point is at the heart of the error of those who reject lordship salvation. They assume that because Scripture contrasts faith and works, faith must be incompatible with works. They set faith in opposition to submission, yieldedness, *[sic]* or turning from sin, and they categorize all the practical fruits of salvation as human works. They stumble over the twin truths that salvation is a gift, yet it costs everything ... .
>
> As a part of His saving work, God will produce repentance, faith, sanctification, yieldedness, *[sic]* obedience, and ultimately glorification. Since He is not dependent on human effort in producing these elements, an experience that lacks any of them cannot be the saving work of God.[173]

While a detailed refuting of the erroneous doctrine of Lordship Salvation is not within the scope of this book, it is proper to recognize that MacArthur's advocacy for Lordship Salvation is the reasonable *and the required* application of his Calvinist doctrine of the Perseverance of the Saints. Though some Calvinists, such as Charles Ryrie, have attempted to distance themselves from Lordship Salvation, it is the logical *and the only consistent* expression of Perseverance.

The doctrine of Lordship Salvation requires that grace be the empowerment to perform the works

---

[173]http://www.gty.org/Resources/Articles/A317

that are the evidence of the true "saving work of God," because the doctrine of Total Inability insists that man has no capability of obeying God until God bestows the grace to accomplish the obedience. Lordship Salvation is only logical when Total Inability is accepted as a true doctrine. In the same manner, it is the doctrine of Total Inability that produces the Calvinist definition of grace.

Grace to the Calvinist is not an attribute or part of the character of God; it is instead "God's sovereign initiative to sinners." Grace is an action that God sovereignly initiates. Grace is the *power* that God gives to the elect so that they may glorify Him. This definition of grace is required because to the Calvinist, man is born in a state of total inability. Therefore, God must regenerate man before man has the ability to exercise the faith, which the Calvinist defines as the gift of God.

It is important to recognize that in Calvinism, faith is the gift of God. This is contrary to the clear reading of the passage (in the Greek[174] of the origi-

---

[174]I borrow this Greek knowledge from the following sources. The first three are frequently cited by Biblical scholars as expert witnesses. The fourth is from a Reformed source and is extensive. None of these who are referenced in this footnote is known as a fundamentalist.

1. I refer the reader to the recognized Greek scholar A. T. Robertson and his often cited *Word Pictures in the New Testament:* **For by grace** (*têi gar chariti*). Explanatory reason. "By the grace" already mentioned in verse **Eph** 2:5 and so with the article. **Through faith** (*dia pisteôs*). This phrase he adds in repeating what he said in verse **Eph** 2:5 to make it plainer. "Grace" is God's part, "faith" ours. **And that** (*kai touto*). Neuter, not feminine *tautê*, and so refers not to *pistis* (feminine) or to *charis* (feminine also), but to the act of being saved by grace conditioned on faith on our part. Paul shows that salvation does not have its source (*ex humôn*, out of you) in men, but from God. Besides, it is God's gift (*dôron*) and not the result of our work. Ephesians 2:8, *A. T. Robertson's Word Pictures*, Sword Searcher, Version 7.0.1.4

2. Agreeing with this understanding of the Greek text is Marvin R. Vincent, *Word Studies in the New Testament*: Verse 8. For by grace, etc. This may truly be called exceeding riches of grace, for ye are saved by grace. Grace has the article, the grace of God, in vers. 5, 7. And that. Not faith, but the salvation. Of God. Emphatic. Of God

nal and in the English of the Authorized Version) from Ephesians that is the center of the argument.

> Ephesians 2:1–10 And you *hath he quickened,* who were dead in trespasses and sins; Wherein in time past ye walked according to the course of this world, according to the prince of the power of the air, the spirit that now worketh in the children of disobedience: Among whom also we all had our conversation in times past in the lusts of our flesh, fulfilling the desires of the flesh and of the mind; and were by nature the children of wrath, even as others. But God, who is rich in mercy,

---

is it the gift. http://www.god-rules.net/library/vincent/vincenteph 2.html

3. Kenneth Wuest, *The New Testament: An Expanded Translation,* translates the verse: "For by the grace have you been saved in time past completely, through faith, with the result that your salvation persists through present time; and this [salvation] is not from you as a source; of God it is the gift, not from a source of works." Kenneth S. Wuest was professor of New Testament Greek at Moody Bible Institute, Chicago, Illinois, until his death in 1962.

4. Reformed Anglican study on verse 8. τη γαρ χαριτι dat. "for [it is] by grace"—The dative is instrumental. Unlike v.5 there is an article, but this simply indicates that the phrase is being repeated. "By the means of grace" we are having been saved. *[sic]*
δια της πιστεως "through faith"—through, by means of the instrumentality of faith. It is always difficult to know how Paul intends us to understand the word "faith." He seems to use it in a technical sense where there is a relationship between Christ's faith/faithfulness, his sacrifice on our behalf, and our faith in Christ's faithfulness. The presence of the article may indicate that both ideas are intended, the preposition ek "out of"/"on the basis of" possibly stresses Christ's faithfulness, while the preposition dia, as here, possibly stresses our reliance/trust. If we take "faith" to mean "reliance on the faithfulness of Christ" we probably come close to what Paul intends.
και τουτο "and this"—Referring to salvation and not faith. Paul is stressing that salvation is achieved apart from works of faithfulness, rather than arguing that faith is not a good work. The "this not from yourselves, it is the gift of God," most likely refers to "the grace of salvation" rather than "faith". In support of "faith," the Westminster Shorted Catechism states that saving faith is a gift of God's grace by which the Holy Spirit acts to "persuade and enable us to embrace Jesus Christ, freely offered to us in the gospel."
θεου το δωρον "the gift of God"—God's the gift. Since God is the predicate, "it is a gift and the gift is God's." http://www.lectionary studies.com/studyn/lent4ben.html

> for his great love wherewith he loved us, Even when we were dead in sins, hath quickened us together with Christ, (by grace ye are saved;) And hath raised *us* up together, and made *us* sit together in heavenly *places* in Christ Jesus: That in the ages to come he might shew the exceeding riches of his grace in *his* kindness toward us through Christ Jesus. For by grace are ye saved through faith; and that not of yourselves: *it is* the gift of God: Not of works, lest any man should boast. For we are his workmanship, created in Christ Jesus unto good works, which God hath before ordained that we should walk in them.

By the rules of English grammar, the word *that* and the word *it* refer to the salvation that is given. This is consistent with Romans 6:23, “For the wages of sin *is* death; but the gift of God *is* eternal life through Jesus Christ our Lord.”

The Calvinist must not only **redefine** the word grace, he must **rearrange** the *whole of the salvation process.* Regeneration, the new birth, to be consistent with the doctrines of Calvinism must occur *before* the person is given faith. Otherwise, the TULIP cannot be sustained.

In a blog post,[175] Dr. R. C. Sproul presents his argument that regeneration precedes faith. He begins by relating the impact on his life when a seminary professor wrote *regeneration precedes faith* on a blackboard. He describes that as “one of the most dramatic moments” of his life and continues by writing that those “words were a shock to my system.”

Sproul writes that when he entered the seminary he thought that “the key work of man to effect[176]

[175]http://www.ligonier.org/blog/regeneration-precedes-faith/

[176]*M-WD* gives: effect, intransitive verb, meaning “to cause to come into being.”

rebirth was faith."[177] He continues that he had assumed that he had a "little island of righteousness, a tiny dose of spiritual power"[178] residing within that would "enable me to respond to the Gospel." He thinks that at that time that he might have been confused by "the teaching of the Roman Catholic Church" and "other branches of Christendom" that teach that regeneration is the result of receiving prevenient grace with which the sinner must cooperate.

> This concept of cooperation is at best a half-truth. Yes, the faith we exercise is our faith. God does not do the believing for us. When I respond to Christ, it is my response, my faith, my trust that is being exercised. The issue, however, goes deeper. The question still remains: "Do I cooperate with God's grace before I am born again, or does the cooperation occur after?" Another way of asking this question is to ask if regeneration is monergistic or synergistic. Is it operative or cooperative? Is it effectual or dependent? Some of these words are theological terms that require further explanation.

He gives definitions for the two words that he deems essential to understanding regeneration.

> A monergistic work is a work produced singly, by one person. The prefix "mono" means one. The word "erg" refers to a unit

---

[177]Dr. Sproul makes what I believe are two critical errors in this sentence. First, he speaks of "the key work of man" in regeneration. This is a serious error, because man has no "key work" to perform; man has no work whatsoever. Second, he speaks of *effecting* rebirth. The word *effect* has the meaning of "to carry out successfully, to accomplish, to get or to attain as the result of exertion." It would appear that Dr. Sproul was somewhat confused in his thinking regarding salvation before the professor wrote on the blackboard.

[178]I submit that having a "little island of righteousness, a tiny dose of spiritual power" residing within is not a reasonable understanding of man having a freewill. Having the ability to reason and to choose is not an equivalent of having righteousness or spiritual power.

> of work. Words like energy are built upon this root. A synergistic work is one that involves cooperation between two or more persons or things. The prefix "syn-" means "together with."

Sproul explains why Calvinism requires regeneration to be given **before** a person has the capacity to do anything spiritually.

> I labor this distinction for a reason. ... Is regeneration a monergistic work of God or a synergistic work that requires cooperation between man and God? ... After a person is regenerated, that person cooperates by exercising faith and trust. But the first step is the work of God and of God alone. ... The reason we do not cooperate with regenerating grace before it acts upon us and in us is because we cannot. We cannot because we are spiritually dead. We can no more assist the Holy Spirit in the quickening of our souls to spiritual life than Lazarus could help Jesus raise him for the dead.

Certainly, all descendents of Adam are spiritually dead; however, spiritual death does not preclude having freewill. The verse that he cites does not carry the battle to a victory for his doctrine.

> The key phrase in Paul's Letter to the Ephesians is this: "... even when we were dead in trespasses, made us alive together with Christ (by grace have you been saved)" (Eph. 2:5). Here Paul locates the time when regeneration occurs. It takes place 'when we were dead.' With one thunderbolt of apostolic revelation all attempts to give the initiative in regeneration to man are smashed. Again, dead men do not cooperate with grace. Unless regeneration takes place first, there is no possibility of faith.

However, when allowed to remain in the context in which the Holy Spirit placed Ephesians 2:5, the verse is speaking of the death, burial, and resurrection of the LORD Jesus: "hath quickened us together with Christ ... quickened us together ... made us sit together in heavenly places in Christ Jesus." The emphasis is that *salvation* is the work of Christ and not the work of the individual believer.

> Ephesians 2:4 But God, who is rich in mercy, for his great love wherewith he loved us, 5 Even when we were dead in sins, hath quickened us together with Christ, (by grace ye are saved;) 6 And hath raised *us* up together, and made *us* sit together in heavenly *places* in Christ Jesus: 7 That in the ages to come he might shew the exceeding riches of his grace in *his* kindness toward us through Christ Jesus.

In what I see as an unintended acknowledgment that this teaching originates with humanity (as do all the doctrines of Calvinism), Sproul generates a list of giants from Reformed history to support his position. Having listed "Augustine, Martin Luther, John Calvin, Jonathan Edwards, [and] George Whitefield," Sproul then adds the curious information that "even the great medieval theologian Thomas Aquinas ... the *Doctor Angelicus* of the Roman Catholic Church." It is as though he is saying, "If Augustine, Luther and Calvin were agreed, how could anyone rise to disagree?" Then, in case someone might be so bold as to do so, he proceeds to interject the information that "even ... Thomas Aquinas ... the Doctor Angelicus of the Roman Catholic Church" held this position.

He will repeat the weighty label of "giants of Christian history" before he closes his writing. It is the authority.

> If we believe that faith precedes regeneration, then we set our thinking and therefore ourselves in direct opposition not only to giants of Christian history but also to the teaching of Paul and of our Lord Himself.

This is the typical Calvinist pattern of argument. The weight of the support for the thesis of Calvinism rests first and primarily in the writings of men. One is always referred to the writings of Augustine, Calvin, Spurgeon, Berkhof, Chafer, Hodge, Warfield, Vos, or the more contemporary Calvinists Driscoll, White, MacArthur, Grudem, Clark, or Horton for study. There is not the direct referral to the Scriptures, because in Calvinism, for the Scriptures to be understood rightly (That is calvinistically.), it is required that the reader or listener has the knowledge of the contrived vocabulary of Calvinism.

As occurred in the case of Sproul, one needs a professor to write on the blackboard, because Calvinism does not come naturally to the mind as the Scriptures are being read. Calvinism has a special vocabulary that must be taught. Special lenses are required to see Scripture as the Calvinist views the text.

The Calvinist carefully interprets the word grace to mean *power and ability.* To do so is crucial to the understanding of Calvinism. Grace is an *ability* or *power* that God gives the elect first *to believe effectively* and then *to live properly.* MacArthur is tediously clear:

> Grace is the power of God to fulfill our New Covenant duties (cf. 1 Cor. 7:19), however inconsistently we obey at times. Clearly, grace does not grant permission to live in the flesh; it supplies power to live in the Spirit (cf. Rom. 6:1–2).
>
> Misunderstanding on that key point is at the heart of the error of those who reject lordship salvation. … .
>
> As a part of His saving work, God will produce repentance, faith, sanctification, yieldedness, *[sic]* obedience, and ultimately glorification. Since He is not dependent on human effort in producing these ele-

> ments, an experience that lacks any of them cannot be the saving work of God.

MacArthur attributes the Christian life to *the action of God that produces* "repentance, faith, sanctification, yieldedness, *[sic]* obedience, and ultimately glorification." He proceeds to say that if even one of these elements is missing it is evidence that the person is not saved: "an experience that lacks any of them cannot be the saving work of God."

He writes that "Saving faith is ... inseparable from repentance, surrender, and a supernatural longing to obey." The longing to obey itself is *supernatural*; the very longing to obey God is given to man by God and without that giving, no man has a true longing to submit to God.

To the Calvinist, *saving* faith is worked by grace, which is imposed upon some and not upon others. This concept of grace makes passages such as Romans 12:1, 2 meaningless.

> I beseech you therefore, brethren, by the mercies of God, that ye present your bodies a living sacrifice, holy, acceptable unto God, *which is* your reasonable service. And be not conformed to this world: but be ye transformed by the renewing of your mind, that ye may prove what *is* that good, and acceptable, and perfect, will of God.

Under the teaching of Calvinism, unless God gives me the grace (desire and power) to do so, I have no genuine desire and I am powerless to perform that which is required. I cannot *present* my body; I cannot *be transformed* by renewing my mind; I cannot *prove* anything! According to Calvinism, I have (within myself and apart from the gift of God) no ability and no power to repent, to exercise faith, to set myself apart for holy purposes, to yield myself to serve God, or to obey God. If I have no such ability and no such power to do those things, why am I to be held responsible for not doing those very things?

That is the underlying folly of Calvinism. In the noble attempt to insure that God receives all the glory, Augustine, Calvin, and all of those who followed or follow the same precepts remove the responsibility of humanity.

This is an assertion that Calvinists are quick to deny. However, the conclusion is inescapable because the Calvinism vividly describes the individual as being dead spiritually. That spiritual deadness is presented in terms that are *total* and absolute in application. The Calvinist theologians do expend great mental energy to manipulate logic and Scripture (*in that order*) to declare that each man is fully responsible for all of his thoughts, words, and deeds; but they so this while insisting that the same man has no ability or power, in the case of sin, to avoid or to alter, or, in the case of righteousness, to accomplish, to attain, to achieve, or *even to desire.*

> We must ask, then: Can the DEAD raise themselves? Can the BOUND free themselves? Can the BLIND give themselves sight, or the DEAF hearing? Can the SLAVES redeem themselves? Can the UNINSTRUCTABLE *[sic]* teach themselves? Can the NATURALLY SINFUL change themselves? Surely not! ... Could the Word of God show more plainly than it does that the depravity is total? and that our inability to desire or procure salvation is also total? The picture is one of death—spiritual death. We are like Lazarus in his tomb; we are bound hand and foot; corruption has taken hold upon us. Just as there was no glimmer of life in the dead body of Lazarus, so there is no 'inner receptive spark' in our hearts. But the Lord performs the miracle—both with the physically dead, and the spiritually dead; for 'you hath he quickened—made alive—who were dead in

> trespasses and sins.' [Eph 2.1]. Salvation, by its very nature, must be 'of the Lord.'[179]

The Calvinist insists that until God exerts grace on the individual that He has elected there is no possibility of that person to respond to God in an acceptable way. Before "God perform the miracle," the person cannot spiritually see *because* he is spiritually blind, cannot hear spiritually *because* he is deaf spiritually, cannot do spiritually *because* he is spiritually bound, and cannot be spiritual *because* he is dead.

Notwithstanding this insistence for Total Inability, the Calvinist passionately asserts that God holds every person fully responsible and *totally* accountable for his every failure to please God. The man who is spiritually dead (blind, deaf, etc.) will be judged as responsible and answerable for being what God made him incapable of performing.

The passage discusses the financial giving of Christians; however, I believe the principle identified is one that is demonstrated throughout Scripture in all of the interaction of God and man.

> 2 Corinthians 8:12 For if there be first a willing mind, *it is* accepted according to that a man hath, *and* not according to that he hath not.

It is uncharacteristic of God for Him to condemn a person for what that person cannot desire to do, let alone attempt to do.

If Scripture is to have precedence over human logic, then this essential premise of Calvinism is untenable. When Scripture is granted that precedence, I believe that Calvinism is unsustainable.

---

[179]Seaton, *The Five Points of Calvinism,* 10.

APPENDIX 3

DOUBLE PREDESTINATION

Dr. R. C. Sproul wrote a meticulous discussion in support of the doctrine of Double Predestination.[180] While the article would seem to require the reader to have a dictionary for the unfamiliar and theological terminology, it is worth the reading, because it is an excellent example of the level of philosophical reasoning that is required to defend Double Predestination. I respect his scholarship; I disagree with and reject his conclusions.

I cited extensively from this article in Chapter 8 however, Double Predestination merits more attention, because the importance to the system of Calvinism of this polarizing doctrine must not be minimized. If *Total Inability* is accepted, then Double Predestination is the logical and mandatory necessity. Rejection of either brings the compulsory refutation of the other.

Sproul's reasoning is a prime illustration of the intellectual maneuvering generated by the attempt

---

[180]http://www.the-highway.com/DoublePredestination_Sproul.html

to have God decree that a particular individual will spend eternity in the Lake of Fire without the possibility of any other destiny, while insisting that God has no responsibility for that reprobation. The damnation of the non-elect is considered the act of preterition, the *passing over*.

An internal debate divides Calvinism between the supporters of Single Predestination and the proponents of Double Predestination. The distinction made between the two might appear to the non-Calvinist as merely an insignificant semantical exercise. However, the contrast between the two as recognized by Calvinists makes the division a deep separation.

The strength of that severance is made evident by Sproul in the following comments:

> I once heard the case for "single" predestination articulated by a prominent Lutheran theologian in the above manner. He admitted to me that the conclusion of reprobation was logically inescapable, but he refused to draw the inference, holding steadfastly to "single" predestination. Such a notion of predestination is manifest nonsense. … .
>
> Thus, "single" predestination can be consistently maintained only within the framework of universalism or some sort of qualified Arminianism.[181] If particular election is to be maintained and if the notion that all salvation is ultimately based upon that particular election is to be maintained, then we must speak of double predestination.[182]

---

[181]When a Calvinist labels another Calvinist as a follower of Arminianism, he is using a pejorative that would be surpassed only by the labels heretic and apostate.

[182]http://www.the-highway.com/DoublePredestination_Sproul.html

Single Predestination is the doctrine that while God actively chose whom He would regenerate, God did not choose whom He would condemn. This concept advocates that God chose to elect certain individuals to salvation but left all others to receive the justice that sin deserves. To the elect, mercy was extended; to the non-elect, mercy was *only* not extended. The reasoning of the Single Predestinarian is that God is not obligated to extend mercy to any and that He has the right not to extend mercy as He might chose. By this verbal maneuvering, in not choosing to extend mercy, it is possible to insist that God did not cause the eternal damnation of the non-elect, but instead, He simply permitted justice to be administered unhindered by the intervention of mercy.

Double Predestination is the position that God decreed that certain individuals will be saved and that certain other individuals will be lost. Those who are elected to salvation are extended mercy and those that are elected to damnation are denied mercy. Salvation and damnation are both entirely the choice of God. The saved believe *solely* because they have been regenerated and have been provided with the gift of faith so that they might believe. The lost are denied regeneration with its accompanying gift of faith so that they are constitutionally unable to believe.

Whether God does or does not *decree* the damnation, the non-elect was destined to Hell and the Lake of Fire before the foundation of the world under either Single or Double Predestination. Moreover, that predestined damnation is irreversible and inescapable and without the possibility of alleviation.

However, the Double Predestinarian advocates are further divided over the question as to whether (1) God has *actively* decreed that certain individuals will be damned or (2) God has *only* withheld the opportunity for salvation from those individuals. The first is described as *positive-positive* in that God has *actively* decreed salvation to some, while He also *actively* decreed reprobation, which is condemnation to damnation, to the rest. The second position is defined as God having decreed salvation to certain individuals and simply not having chosen to decree salvation to the rest.

While it must be obvious to all intelligent thought that *the consequences for the condemned remains the same*, in the later, the argument is made that by the use of this choice of precision wordage, God is not responsible for the damnation, *because* God *only* decreed *not* to elect them to salvation; therefore, it is asserted that God did not decree to elect them to damnation. After this fashion of reasoning, the damnation of the non-elect is declared justified because they are receiving justice and not mercy.

A philosophical concept daring to pass itself as doctrinal teaching that requires the necessity of that level of splitting the proverbial theological hair is hardly worthy of consideration. I believe that it falls within that warning of the apostle against the enticement of "the words of man's wisdom" that corrupt "from the simplicity that is in Christ" through "strifes of words." Calvinism can never be described with the title of simplicity nor is it ever conveyed "in words that are easy to be understood."[183]

---

[183]2 Corinthians 11:2 For I am jealous over you with godly jealousy: for I have espoused you to one husband, that I may present *you as* a chaste virgin to Christ. 3 But I fear, lest by any means, as the serpent beguiled Eve through his subtilty, so your minds should be corrupted from the simplicity that is in Christ. 4 For if he that cometh preacheth another Jesus, whom we have not preached, or *if* ye receive another spirit, which ye have not received, or another gospel, which ye have not accepted, ye might well bear with *him*.
1 Corinthians 2:4 And my speech and my preaching *was* not with enticing words of man's wisdom, but in demonstration of the Spirit and of power:
1 Timothy 6:4–5 He is proud, knowing nothing, but doting about questions and strifes of words, whereof cometh envy, strife, railings, evil surmisings, Perverse disputings of men of corrupt minds, and destitute of the truth, supposing that gain is godliness: from such withdraw thyself.

Sproul has a disdain for the doctrine of Single Predestination, believing that it is a distortion of Calvinism.

> The use of the qualifying term "double" has been somewhat confusing in discussions concerning predestination. The term apparently means one thing within the circle of Reformed theology and quite another outside that circle and at a popular level of theological discourse. The term "double" has been set in contrast with a notion of "single" predestination. It has also been used as a synonym for a symmetrical view of predestination which sees election and reprobation being worked out in a parallel mode of divine operation. Both usages involve a serious distortion of the Reformed view of double predestination.[184]

Following a lengthy citation from *The Christian Doctrine of God,* written by Emil Brunner, that advocates the doctrine of Single Predestination, Sproul counters with a strongly worded rebuttal.

> ... Brunner argues passionately, though not coherently, for "single" predestination. There is a decree of election, but not of reprobation. Predestination has only one side—election. In this context, double predestination is "avoided" (or evaded) by the dialectical method. The dialectical method which sidesteps logical consistency has had a pervasive influence on contemporary discussions of double predestination. A growing antipathy to logic in theology is manifesting itself widely. ... .
>
> It is one thing to construct a theology of election (or any other kind of theology)

---

1 Corinthians 14:9 So likewise ye, except ye utter by the tongue words easy to be understood, how shall it be known what is spoken? for ye shall speak into the air.

[184]http://www.the-highway.com/DoublePredestination_Sproul.html

> purely on the basis of rational speculation. It is quite another to utilize logic in seeking a coherent understanding of biblical revelation. Brunner seems to abhor both.[185]

Sproul is unquestionably correct in affirming that the doctrine of Single Predestination is nothing other than an attempt to evade the harshness of God having decreed the eternal damnation of the non-elect. He then rebukes Brunner, and through him, all other advocates of Single Predestination for shrinking from following consistent *logic.*

> If, as Brunner maintains, *all* salvation is based upon the eternal election of God and not all men are elect from eternity, does that not mean that from eternity there are non-elect who most certainly will not be saved? Has not God chosen from eternity not to elect some people? If so, then we have an eternal choice of non-election which we call reprobation. The inference is clear and necessary, yet some shrink from drawing it.[186]

To the Calvinist, the battle is always based upon and rises from *logic.* The foundation is laid and the superstructure must be logically constructed and defended. I submit that the battle is in actuality *Biblical* and not *logical.* It is the fatal flaw of accepting the initial fallacy of Total Inability that makes the system of Calvinism *appear* logical. Without Total Inability, the philosophical theological system of Calvinism is patently illogical.

The framework of all Christian heresies, cults, and factions rises from similar kinds of faulty foundations. It is only when the first premise is accepted that the rest of the multiple doctrinal errors are made to have a semblance of being *logical.*

---

[185]http://www.the-highway.com/DoublePredestination_Sproul.html
[186]http://www.the-highway.com/DoublePredestination_Sproul.html

Disprove the contention that Jesus is not God and the Watchtower Society and its alleged witnesses to Jehovah cannot exist. Reject Joseph Smith as a prophet and Mormonism in all of its permutations falls. Accept the Biblical record that Joseph and Mary had children following the birth of Jesus and Roman Catholicism has suffered an incapacitating blow. Discard the unique definition that total depravity is Total Inability and Calvinism is a building constructed on sand. It cannot stand.

In his effort to justify Double Predestination, Sproul introduces the contrast between a *positive-positive* view of predestination and a *positive-negative* view. The discussion is far too complicated and lengthy for inclusion. Sproul rejects the *positive-positive* position to advance the *positive-negative* position. He continues:

Positive-positive:

> God *positively* and *actively* intervenes in the lives of the elect to bring them to salvation. In the same way God *positively* and *actively* intervenes in the life of the reprobate to bring him to sin. [187]

Positive-negative:

> In sharp contrast to the caricature of double predestination seen in the positive-positive schema is the classic position of Reformed theology on predestination. In this view predestination is double in that it involves both election and reprobation but is not symmetrical with respect to the mode of divine activity. A strict parallelism of operation is denied. Rather we view predestination in terms of a positive-negative relationship.
>
> In the Reformed view God from all eternity decrees some to election and positively in-

[187]http://www.the-highway.com/DoublePredestination_Sproul.html

> tervenes in their lives to work regeneration and faith by a monergistic work of grace. To the non-elect God withholds this monergistic work of grace, passing them by and leaving them to themselves. He does not monergistically work sin or unbelief in their lives. [188]

Sproul advances the following rationalization to prove his proposal for the *positive-negative* concept of Double Predestination.

> God shows mercy sovereignly and unconditionally to some, and gives justice to those passed over in election. That is to say, God grants the mercy of election to some and justice to others. No one is the victim of injustice. To fail to receive mercy is not to be treated unjustly. God is under no obligation to grant mercy to all—in fact He is under no obligation to grant mercy to any. [189]

In this concept of the actions of God, God (positively) redeems those whom He chooses and (negatively) does not redeem those that He does not choose to redeem. He does not positively condemn them; He allows the condemnation to stand without the extension of mercy.

Sproul adds a mystifying statement that would seem to conflict with his explanation.

> If God foreordains anything, it is absolutely certain that what He foreordains will come to pass. The purpose of God can never be frustrated. Even God's foreknowledge or prescience makes future events certain with respect to time. That is to say, if God knows on Tuesday that I will drive to Pittsburgh on Friday, then there is no doubt that, come Friday, I will drive to

---

[188] http://www.the-highway.com/DoublePredestination_Sproul.html
[189] http://www.the-highway.com/DoublePredestination_Sproul.html

> Pittsburgh. Otherwise God's knowledge would have been in error. Yet, there is a significant difference between God's knowing that I would drive to Pittsburgh and God's ordaining that I would do so. Theoretically He could know of a future act without ordaining it, but He could not ordain it without knowing what it is that He is ordaining. But in either case, the future event would be certain with respect to time and the knowledge of God. ... .

In simplistic words, the assertion is that God knows all and but that He does not ordain all. Even though God knew about sin, He did not ordain sin. "The purpose of God can never be frustrated." The obvious question that begs to be asked is "Since sin is obviously existing and since 'the purpose of God *can never* be frustrated, what is the origin of sin?'" The answer that Sproul provides seems to be rather a strained attempt at reasoning. He will say that what God foreknows must come to pass, but that what He foreknows is not necessarily foreordained.

> We see then, that what God knows in advance comes to pass by necessity of infallibly or necessity of immutability. But what about His foreordaining or predestinating what comes to pass? If God foreordains reprobation does this not obliterate the distinction between positive-negative and involve a *necessity of force*? If God foreordains reprobation does this not mean that God forces, compels, or coerces the reprobate to sin? Again the answer must be negative ...
>
> If God, when He is decreeing reprobation, does so in consideration of the reprobate's being already fallen, then He does not coerce him to sin. To be reprobate is to be left in sin, not pushed or forced to sin. If the decree of reprobation were made without a view to the fall, then the objection to double predestination would be valid and God would be properly charged with being

> the author of sin. But Reformed theologians have been careful to avoid such a blasphemous notion.

Apparently, God foreknew the Fall, but He did not foreordain the Fall while He was foreordaining reprobation as a result of the Fall. It seems that the Fall is the key issue for Sproul's explanation; however, dating all things from the Fall is an attempt to avoid the issues of the Fall. Responsibility for the Fall is the critical issue. Was Adam able not to sin or not to sin? Was Adam required to sin? Was the Fall decreed? Those are the defining questions and they are avoided entirely.

> God's decree of reprobation, given in light of the fall, is a decree to justice, not injustice. In this view the biblical *a priori* that God is neither the cause nor the author of sin is safeguarded.

While it is evident that this verbal maneuvering satisfies Sproul, it does not satisfactorily answer the questions. In fact, it seems that what he denies the Single Predestinarian the right to claim becomes the very argument that he uses to explain his *positive-negative* position. I am unable to see a substantial difference in the two doctrines. The non-elect is destined to perdition because of either a direct act of God consigning the non-elect to eternal damnation *or* a direct act of only not assigning the non-elect to eternal life.

Whichever side of Calvinism's internal argument is taken, it is the action of God that is the cause of the eternal death of the non-elect. In all forms of Calvinism, God alone determines the eternal destiny of every person. That is the undeniable result of the doctrine of Unconditional Election.

The great doctrine of Scripture that Calvinism *totally* omits is that of the *love of God*. The emphasis of Calvinism is placed on the glory of God and, even more so, on the sovereignty of God, to the near exclusion of the love of God.

Though *The Institutes of the Christians Religion.*[190] were not written as evangelizing sermons, they were written to provide a systematic theological defense of the Reformation; therefore, I found it revealing that a series of word searches by computer could not find the phrase "the love of God." A visual scanning of the paragraphs where the words *love, loves, loved,* were located found no clear reference to the love of God for general humanity. The same readings found that the use of the word in relation to the elect is a rare occasion when speaking of the love that *comes from* God; the far more frequent use is the love of the elect that is *directed toward* God.

This is disturbing, since the Scriptures contain the direct statement that "God is love."[191] I have noted before and repeat it here because repetition aids learning. The emphasis in Calvinism is placed on the glory of God and, even more so, on the sovereignty of God, to the near exclusion of the love of God.

Consider the firmness with which John Calvin wrote the following sentences in *The Institutes,* Book 3, Chapter 21.

> CHAPTER 21. —OF THE ETERNAL ELECTION, BY WHICH GOD HAS PREDESTINATED SOME TO SALVATION, AND OTHERS TO DESTRUCTION.

---

[190]"*The Institutes of the Christian Religion* is John Calvin's seminal work of Protestant systematic theology ... published in Latin in 1536 ... French in 1541, with the definitive editions appearing in 1559 and in 1560. The book was written as an introductory textbook on the Protestant faith for those with some previous knowledge of theology and covered a broad range of theological topics from the doctrines of church and sacraments to justification by faith alone and Christian liberty." http://www.definitions.net/definition/institutesofthechristian religion.

[191]1 John 4:16 And we have known and believed the love that God hath to us. God is love; and he that dwelleth in love dwelleth in God, and God in him.

> 5. The predestination by which God adopts some to the hope of life, and adjudges others to eternal death, no man who would be thought pious ventures simply to deny; but it is greatly caviled at, especially by those who make prescience its cause. We, indeed, ascribe both prescience and predestination to God; but we say, that it is absurd to make the latter subordinate to the former. When we attribute prescience to God, we mean that all things always were, and ever continue, under his eye; that to his knowledge there is no past or future, but all things are present, and indeed so present, that it is not merely the idea of them that is before him (as those objects are which we retain in our memory), but that he truly sees and contemplates them as actually under his immediate inspection. This prescience extends to the whole circuit of the world, and to all creatures. By predestination we mean the eternal decree of God, by which he determined with himself whatever he wished to happen with regard to every man. All are not created on equal terms, but some are preordained to eternal life, others to eternal damnation; and, accordingly, as each has been created for one or other of these ends, we say that he has been predestinated to life or to death.

The next citation is taken from *The Institutes*, Book 3, Chapter 24.

> Wherefore, let us not decline to say with Augustine, "God could change the will of the wicked into good, because he is omnipotent. Clearly he could. Why, then, does he not do it? Because he is unwilling. Why he is unwilling remains with himself," (August. de Genes. ad Lit. Lib. 2). We should not attempt to be wise above what is meet, and it is much better to take Augustine's explanation, than to quibble with Chrysostom, "that he draws him who is

> willing, and stretching forth his hand," (Chrysost. Hom. de Convers. Pauli), lest the difference should seem to lie in the judgment of God, and not in the mere will of man.

Calvin believed this doctrine so strongly that he devoted three chapters to the subject: Chapter 21 (OF THE ETERNAL ELECTION, BY WHICH GOD HAS PREDESTINATED SOME TO SALVATION AND OTHERS TO DESTRUCTION.), Chapter 22 (THIS DOCTRINE CONFIRMED BY PROOFS FROM SCRIPTURE.), and Chapter 23 (REFUTATION OF THE CALUMNIES BY WHICH THIS DOCTRINE IS ALWAYS UNJUSTLY ASSAILED.).[192] It is indisputable that Calvin taught that God created some individuals for the purpose of eternal damnation. It is impossible to reconcile that heinous malevolent action with the love of God.

In response to the assertion by Calvinism that predestination means that "some individuals are created to spend eternity in the presence of God and some individuals are created to spend eternity in the Lake of Fire," may I submit this is not only an error that slanders the character of God, but it is an error of misusing Bible words. The word predestine as used in the Scriptures has nothing to do with where anyone spends eternity.

In the three passages where the term predestination is found, the word clearly is used in relationship to what the believer receives in Christ. The believer[193] is destined to be conformed to the image of Christ, to receive the adoption of children, and to obtain an inheritance.

> Romans 8:29–30 For whom he did foreknow, he also did predestinate *to be* conformed to the image of his Son, that he might be the firstborn among many breth-

---

[192]The use of capitals is in the original.

[193]Romans 10:14 How then shall they call on him in whom they have not believed? and how shall they believe in him of whom they have not heard? and how shall they hear without a preacher?

> ren. Moreover whom he did predestinate, them he also called: and whom he called, them he also justified: and whom he justified, them he also glorified.
>
> Ephesians 1:5 Having predestinated us unto the adoption of children by Jesus Christ to himself, according to the good pleasure of his will,
>
> Ephesians 1:11 In whom also we have obtained an inheritance, being predestinated according to the purpose of him who worketh all things after the counsel of his own will: 12 That we should be to the praise of his glory, who first trusted in Christ. 13 In whom ye also *trusted*, **after** that ye heard the word of truth, the gospel of your salvation: in whom also **after** that ye believed, ye were sealed with that Holy Spirit of promise, 14 Which is the earnest of our inheritance until the redemption of the purchased possession, unto the praise of his glory.

I call attention to the clarity of the statements in verse 13 of Ephesians 1. It is evident that the trust came ***after*** they heard. The order is specific that ***after*** they heard, trusted, and believed, they were sealed. They could not believe until they heard. They were not sealed until ***after*** they heard trusted, and believed.

> "In whom ye also *trusted*, ***after that ye heard*** the word of truth, the gospel of your salvation: in whom also ***after that ye believed***, ye were sealed with that Holy Spirit of promise." [Emphasis is added.]

I believe that John Calvin would have been far wiser to have devoted more time to the reading of the Scriptures and less time to the study of the writings of Augustine and Martin Bucer. Calvin seems to have accepted and even expanded their concept of predestination.

The words that the Holy Spirit gave to the writers of Scripture must be allowed to stand as they are found and not adjusted by the assignment of special, secret, or unusual definitions to fit a preconceived system of theology.

APPENDIX 4

MANIPULATED WORDS

This excerpt from Calvin's unfinished Commentary on Ezekiel[194] provides an example of how minor concessions on the meanings of words lead to major deviations in doctrines. John Calvin was gifted with a brilliant intellect. That he was supremely confident regarding the rightness of his thinking is unchallengeable. No one has ever attempted to match intellect with John Calvin and be able to walk away unscathed.

Read the following carefully and slowly with an open Bible to verify the Scriptures cited. I do not recommend scanning Calvin. He is tedious to read; and while skimming through the works of Calvin is tempting, he must be read carefully or else misconceptions will occur that may open the door for the infiltration of error.

> Ezekiel 18:23 Have I any pleasure at all that the wicked should die? saith the Lord GOD: and not that he should return from his ways, and live?

---

[194]http://www.ccel.org/ccel/calvin/calcom23.i.html

He confirms the same sentiment in other words, that God desires nothing more earnestly than that those who were perishing and rushing to destruction should return into the way of safety. And for this reason not only is the Gospel spread abroad in the world, but God wished to bear witness through all ages how inclined he is to pity. For although the heathen were destitute of the law and the prophets, yet they were always endued with some taste of this doctrine. Truly enough they were suffocated by many errors: but we shall always find that they were induced by a secret impulse to seek for pardon, because this sense was in some way born with them, that God is to be appeased by all who seek him. Besides, God bore witness to it more clearly in the law and the prophets. In the Gospel we hear how familiarly he addresses us when he promises us pardon. (Luke 1:78.) And this is the knowledge of salvation, to embrace his mercy which he offers us in Christ. It follows, then, that what the Prophet now says is very true, that God wills not the death of a sinner, because he meets him of his own accord, and is not only prepared to receive all who fly to his pity, but he calls them towards him with a loud voice, when he sees how they are alienated from all hope of safety. But the manner must be noticed in which God wishes all to be saved, namely, *when they turn themselves from their ways*. God thus does not so wish all men to be saved as to renounce the difference between good and evil; but repentance, as we have said, must precede pardon. How, then, does God wish all men to be saved? By the Spirit's condemning the world of sin, of righteousness, and of judgment at this day, by the Gospel, as he did formerly by the law and the prophets. (John 16:8.) God makes manifest to mankind their

> great misery, that they may betake themselves to him: he wounds that he may cure, and slays that he may give life. We hold, then, that; God wills not the death of a sinner, since he calls all equally to repentance, and promises himself prepared to receive them if they only seriously repent.

What Calvin has written in the paragraph down through this sentence would convey the impression that the invitation of salvation is being extended to all men and may be accepted by all men. However, he will immediately proceed to correct that impression. Notice that he speaks of "God's secret counsel" and of God acting in "a manner inscrutable to us."

> If any one *[sic]* should object—then there is no election of God, by which he has predestinated a fixed number to salvation, the answer is at hand: the Prophet does not here speak of God's secret counsel, but only recalls miserable men from despair, that they may apprehend the hope of pardon, and repent and embrace the offered salvation. If any one again objects—this is making God act with duplicity, the answer is ready, that God always wishes the same thing, though by different ways, and in a manner inscrutable to us. Although, therefore, God's will is simple, yet great variety is involved in it, as far as our senses are concerned. Besides, it is not surprising that our eyes should be blinded by intense light, so that we cannot certainly judge how God wishes all to be saved, and yet has devoted all the reprobate to eternal destruction, and wishes them to perish.

It is tempting to scan Calvin's comments, but that allows the potential of not grasping that last sentence. I will interrupt this continuing long paragraph to call attention to what was in fact written. Calvin was so moved by his doctrine that he wrote,

"God ... has devoted all the reprobate to eternal destruction, and ***wishes them to perish***. This is after he had written that "It follows, then, that what the Prophet now says is very true, that God wills not the death of a sinner, because he meets him of his own accord, and is not only prepared to receive all who fly to his pity, but he calls them towards him with a loud voice, when he sees how they are alienated from all hope of safety." [Emphasis is mine.]

Having described God with terms that undeniably appear to portray Him as compassionate and receptive to sinners, the God that "wills not the death of a sinner," Calvin then boldly declares that God "has devoted all the reprobate to eternal destruction, and wishes them to perish." Calvin never saw his statements as irreconcilable, but instead he devoted his great skills to shameless revisions of Scripture that resulted in amazing inversions that were constructed for the singular purpose to support his doctrine.

These extensive comments by Calvin are on one verse of Scripture and that verse reads *exactly the opposite* of how he reconstructs the verse to mean. He skillfully accomplishes this transformation from the positive to the negative by carefully maneuvering the words.

Ezekiel 18:23 reads, "Have I any pleasure at all that the wicked should die? saith the Lord GOD: and not that he should return from his ways, and live." To the contrary, Calvin is determined to argue that God "wishes them to perish." The verse as written does not fit the construct of Calvinism.

Such is the firmness of his belief system that he is compelled to work diligently to alter the meaning of the words of that Scripture to conform to meet that system to which he is committed. He justifies this manipulation of the words of Scripture by the convenient appeal to "God's secret counsel" that God achieves in "a manner inscrutable to us."

He continues:

> While we look now through a glass darkly, we should be content with the measure of our own intelligence. (1 Corinthians 13:12.) When we shall be like God, and see him face to face, then what is now obscure will then become plain. But since captious men torture this and similar passages, it will be needful to refute them shortly, since it can be done without trouble.

My interjections may have obscured it, but that sentence concludes the first paragraph. We are simply to accept Calvinism and wait until we see God for the answers to our objections, because then we will understand why He created some men for the purpose of eternal damnation. However, Calvin assures his readers that he could answer any challenge "without trouble."

The next paragraph proceeds to provide his answers to the teaching that God "is longsuffering, not willing that any should perish" by emphasizing that God does not wish to convert the reprobate. The reasoning is difficult to follow, because it is continuously presenting the words of Scripture as requiring his intervention in order for those words to be understood in accordance with his predetermined system of interpretation. The words of Scriptures are not allowed to stand as they are written. You must read carefully to follow his reasoning. The bold font is my emphasis.

> God is said *not to wish the death of a sinner.* How so? since he wishes all to be converted. Now we must see how God wishes all to be converted; for repentance is surely his peculiar gift: as it is his office to create men, so it is his province to renew them, and restore his image within them. For this reason we are said to be his workmanship, that is, his fashioning. (Ephesians 2:10.) **Since, therefore, re-**

> **pentance is a kind of second creation, it follows that it is not in man's power; and if it is equally in God's power to convert men as well as to create them, it follows that the reprobate are not converted, because God does not wish their conversion; for if he wished it he could do it: and hence it appears that he does not wish it.** But again they argue foolishly, since God does not wish all to be converted, he is himself deceptive, and nothing can be certainly stated concerning his paternal benevolence. But this knot is easily untied; for he does not leave us in suspense when he says, that he wishes all to be saved. Why so? for if no one repents without finding God propitious, then this sentence is filled up. But we must remark that God puts on a twofold character: for he here wishes to be taken at his word. As I have already said, the Prophet does not here dispute with subtlety about his incomprehensible plans, but wishes to keep our attention close to God's word. Now, what are the contents of this word? The law, the prophets, and the gospel. Now all are called to repentance, and the hope of salvation is promised them when they repent. This is true, since God rejects no returning sinner: he pardons all without exception: meanwhile, this will of God which he sets forth in his word does not prevent him from decreeing before the world was created what he would do with every individual: and as I have now said, the Prophet only shows here, that when we have been converted we need not doubt that God immediately meets us and shows himself propitious. The remainder tomorrow.

It is not practical in the scope of this book to analyze each word of every sentence of the multiple works of John Calvin, not even those of this small portion of his commentary on Ezekiel. However, it is profitable to attempt to show the reader how Calvin must be read to understand what he intends to convey. The words have special definitions. If you scanned that paragraph instead of reading it, then you likely missed in line five that he terms repentance as the gift of God; that is why Calvin can affirm that all who repent are received by God.

The following paragraph is my attempt to show how Calvin must be understood.

> "Now all are called to repentance, and the hope of salvation is promised [*to all of*] them ***when*** they repent [*which only the elect can do*]. This is true, since God rejects no returning sinner [*because His election and regeneration of them causes them to return and to repent and because only those so elected will truly return and repent*]: he pardons all [*elected returning sinners*] without exception [*because He elected them*]: meanwhile, this will of God which he sets forth in his word does not prevent him from decreeing before the world was created what he would do with every individual [*which is that He elects particular individuals to salvation and the rest of humanity, whom He did not elect, are those that therefore do not return repenting, because they cannot either return or repent, because God wishes them to perish eternally.*]

One must read Calvin as Calvin intended that he be understood. That is accomplished only by using Calvin's definitions of his words. It is tedious work to labor over every word proceeding from the pen of Calvin. **However, it is, in my view, exceeding dangerous not to do so**. He manipulates the words to make the Scriptures and those of his opponents to mean whatever it is that he desires these words to mean. This is clearly evidenced in the next section. [All emphasis and parentheses in these paragraphs are in the original.]

Ezekiel 18:32 For I have no pleasure in the death of him that dieth, says the Lord GOD: wherefore turn *yourselves*, and live ye.

We see, therefore, how God throws off that false reproach from himself with which the children of Israel taunted him, saying, that they perished by his immoderate rigor, and could find no reason for his severity against them. He announces, on the other hand, that the cause of death rested with themselves; and then he points out the remedy, that they should amend their life, not only in outward appearance, but in sincerity of heart: and at the same time he testifies of his willingness to be entreated; nay, he meets them of his own accord, if they only repent heartily and unfeignedly. We now understand the Prophet's meaning. We said, that we are admonished in this way, that if we desire to return to God we must begin at the beginning, namely, renewal of the heart and spirit; because, as Jeremiah says, he looks for truth and integrity, and does not value outward disguises. (Jeremiah 5:3.) But it may seem absurd for God to exhort the Israelites *to form their hearts anew*: and men badly trained in the Scriptures erect their crests under the pretense of this passage, as if it were in the power of man's free will to convert himself. They exclaim, therefore, either that God here exhorts his people deceitfully, or else that when alienated from him we can by our own movement repent, and return into the way. But the whole Scripture openly refutes this. It is not in vain that the saints so often pray that God would renew them; (Psalm 51:12, and very often elsewhere;) for it would be a feigned and a lying prayer, if newness of heart were not his gift. If any one requests of God what he is persuaded that he has already, and by his own inherent virtue, does he not trifle with

God? But nothing occurs more frequently than this mode of entreaty. Since therefore, the saints pray to God to renew them, they doubtless confess that to be his peculiar gift; and unless he moves his hand, they have no strength remaining, so that they can never rise from the ground. Besides, in many passages God claims the renewal of the heart as peculiar to himself. We noticed that remarkable passage in the eleventh chapter of this Prophet, (Ezekiel 11:19,) he will repeat the same in the thirty-sixth chapter, (Ezekiel 36:26, 27;) and we know what Jeremiah says in his thirty-first chapter, (Jeremiah 31:33.) But Scripture is everywhere full of testimonies of this kind, so that it would be superfluous to heap together many passages; nay, if any one denies that regeneration[195] is a gift of the Holy Spirit, he will tear up by the roots all the principles of piety. We have said that regeneration is like another

[195]It cannot be overly emphasized that Calvin must be read with his definitions readily available. Calvin taught that regeneration *precedes* faith. He insisted that until a person is regenerated that person is incapable of exercising faith. Faith to Calvin was the gift of God, which is received after regeneration. This is a hallmark of Calvinism. In his commentary on the Gospel of John, he recorded his reasoning:
"Hence it follows, first, that faith does not proceed from ourselves, but is the fruit of spiritual regeneration; for the Evangelist affirms that no man can believe, unless he be begotten of God; and therefore faith is a heavenly gift. It follows, secondly, that faith is not bare or cold knowledge, since no man can believe who has not been renewed by the Spirit of God.
It may be thought that the Evangelist reverses the natural order by making regeneration to precede faith, whereas, on the contrary, it is an effect of faith, and therefore ought to be placed later. I reply, that both statements perfectly agree; because by faith we receive the *incorruptible seed,* (1 Peter 1:23) by which we are born again to a new and divine life. And yet faith itself is a work of the Holy Spirit, who dwells in none but the children of God. So then, in various respects, faith is a part of our regeneration, and an entrance into the kingdom of God, that he may reckon us among his children. The illumination of our minds by the Holy Spirit belongs to our renewal, and thus faith flows from regeneration as from its source; but since it is by the same faith that we receive Christ, who sanctifies us by his Spirit, on that account it is said to be the beginning of our adoption." http://www. ccel.org/ccel/Calvin/cal com34.pdf

creation; and if we compare it with the first creation, it far surpasses it. For it is much better for us to be made children of God, and reformed after his image within us, than to be created mortal: for we are born children of wrath, corrupt and degenerate; (Ephesians 2:3;) since all integrity was lost when God's image was removed. We see, then, the nature of our first creation; but when God refashions us, we are not only born sons of Adam, but we are the brothers of angels,[196] and members of Christ; and this our second life consists in rectitude, justice, and the light of true intelligence.

We now see that if it had been in man's free will to convert himself, much more would be ascribed to him than to God, because, as we have said, it was much more valuable to be created sons of God than of Adam. It ought, then, to be beyond all controversy with the pious that men cannot rise again when they are fallen, and turn of themselves when alienated from God; but this is the peculiar gift of the Holy Spirit. And the sophists, who in all ways endeavor to obscure God's grace, confess that half the act of conversion is in the power of the Holy Spirit: for they do not say that we are simply and totally con-

---

[196]"... when God re-fashions *[sic]* us, we are not only born sons of Adam, but we are the brothers of angels ..." While this "brothers of angels" is a very strange statement, it is not isolated. In his commentary on Daniel, Calvin wrote the following 7:25: "By saints he doubtless means sons of God, or his elect people, or the Church. He calls these "saints of lofty ones," because as elect they depend upon heaven; and although they are pilgrims in the world, yet their life is in heaven, where the eternal inheritance remains for them which was obtained by Christ. As, therefore, their treasure is now heaven, they deservedly boast of being citizens of heaven, and allies and brethren of angels."
I have not yet discovered an explanation from any Calvinist as to what John Calvin intended to convey by this assertion that Christians are "brothers of angels." I will not speculate what he intended beyond the meaning of the words. The statement has no possible basis in Scripture and must be rejected.

verted by the motion of our own free will, but they imagine a concurrence of grace with free will, and of free will with grace. Thus they foolishly represent us as cooperating with God: they confess, indeed, that God's grace goes before and follows; and they seem to themselves very liberal towards God when they acknowledge this twofold grace in man's conversion. But God is not content with that partition, since he is deprived of half his right: for he does not say that he would assist men to renew themselves and to repent; but he attributes the work to himself entirely: I will give you a new heart and a new spirit. (Ezekiel 36:26.) If it is his to give, it follows that the slightest portion of it cannot be transferred to man without diminishing something from his right. But they object that the following precept is not in vain, *that men should make for themselves a new heart*. Now their deception arises through ignorance, from their judging of the powers of men by the commands of God; but the inference is incorrect, as we have said elsewhere: for when God teaches what is right, he does not think of what we are able to do, but only shows us what we ought to do. When, therefore, the power of our free will is estimated by the precepts of God, we make a great mistake, because God exacts from us the strict discharge of our duty, just as if our power of obedience was not defective. We are not absolved from our obligation because we cannot pay it; for God holds us bound to himself, although we are in every way deficient.

They object again, God then deludes men when he says, *make yourselves a new heart*. I answer, we must always consider to what purpose God thus speaks, namely, that men convicted of sin may cease to throw the blame on any one *[sic]* else, as they often endeavor to do; for nothing is more natural than to transfer the cause of our condemnation away from ourselves, that we may seem just, and God appear unjust. Since, then, such depravity reigns among men, hence the Holy Spirit demands from us what all acknowledge they ought to pay: and if we do not pay it, still we are bound to do so, and thus all strife and complaint should cease. Thus, as it concerns the elect, when God shows them their duty, and they acknowledge that they cannot discharge it, they fly to the aid of the Holy Spirit, so that the outward exhortation becomes a kind of instrument which God uses to confer the grace of his Spirit. For although he gratuitously goes before us, and does not need outward channels, yet he desires exhortations to be useful to this end. Since, therefore, this doctrine stirs up the elect to deliver themselves up to be ruled by the Holy Spirit, we see how it becomes fruitful to us. Whence it follows, that God does not delude or deceive us when he exhorts *each of us to form his heart and his spirit afresh.* In fine, Ezekiel wished by these words to show that pardon would be prepared for the Israelites if they seriously repented, and showed its effects through their whole life. That was most true, because the elect did not embrace this doctrine in vain, when at the same time God worked in them by his Spirit, and so turned them to himself. But the reprobate, though they do not cease to murmur, yet they are rendered ashamed, since all excuse has been removed, and they must perish through their own fault, since they willingly remained in their wickedness, and by self-indulgence they cherished the old man within themselves,—a fountain of all injustice. Whenever such passages occur, let us remember that celebrated prayer of Augustine: grant us what you command, and command what you wish, (Epist. 24;) for otherwise, if God should lay upon us the slightest burden, we should be unable to bear it. Besides, our strength will be sufficient to fulfill his requirements, if only he supply it, and we are not so foolish as to think anything comprehended in his precepts which he has not granted to us; because, as I have said before, nothing is more perverse than to measure the angelic righteousness of the law by our strength. By the word *heart*, I understand him to mean the seat of all the affections; and by *spirit*, the intellectual part of the soul. The heart is often taken for the reason and intelligence; but when these two words are joined together, the spirit relates to the mind, and so it is the intellectual faculty of the soul; but the heart is taken for the will, or the seat of all the affections. Hence we see how very corrupt the Israelites were, since they could not be otherwise reconciled to God, unless by being renewed in both heart and mind. Hence also we my gather the general doctrine, that nothing in us is sound and perfect, and hence all entire renovation is necessary that we may please God.

The subjoined phrase, *why will ye die, O house of Israel?* suggests many questions. Here unskillful men think that God speculates on what men will do, and that the salvation or destruction of each depends on themselves, as if God had determined nothing concerning us before the foundation of the world. Hence they set him at naught, since they fancy that he is held in suspense and doubt as to the future end of every one, and that he is not so anxious for our salvation, as to wish all to be saved, but leaves it in the power of every one to perish or to be saved as he pleases. But as I have said, this would reduce God to a specter. But we have no need of a long dispute, because Scripture everywhere declares with sufficient clearness that God has determined what shall hap-

> pen to us: for he chose his own people before the foundation of the world and passed by others. (Ephesians 1:4.)

Reread that last sentence and then take notice that he amplifies the position in the next sentences.

> Nothing is clearer than this doctrine; for if there had been no predestination on God's part, there had been no deity, since he would be forced into order as if he were one of us: nay, men are to a certain extent provident, whenever God allows some sparks of his image to shine forth in them. If, therefore, the very smallest drop of foresight in men is laid hold of, how great must it be in the fountain itself? Insipid indeed is the comment, to fancy that God remains doubtful and waiting for what will happen to individuals, as if it were in their own power either to attain to salvation or to perish. But the Prophets words are plain, for God testifies with grief that he *willeth not the death of a mortal.* I answer, that there is no absurdity, as we said before, in God's undertaking a twofold character, not that he is two-faced himself, as those profane dogs[197] blurt out against us, but because his counsels are incomprehensible by us. This indeed ought to be fixed, that before the foundation of the world we were predestinated either to life or death. Now because we cannot ascend to that height, it is needful for God to conform himself to our ignorance, and to descend in some way to us since we cannot ascend to him. When Scripture so often says that God has heard, and inquires, no one is offended: all pass over those forms of speech securely, and confess them adopted from human language. (Genesis 16:11, and often.) Very often, I say, God

---

[197]Calvin did not hesitate to demean and persecute those who challenged his approach to Scripture.

> transfers to himself the properties of man, and this is admitted universally without either offense or controversy. Although this manner of speaking is rather harsh: God came to see, (Genesis 11:5,) when he announces that he came to inquire about things openly known; it is easily excused, since nothing is less in accordance with his nature: for the solution is at hand, namely, that God speaks metaphorically, and adapts his speech to the convenience of men. Now why will not the same reasoning avail in the present case? for with respect to the law and the whole teaching of the prophets, God announces his wish that all should be saved. And surely we consider the tendency of the heavenly teaching, we shall find that all are promiscuously called to salvation. For the law was a way of life, as Moses testifies, This is the way, walk you in it: again, Whosoever has done those things shall live in them: and, again, This is your life. (Deuteronomy 30:15, 19; Deuteronomy 32:47; Leviticus 18:5; Isaiah 30:21.) Then of his own accord God offers himself as merciful to his ancient people, so that this heavenly teaching ought to be life-giving. But what is the Gospel? It is God's power unto salvation to every believer, says Paul. (Romans 1:16.) Therefore God *delighteth not in the death of him who dieth,* if he repent at his teaching.

[A reminder that all emphasis and parentheses in those paragraphs are in the original.]

This last sentence is a prime example of where scanning or skimming the writings of Calvin is apt to introduce error. Calvin is carefully rewording the text of Scripture by placing a condition that can only be fulfilled *by* the elect *after* those elected have been regenerated.

> But if we wish to penetrate to his incomprehensible counsel, this will be another

> objection: Oh! but in this way God is chargeable with duplicity;—but I have denied this, though he takes up a twofold character, because this was necessary for our comprehension. Meanwhile Ezekiel announces this very truly as far as doctrine is concerned, *that God wills not the death of him that perishes*: for the explanation follows directly afterwards, *be you converted and live.* Why does not God delight in the death of him who perishes? Because he invites all to repentance and rejects no one.

Calvin insists that the invitation to repent may be extended to all with the qualification that God *rejects no one that repents.* Calvin, the two-fold predestinarian may write this, because he is confident that only the elect will repent. Contrary to Calvin's accusatory challenge to those of us who reject his doctrines, I do not charge God with duplicity; I charge Calvin with duplicity.

> Since this is so, it follows that he is not delighted by the death of him who perishes: hence there is nothing in this passage doubtful or thorny, and we should also hold that we are led aside by speculations too deep for us. For God does not wish us to inquire into his secret. Counsels: His secrets are with himself, says Moses, (Deuteronomy 29:29,) but this book for ourselves and our children. Moses there distinguishes between the hidden counsel of God, (which if we desire to investigate too curiously we shall tread on a profound abyss,) and the teaching delivered to us. Hence let us leave to God his own secrets, and exercise ourselves as far as we can in the law, in which God's will is made plain to us and to our children. Now let us go on.

These lengthy, tedious paragraphs are provided to allow the words of John Calvin to stand in their context and to defeat the assertion that I have twisted those words to mean something that he did not intend.

Since I made some interruptions of his presentation, I wish to revisit certain paragraphs for emphasis and clarity. The first paragraph of this Commentary implies that there is an openness to the Gospel invitation that includes everyone.

> He confirms the same sentiment in other words, that God desires nothing more earnestly than that those who were perishing and rushing to destruction should return into the way of safety. And for this reason not only is the Gospel spread abroad in the world, but God wished to bear witness through all ages how inclined he is to pity. For although the heathen were destitute of the law and the prophets, yet they were always endued with some taste of this doctrine. Truly enough they were suffocated by many errors: but we shall always find that they were induced by a secret impulse to seek for pardon, because this sense was in some way born with them, that God is to be appeased by all who seek him.

Calvin proceeds to declare that God uses a loud voice to call all to repentance.

> It follows, then, that what the Prophet now says is very true, that God wills not the death of a sinner, because he meets him of his own accord, and is not only prepared to receive all who fly to his pity, but he calls them towards him with a loud voice, when he sees how they are alienated from all hope of safety. But the manner must be noticed in which God wishes all to be saved, namely, when they turn themselves from their ways. God thus does not so wish all men to be saved as to renounce the difference between good and evil; but repentance, as we have said, must precede pardon.

However, he grows bold as he continues:

> ... the Prophet does not here speak of God's secret counsel, but only recalls miserable men from despair, that they may apprehend the hope of pardon, and repent and embrace the offered salvation. If any one *[sic]* again objects—this is making God act with duplicity, the answer is ready, that God always wishes the same thing, though by different ways, and in a manner inscrutable to us. Although, therefore, God's will is simple, yet great variety is involved in it, as far as our senses are concerned. Besides, it is not surprising that our eyes should be blinded by intense light, so that we cannot certainly judge how God wishes all to be saved, and yet has devoted all the reprobate to eternal destruction, and wishes them to perish.

In one sentence, with one breath as it were, John Calvin is able to write, "God wishes all to be saved, and yet God has devoted all of the reprobate to eternal destruction, because God wishes them to perish." As his commentary receives a further reading, it becomes apparent that John Calvin outperforms a circus contortionist in twisting the plain words of Scripture into a jumbled mess decipherable only by the application of his special definitions. He then makes what I consider a futile appeal to accept what he has written as the last word of interpretation: "*For God does not wish us to inquire into his secret.*"

It is true the "secret things belong unto the LORD," but it is also true that "those things which are revealed belong unto us and to our children for ever, that we may do all the words of this law." (Deuteronomy 29:29) Surely, salvation has been revealed unto us and is certainly within the purview of the believer to understand his salvation.

Solomon wrote that "It is the glory of God to conceal a thing: but the honour of kings is to search out a matter." (Proverbs 25:2) The LORD Jesus encouraged the searching of the Scriptures (John 5:29) and the Bereans were declared to be" more noble than those in Thessalonica, in that they received the word with all readiness of mind, and searched the scriptures daily, whether those things were so." (Acts 17:11)

I do not believe that Calvin has proven the validity of his system of theology by declaring that God does not wish us to inquire into his secret." Instead, that appeal for secrecy indicates that Calvinism will not endure diligent comparison with Scripture.

The God of Heaven is not duplicitous, but the reasoning of John Calvin would make Him to be so. One example of the reasoning required to support Calvinism should be sufficient to cause a sincere seeker of truth to reject Calvinism.

> Besides, it is not surprising that our eyes should be blinded by intense light, so that we cannot certainly judge how God wishes all to be saved, and yet has devoted all the reprobate to eternal destruction, and wishes them to perish.

How can it be sensible to believe that "God wishes all to be saved" while God "wishes" the reprobate "to perish"? It is assuredly not a belief based upon Scripture, because it conflicts with the word of God. To accept that confliction requires more than blinded eyes; it necessitates a mental deadness.

The words of John Calvin have insufficient authority to compel me to set aside the words of the word of God to follow his reasoning that declares *the exact opposite* of the written text.

APPENDIX 5

PREDESTINATED RAINDROPS

Earlier, I suggested that I found an occasion of some humor in the use of the phrase "an accident of history" by Elder Seaton. In that footnote, I provided the following quotation, which is an affirmation that **everything** is divinely decreed.

> "In other words, no occurrence, large or small, occurs outside the sovereignty of God—from the number of rain drops falling on your lawn during an afternoon thunder storm *[sic]*, to the dramatic events of the Desert Storm war, all are within, and part of, God's divine decree. As often commented, even if one molecule is roaming free in the universe, God is not sovereign." If the God of Heaven decreed before the foundation of the world that the precise "number of rain drops" that would fall upon my front lawn during a particular thunderstorm on a specific afternoon, then it is an absolute[198] that there is no

---

[198]The *M-WD* definition is "having no restriction, exception, or qualification."

> possibility of an accident[199] at any time in any place.

Should this assertion of absolute determinism (foreordained predestination) be actually true then every possible permutation of all potential possibilities have been restricted to one and only one result, with only one resultant consequence. The prospect of existing alternatives or the existence of even one alternative would be eliminated. To the Calvinist, all things of every nature were established immutably, unalterably, and eternally before the Creator ever created.

No true Bible believer, be he Calvinist or not, would challenge the statement that God is omnipotent, unlimited in power, and omniscient, unlimited in knowledge. Since those descriptions of God are accepted without qualification, the logical question becomes, "Would God choose to be the Author of sin?"

Without describing all of the natural and human-caused occasions of tears and sorrows, without rehearsing any of the horrific sins and their infliction of injuries and pain, and without considering the eternal torments of the lost souls in the eternal Lake of Fire, I insist that for the Calvinist to portray God, as having full knowledge of all complications eventuating and with complete responsibility for all attendant consequences, thereby making God the proximate cause of all these things **is the untenable vilification of the holiness, the love, the mercy, and the kindness of God.** Moreover, to attribute all of the obvious consequences of the fall of Adam to the ***grace*** of God is unspeakable. Further, for God

---

[199]The *M-WD* defines accident as "an unforeseen and unplanned event or circumstance b: lack of intention or necessity: CHANCE 'met by accident rather than by design.'" The *Merriam-Webster Thesaurus* adds "absence of positive plan or intent 'we stopped there by accident'; Synonyms: chance, fortuity, hap, luck; Related Word: fluke, fortune, hazard; Contrasted Words: design, premeditation; Antonym: intent."

the Father to be made the sole cause of the sufferings of the LORD Jesus Christ is atrocious.

To show the logic used by the Calvinist to reach this conclusion of absolute determinism (foreordained predestination), I submit the following two articles; the first is from a Calvinist website and the second is from a sermon by Charles Spurgeon.

The following excerpts are taken from an article written by Michael Bremmer and titled, *The Sovereignty of God and Human Freewill,*[200] containing the comment regarding "raindrops" referenced previously. It is found on the website *Sola Scriptura!*, which is self-described as "a Reformed Theology Resource with many articles and links on Reformed Theology." I am providing the introductory paragraphs to the article.

> By sovereignty of God I mean that God has ordained (or decreed), by an act of His sovereign will, all that has come to pass, all that is, and all that will come to pass, and apart from His knowledge, purpose, and predetermined plan, nothing will come to pass. God, says the Scriptures, "Works all things after the counsel of His will" (Eph. 1.11). The Scriptures do not say God works some things, or most things. Much less does it say only the good things—it says all things. "Scripture everywhere affirms that whatsoever is and comes to pass is the realization of God's thought and will ..." (Bavinck, The Doctrine of God. P. 369). In other words, no occurrence, large or small, occurs outside the sovereignty of God—from the number of rain drops falling on your lawn during an afternoon thunder storm *[sic]*, to the dramatic events of the Desert Storm war, all are within, and part of, God's divine decree. As often commented, even if one

---

[200]http://www.mbrem123.com/calvinism/free-will.php

molecule is roaming "free" in the universe, God is not sovereign.

Ten thousand ages ere the skies, Were into motion brought, All the long years and worlds to come, Stood present to His thought; There's not a sparrow or a worm, But is found in His decrees, He raises monarchs to their throne, and sinks them as He pleases. - Issac *[sic]* Watts

If God ordains all things, then he not only ordains the ends, He also ordains the means. As R. B. Kuiper has pointed out (The Bible Tells Me So, P. 37), not only does God ordain that a farmer's field yield so many bushels of wheat, God also ordains that the farmer plow and sow the field. Not only does God ordain a child's recovery of a serious illness, God also ordains that the child recovers because of the parent's prayers. Realizing God ordains the means and the ends helps us to comprehend how our responsibility works within God's sovereignty. For example, Arminians object to the doctrine of election because it makes the preaching of the gospel unnecessary. However, God not only ordained who will be saved, God also ordained the preaching of the gospel to accomplish the salvation of His elect.

Furthermore, the sovereignty of God means all that He decreed will come about, and in the precise manner that He decreed. No one can ignore or reject His decree. Again, this does not suggest God compels anyone to act against their *[sic]* will. Man's freedom to act according to his choice is within God's decree. What it does mean is, all of what God has ordained will surely come to pass, and in the manner that God ordains. The Scriptures say, "The counsel of the Lord stands forever, the plans from His heart from generation to generation" (Ps. 33.11). (Isa. 14.27; Ps.

> 115.3; 135.6; Job 23.13–14; 42.2–3; Isa. 46.10).
>
> God's sovereignty encompasses all that comes to pass, even sin; however, God never forces anyone to act contrary their will; therefore, He is not the author of sin. When we sin, we do so because we choose to sin. That God has even ordained sin will not sit well with everyone. Yet, if Jesus is in fact the "Lamb slain before the foundation of the world" (Rev. 13.8) then sins *[sic]* appearance into the world and our redemption through the atonement, were decreed by God before creation and the fall; however, Scripture is clear that God is not the author of sin (Ja. 1.13). [The emphasis and parentheses are in the original.]

I must confess to deep mystification at the strange logic demonstrated in these comments in general; and, in particular, in the strain placed upon the English language (not to mention Biblical truth) to declare that God "even ordained sin" and yet also to declare that "God is not the author of sin." It is impossible to proclaim that "all of what God has ordained will surely come to pass, and in the manner that God ordains," while defining that to include sin, and nevertheless pretend that this does not lay the authorship of sin as the responsibility of God.

> That God has even ordained sin will not sit well with everyone. Yet, if Jesus is in fact the "Lamb slain before the foundation of the world" (Rev. 13.8) then sins *[sic]* appearance into the world and our redemption through the atonement, were decreed by God before creation and the fall; however, Scripture is clear that God is not the author of sin (Ja. 1.13).

Bremmer acknowledges that his assertion, "God has even ordained sin" as an affirmation of truth, "will not sit well with everyone." I place my name on the list of those with whom it does not sit well and I wish to do so in letters sized to rival those of John Hancock's intent as he signed the Declaration of Independence. I find the assertion of the article to be irreconcilable with the clarity of the Biblical proclamations.

> Psalm 145:17 The LORD is righteous in all his ways, and holy in all his works.
>
> Daniel 9:14 ... for the LORD our God is righteous in all his works which he doeth:

Not only does God do right in all His ways, but God is holy in all His works. He is both holy and righteous. It is impossible to reconcile those truths and then make God the ordainer of sin.

> 1 Corinthians 14:33 For God is not the author of confusion, but of peace, as in all churches of the saints.

If God is specifically declared not to be the author of confusion, how could He be described as the author of sin?

> 1 John 1:5 This then is the message which we have heard of him, and declare unto you, that God is light, and in him is no darkness at all.

The light and darkness that is in view in this passage is not physical light and darkness, but moral or spiritual light and darkness. God has no moral or spiritual darkness in Him "at all."

I am constrained to ask a question, but I first need to establish the premise for that question. The concept that is the foundation of Calvinism was well summarized in the first sentence of this article.

> By sovereignty of God I mean that God has ordained (or decreed), by an act of His sovereign will, all that has come to pass, all that is, and all that will come to pass, and apart from His knowledge, purpose, and predetermined plan, nothing will come to pass.

That statement affirms that nothing will ever occur that God did not ordain by decree to happen by an act of His sovereign will. This is precisely what Calvin taught. Two quotations from the *Institutes of the Christian Religion* and one from his *Commentary on Romans* should be sufficient to illustrate his teaching.

> By predestination we mean the eternal decree of God, by which he determined with himself whatever he wished to happen with regard to every man. All are not created on equal terms, but some are preordained to eternal life, others to eternal damnation; and, accordingly, as each has been created for one or other of these ends, we say that he has been predestinated to life or to death.[201]

> We say, then, that Scripture clearly proves this much, that God by his eternal and immutable counsel determined once for all those whom it was his pleasure one day to admit to salvation, and those whom, on the other hand, it was his pleasure to doom to destruction. We maintain that this counsel, as regards the elect, is founded on his free mercy, without any respect to human worth, while those whom he dooms to destruction are excluded from access to life by a just and blameless, but at the same time incomprehensible judgment.[202]

> Though they indeed, whom God in his eternal counsel has destined as sons to himself, are perpetually his sons, yet Scripture in many parts counts none to be God's children but those the election of whom has been proved by their calling: and hence he teaches us not to judge, much less to decide, respecting God's elec-

---

[201]Calvin, *Institutes*, Book 3, chapter 21, section 5.
[202]Calvin, *Institutes*, Book 3, chapter 21, section 7.

> tion, except as far as it manifests itself by its own evidences. Thus Paul, after having shown to the Ephesians that their election and adoption had been determined by God before the creation of the world, shortly after declares, that they were once alienated from God, (Eph 2:12,) that is, during that time when the Lord had not manifested his love towards them; though he had embraced them in his eternal mercy.[203]

Calvinism teaches that God determined in His eternal counsel to elect, to adopt, and to choose certain individuals for the determinative purpose of preordaining them to eternal life **and** that He determined in His eternal counsel to elect and to choose other individuals for the discriminative purpose of preordaining those individuals to eternal death.

Now we come to my question. It is alleged by Calvinism that "God has ordained or decreed, by an act of His sovereign will, all that has come to pass, all that is now occurring, and all that will come to pass in the future, and that apart from His knowledge, purpose, and predetermined plan, nothing will come to pass." Therefore, I must ask this question, "Did God ordain or decree in His eternal counsel that He would ordain or decree that He would determine in His eternal counsel to elect, to adopt, and to choose some to preordain them to eternal life and did God ordain or decree that He would ordain or decree that He would determine in His eternal counsel to elect and to choose some to preordain them to doom them to eternal death?"

My question is convoluted, but so is the system that I am challenging. In the simplest of terms, "Does not Calvinism of necessity require that we believe that God ordained that He would ordain?" Calvinism complicates the simple and encumbers

---

[203]http://www.sacred-texts.com/chr/calvin/cc38/cc38012.htm

the complex. This becomes a tortuous manipulation of reason. It seems to me that Calvinism is asking that the illogical be accepted in the name of following logic. This logical procession of this illogical circuitous reasoning becomes an impossibility to restrain. The attempt to follow this progression would lead to insanity or to atheism.

APPENDIX 6

PROVIDENCE

A Sermon Published On Thursday, October 15TH, 1908 as NO. 3114. The Date Delivered by C. H. Spurgeon is Unknown, At New Park Street Chapel, Southwark.

> Now as I beheld the living creatures, behold one wheel upon the earth by the living creatures, with his four faces. The appearance of the wheels and their work was like unto the color of a beryl: and they tour had one likeness: and their appearance and their work was as it were a wheel in the middle of a wheel. Where they went, they went upon their four sides: and they turned not when they went. As for their rings, they were so high that they were dreadful; and their rings were full of eyes round about them four. And when the living creatures went, the wheels went by them, and when the living creatures were lifted up from the earth, the wheels were lifted up.—Ezekiel 1:15–19.

In my preaching, I am constantly talking about Providence, so I thought it would be well to devote a whole sermon to explain-

> ing what I believe are God's great wonder-working processes which we call "Providence." In looking for a suitable text, I found this one. These "wheels" signify Divine Providence; and I trust, while explaining them, I may be so assisted by God's Spirit that I may say many things to you concerning God's government which may rejoice any who are despondent, and lift up the souls of many who are distressed.

Spurgeon continues:

> VIII. Another thought is, that PROVIDENCE IS AMAZING.
>
> I shall not dwell on this point, but just remind you that the text says it is so: "As for their rings, they were so high that they were dreadful; and their rings were full of eyes round about them four." Even the man who knows that every wave that dashes against the ship is washing him nearer home, —that every breath of wind that rises comes to his sail, and fills it, and sends it to the white cliffs of his native Albion, —even the man who feels that everything is working for him, —even he must say that Providence is amazing. Oh, that thought, it staggers thought! It is an idea that overwhelms me, —that God is working in all that happens! The sins of man, the wickedness of our race, the crimes of nations, the iniquities of kings, the cruelties of wars, the terrific scourge of pestilence—all these things are, in some mysterious way, working the will of God!
>
> I cannot explain this. I cannot tell you where human will and free agency unite with God's sovereignty and with his unfailing decrees. This has been the place where intellectual gladiators have fought with each other since the time of Adam. Some have said, "Man does as he likes;" and others have said "God does as he pleases." In one sense they are both true;

but there is no man who has brains or understanding enough to show where they meet.

We cannot tell how it is that I do just as I please as to which street I shall go home by; and yet I cannot go home except through a certain road. John Newton used to say that there were two streets by which he could go to St. Mary Woolnoth; but Providence directed him as to which he should use. Last Sabbath-day, I came down a certain street—I do not know why, —and there was a young man who wished to speak to me. I say that was God's Providence, —that I might meet that young man. Here was Providence, and yet there was my choice; how, I cannot tell. I cannot comprehend it.

I believe that every particle of dust that dances in the sunbeam does not move an atom more or less than God wishes—that every particle of spray that dashes against the steamboat has its orbit as well as the sun in the: heavens, —that the chaff from the hand of the winnower is steered as surely as the stars in their courses, —that the chirping of an aphis over a rosebud is as much fixed as the march of the devastating pestilence, and the fall of sere leaves from the poplar is as fully ordained as the tumbling of an avalanche. He who believes in God must believe this truth. There is no standing point between this and atheism. There is no half way between an almighty God who worketh all things according to the good pleasure of his own will and no god at all. A god who cannot do as he pleases, —a god whose will is frustrated, is not a God, and cannot be a God; I could not believe in such a god as that.

IX. My closing idea is, that PROVIDENCE IS FULL OF WISDOM.

> You will see this by the last part of the 18th verse: "and their rings were full of eyes round about them four." You will say, this morning, "Our minister is a fatalist." Your minister is no such thing. Some will say, "Ah! he believes in fate." He does not believe in fate at all.
>
> What is fate? Fate is this, *Whatever is, must be.* But there is a difference between that and Providence. Providence says, *Whatever God ordains, must be;* but the wisdom of God never ordains anything without a purpose. Everything in this world is working for some one great end. Fate does not say that. Fate simply says that the thing must be; Providence says that God moves the wheels along, and there they are. If anything would go wrong, God puts is right; and if there is anything that would move awry, he puts forth his hand, and alters it. It comes to the same thing; but there is a difference as to the object. There is all the difference between fate and Providence that there is between a man with good eyes and a blind man. Fate is a blind thing: it is the avalanche crushing the villages down below the mountain and destroying thousands of lives. Providence is not an avalanche, it is a rolling river, rippling at the first like a rill down the sides of the mountain, followed by minor streams, then it rolls in the broad ocean of everlasting love, working for the good of the human race. **The doctrine of Providence is not that *what is, must be;* but that, what is, works together for the good of our race, and especially for the good of the chosen people of God**. The wheels were full of eyes, they were not blind wheels. [Emphasis is mine.]

In these paragraphs, Charles Haddon Spurgeon touches on the theme of the control of God over all things. Spurgeon's examples are as strong as that of the raindrops in the previously cited article by Michael Bremmer; however, his presentation has a gentler tone to it. I have not throughly searched my Spurgeon resources for each of his comments on the eternal decrees of God; and, therefore, I am not alleging that he would or would not have disagreement with Bremmer's example.

I will testify that these particular words of Spurgeon concerning the particle of dust have been used to support exactly the exact position that Bremmer proposed. I recall an occasion that it was used by a Calvinist pastor to describe the journey of a particular drop of rainwater down the windshield of my car. The preacher confidently assured me that he found comfort in the knowledge that the journey of that single raindrop was *determined by a decree of God before the foundation of the world.*

Spurgeon attributes the pattern of dust motes in a sunbeam to the providence of God. I understand the providence of God to be something entirely different from a decree of God. I believe the providence of God is His watchcare.[204]

The providence of God encompasses the laws established and the bounds set by the LORD. By way of example, consider the statements regarding to the bounds of the sea and those bounds being compared to human will.

> Jeremiah 5:20–25 Declare this in the house of Jacob, and publish it in Judah, saying, 21 Hear now this, O foolish people, and without understanding; which have eyes, and see not; which have ears, and hear not: 22 Fear ye not me? saith the LORD: will ye not tremble at my presence, which have placed the sand *for* the bound

[204] *M-WD* definition: "often capitalized: divine guidance or care; capitalized: God conceived as the power sustaining and guiding human destiny."

> of the sea by a perpetual decree, that it cannot pass it: and though the waves thereof toss themselves, yet can they not prevail; though they roar, yet can they not pass over it? 23 But this people hath a revolting and a rebellious heart; they are revolted and gone. 24 Neither say they in their heart, Let us now fear the LORD our God, that giveth rain, both the former and the latter, in his season: he reserveth unto us the appointed weeks of the harvest. 25 Your iniquities have turned away these *things*, and your sins have withholden good *things* from you.
>
> Proverbs 8:28–29 When he established the clouds above: when he strengthened the fountains of the deep: 29 When he gave to the sea his decree, that the waters should not pass his commandment: when he appointed the foundations of the earth:

I would not dare to question the omniscience of God or His omnipotence; instead, I unquestioningly affirm my complete reliance on both. Those are foundational truths to any understanding of the validity of the claims of the God of the Bible.

> Omnipotence: God, as revealed in the Scriptures, has the power, *both the strength and the authority,* to do whatsoever He wills to do, whenever, and however, He wills.
>
> Omniscience: the God of the Bible has the fullness of all knowledge; there is nothing that is beyond the capability of His knowing. Those are unchallengeable statements. One has to reject the inspiration and the inerrancy of Scripture and its literalness to disbelieve either omnipotence or omniscience.

Those who are Process Theologians believe that God is learning what will be as the events play themselves out. This would undermine the very essence of Deity. A god that is not omniscient and omnipotent is nothing more than the gods of ancient peoples were—mere demigods: more than mortal men, but something less than and other than JEHOVAH, the God of the Bible. Some of those who have adopted Process Theology have gone on to deny all that is considered Christian theology. To them, all of Scripture must be stripped of authority beyond that of history, because prophecy is not acceptable as a possibility.[205]

Amazingly, some scholars and preachers within (or at least who were considered at one time to have been within) the ranks of evangelical Calvinists have left their orthodox roots and have adopted Process Theology. Among those are some that have continued in their *process* of rethinking theology to adapt themselves into a new theology, generally under the names of Free Will Theism, Open View of God, Relational Theism, Personal Theism, Openness, Open Theism, or Open Theology.[206]

---

[205]http://carm.org/questions-process-theology
"Process theology is the philosophical and theological position that God is changing, as is the universe. Therefore, our knowledge of God must be progressing as we learn more about him and it can never rest in any absolutes, which is why process theologians deny the absolutes of God's immutability and truth. Furthermore, this would mean that absolute knowledge of God would not be achievable, and a self-revelation of God (in the person of Jesus Christ and the Bible) would also not be possible."
"Logically speaking, if process theology maintains that God is progressing and changing, then given an infinite amount of time in the past, God may not have actually been God. Also, it could be argued from this perspective that there is something outside of God that works upon him, bringing him into a greater knowledge and increased greatness. This would be problematic because it would need to study what that 'something' is."
"In process theology, God does not know the future exhaustively. He can guess at what may or may not happen, but absolute knowledge is not attainable until events actually occur."

[206] "... open theists would not say that God is weak or powerless. They say that God is capable of predicting and ordaining certain future events because He is capable of working in the world and bringing certain events to pass when the time is needed. Therefore, God could inspire the Old Testament writers to prophesy certain events and then He could simply ensure that those events occurred at the right time."
"Furthermore, open theists claim that they do not deny the omniscience of God. They, like classical theologians, state that God is indeed all-

Dr. Clark Pinnock is an intriguing case study of a theologian that abandons his strong advocacy for the TULIP and develops Open Theology in its place. An interview that Pinnock gave to the website HOMILETICS Online,[207] gives a brief history of why he left Calvinism and how he labored with others to develop Open Theology.

The first question given him was "What is Open Theism?" Pinnock responded by explaining Openism as "a variant of Wesleyan-Arminian thinking" in which God is "essentially relational himself" *[sic]* and "who treasures *relationships of love* with his creatures." In this brief explanation, he has singularly focused on the great omission of Calvinism—the love of God. [Emphasis is mine.]

I am fascinated by the transitional thinking that led him to move from a position of Determinism to one of Openness. In Determinism, God decreed all things before the foundation of the world. With Openness God is experiencing a process whereby He is learning and adapting as we humans make decisions and He is observing and adjusting Himself as the laws of nature that He established create consequences unforeseen to Him when He set the laws in motion. Those two concepts, Determinism and Openness, are polar opposites.

---

knowing. But they differ in that God can only know that which is knowable and since the future has not yet happened, it cannot be exhaustively known by God. Instead, God only knows the present exhaustively, including the inclinations, desires, thoughts, and hopes of all people."

"In Open Theism God can make mistakes because He does not know all things that will occur in the future. According to them, God also takes risks and adapts to the free-will choices of people. They claim biblical support for their position by citing Scripture where God changes His mind (Exodus 32:14), is surprised (Isaiah 5:3–7), and tests people to see what they will do (Genesis 22:12)." http://carm.org/what-is-open-theism

[207]http://www.homileticsonline.com/subscriber/interviewsPinnock.asp All statements identified by quotation marks in these following paragraphs are attributed to Dr. Pinnock in the article found on the website.

His candid reply to the question is "Well, I used to be a five-point Calvinist in the late '60s and then I came to read Hebrews and noticed how it appears our relationship to God is conditional upon faith, so I was intrigued by the idea that God is conditioned by some of the things that creatures do." His thinking as a Calvinist, with "a high doctrine of predestination," had "made it hard to see how God was relational."

Pinnock rightly identifies a critical failure of Calvinism. Within the doctrines of Calvinism, there is, according to Pinnock, no provision for God to "respond to what we do because it's not really a part of his *[sic]* own decree for the world." Moreover, he continued, Calvinism insists that "God cannot have real relations, because that would imply that aspects of God's experience depend on something else."

I marvel at what the route might have been that led him to his original acceptance of Calvinism. Apparently, it was not from reading the Bible, because it is his reading of the Epistle to the Hebrews that first challenged and then shattered his Calvinism. His faith in the TULIP was shaken when he began to take notice of the importance of faith. He *read* and *noticed* and that "relationship to God is conditioned upon faith." Apparently, he had never recognized that during his days as a Calvinist.

The pattern of the Calvinist is to choose words and to make those words the essence of their doctrine as in the *total* of Total depravity. Pinnock settles upon the word *condition*. It seems that he uses the word as the transitive verb with the meaning "to adapt, modify, or mold so as to conform to an environing culture" or "to modify so that an act or response previously associated with one stimulus becomes associated with another."[208] Pinnock

---

[208]The *M-WD* entry for condition.

speaks of the exercise of faith by a person as being the *condition* of a relationship with God. However as he quickly explains, it is God that is conditioned and not man.

> The old view [Calvinism] is that God is not conditioned by anything his *[sic]* creatures do because he has determined what they do. But if, in fact, God's will is affected by what his *[sic]* creatures decide, then that calls for a personal theism, relational theism, open theism. So in a way open theism goes right back to the early '70s when I realized the weakness of deterministic thinking.[209]

The *if-then either-or* reasoning of his Calvinism betrays the learned Pinnock. It is as though he only sees two possibilities: either God determines or man determines. That is the standard justifying argument used by generations of Calvinists to rationalize their determinism: *If God is not the determiner of all things, then man or a combination of creation, Satan, and humanity must be the determiner.* Pinnock simply shifts from one determiner to another. He could not find a possibility of balance between the sovereignty of God and the freewill of humanity.

I do not mean to suggest that the emotional, mental, spiritual procedures through which Pinnock travelled was simple, quick, or easy. I do say that his destination was uncomplicated in the sense that he seemed to be able to conceive of only two alternatives. In his reasoning, *if* he rejects the uncaring determinism of Calvinism, *then* the opposite of Calvinism must be true. It is the *if-then* argument restricted to the possibility of only two alternatives.

Pinnock was gifted with a brilliant intellect that led him on an eclectic theological journey that

---

[209]http://www.homileticsonline.com/subscriber/interviews/Pinnock.asp

continued until his forced withdrawal from public life in March of 2010 because of a diagnosis of Alzheimer's. Mercifully, he died of a heart attack just over six months later.

I use the term *eclectic*, though I might also use *eccentric*, because he was raised in a liberal Baptist home, became conservative, fought for inerrancy within the southern Baptist convention, moved through Calvinism to toleration of the excesses of the charismatic chaos in the Toronto Airport Christian Fellowship with its holy laughter, and progressed from Process Theology until he came to rest in the doctrinal philosophy of Openness. Stanley Grenz described Pinnock as a man that took the "intellectual journey from quintessential evangelical apologist to anti-Augustinian theological reformist."[210]

To convey the extent of the radical change in the thinking of Pinnock, I submit these additional comments also from this article. "Traditionally [in Calvinism], "God knows everything that will ever happen certainly, so it must happen exactly that way. Whereas we're saying that God appears in the Bible to know some things for certain because he *[sic]* planned them or because they're going to happen definitely, but aspects of the future may surprise him. *[sic]*"

That is a stunning divergence from the doctrine of meticulous providence where all that transpires is decreed by God to a position where God might be surprised by something man or nature might do.

How often we humans become either revolutionaries or reactionaries. Either we enthusiastically embrace a cause or we reject it completely and accept the exact opposite. It appears to me that

---

[210]http://www.christianitytoday.com/ct/2010/augustweb-only/43-22.0.html

Pinnock, for all of his intellectual brilliance, threw out the God of the Bible when he pitched the bath-water of the TULIP.

APPENDIX 7

INVITED

The Associated Baptist Press website[211] carried an article with the bold title, *Pastor Says God Chooses Who Will Be Saved.* The sermon referenced is an unintended illustration of classic circuitous Calvinistic reasoning.

With typical logical eloquence, the Calvinist pastor devotes an entire sermon to the attribution of salvation as being completely the *determinative, discriminative choice* by God. He declares "God the Father drew a circle around our names in eternity past and passed over other names and left them to their just condemnation." Expanding, he proclaims, "God could have chosen none and we would have all gone to hell and God would have been just and perfect in his holiness, for the wages of sin is death." This dogmatic edict is pronounced in the context of "every molecule in this universe was pre-scripted *[sic]* by God in this eternal, sovereign will." With true Calvinistic logic, the affirmation is made that God "pre-scripted" *[sic]* any given individual man to be a

---

[211] http://www.abpnews.com/content/view/6544/53/

sinner; thereby making God the *pre-scripter [sic]* of the sin of the sinners: "God has predetermined and pre-scripted *[sic]* everything that would come to pass." *God wrote the script; man is merely the actor fulfilling the assigned role in the play.*

Therefore, man is totally removed from responsibility because man has a "moral inability to believe upon the Lord Jesus Christ." The Calvinist's *Pre-scripter [sic]* "pre-scripted" *[sic]* man to be unable to believe by His *determinative, discriminative choice* not to give man the capacity to believe.

Even so, with sincerity, Pastor Steve Lawson,[212] true to his Calvinistic persuasion, closes "the sermon with an invitation to anyone in the audience under conviction to accept Christ" with the following instruction:

> "You may say I don't know if I was chosen, I don't know if I was predestined," he said. "You may know that you are chosen and you may know that you are predestined if you will believe upon his Son, the Lord Jesus Christ."

I have no doubt that the speaker would deny the inconsistency that I see in the ***if*** of his invitation: "You may know that you are chosen and you may know that you are predestined **if** you will believe upon his Son, the Lord Jesus Christ." In his understanding, no individual in that audience has the natural capacity, the ability, to believe; yet he tells

---

[212]Dr. Steven J. Lawson is senior pastor of Christ Fellowship Baptist Church in Mobile, Alabama, a graduate of Texas Tech University (B.B.A.), Dallas Theological Seminary (Th.M.), and Reformed Theological Seminary (D.Min.), President of New Reformation, member of the Executive Board of The Master's Seminary and College, teaches expository preaching at The Master's Seminary in the doctor of ministry program, teaches in The Expositor's Institute at Grace Community Church, and is a teaching fellow of Ligonier Ministries. He has written extensively and has an international preaching ministry. I respect his scholarship; I reject his interpretation of Scripture.

the assembled souls that all that any one of them must do is to believe.

He is able to justify this offer of salvation, because in Calvinism, God regenerates the chosen so that the elect may be given the gift of faith that will then enable the predestinated to believe. Further, he is not required under Calvinistic logic to explain, at this step of engagement with an individual, that the ultimate perseverance of that individual who claims to believe will be the proof that he is one of the foreordained, predestinated, chosen elect of God. He is able to do all of this without any sense of deceitfulness, because *if* an individual does or does not respond with belief, that choice was made for them by God before creation. He therefore offers what a person cannot receive because God is holy and would not do anything unholy. I see this as circuitous reasoning.

The "you may know" is qualified in Calvinism with the conditional clause "*if you are one of the elect.*" The Calvinist is enabled to profess sincerity, "since humans cannot know which people are predestined, they have a responsibility to preach the gospel to all people." The sincerity of no Calvinist is challenged; the doctrine is.

Sincerity does not atone for the deceptive practices of Calvinism toward the believer or for the destructive precepts of his Calvinism upon the hearers. Some will conclude that they are not of the one of the elect and turn a deafened ear to the Gospel—*deafened by this doctrine.* Some will attempt to persuade themselves of feeling the conviction—"anyone in the audience under conviction"—only to doubt through life whether the feeling was real or unreal.

At the same time, I can be thankful that he preached salvation through the LORD Jesus. My thankfulness is the same as that of the apostle: "What then? notwithstanding, every way, whether in pretence, or in truth, Christ is preached; and I therein do rejoice, yea, and will rejoice." (Philippians 1:18)

Even so, the *Pre-scripter [sic]* of the Calvinist is not a true representation of the God of the Bible.

Do not infer that what you read are extreme, radical, rare, fringe element, hyper-Calvinist statements. These statements are simply Calvinism expressed openly in the pulpit without the typical codeword camouflage.

> A Southern Baptist pastor told a California audience ... that the notion that God foreknew which believers would freely choose to accept Christ is false. ... it is, theologically speaking, "grossly ignorant" to believe that "God looked down the proverbial tunnel of time to see who would choose his Son" and then "in a reflexive manner" chose them for election. "God has never looked down the tunnel of time and learned anything," ... "God knows everything immediately, eternally, perfectly, completely." ... "God has never received a report from anything that is going on on the earth. God's knowledge is infinite. It is perfect. So God has never looked down the tunnel of time to see anything, and whatever God does foreknow, it is only because he has already foreordained it.

Having defined his understanding of foreknowledge and foreordination, he continued by describing God the Father as having drawn a "circle around our names in eternity past and passed over other names and left them to their just condemnation." As a proper Calvinist, he informed those in his hearing that "God could have chosen none and we would have all gone to hell and God would have been just and perfect in his holiness, for the wages of sin is death."

However, in the same Calvinist propriety, he assured his audience that God had actually "a vast multitude of sinners" to elect to give them salvation. In eternity, before the creation of the world, God Himself made the "determinative, discriminative" choice that He loved a "peculiar people." All of the choices were made before the creation began. Even so, he would assure the hearers that the word predestination or predestined is not a negative concept, because it only means that "God has marked out on the horizon of time the destination by which he is bringing all of human history to an appointed end, and God has predetermined and prescripted *[sic]* everything that would come to pass."

He answers the heart-wrenching question of the destiny of the non-elect by not answering it. By that, I mean that he asks the question, but his answer only discusses the elect.

> "Why is it that you have believed and others in your family have not believed? Why is it that you have believed and others who are friends or classmates have not believed? Is it because you are smarter? Is it because you have a higher IQ? Is it that you were more spiritual when you were lost? Is it that you are wiser? Do you have greater insight? The answer to all of these is no. The reason that you have belief is because of the grace of our God and the saving work of the Holy Spirit of God."

According to Calvinism, the grace of God is also the reason that some do not believe. Yet, he affirms that there is "nothing harsh or offensive" conveyed by the doctrine of predestination, which is "God exalting," "joy producing" and "humbling." Those who are of the non-elect will be exalting God by their perdition—their eternal damnation. I understand the joy in the elect after they persevere and arrive in Heaven, but I do not see how the non-elect find any joy or humility in the doctrine. Nor do I see why they should do so.

In this one sermon, he touches all of the essential doctrines of the Calvinist TULIP as he proceeds to the doctrine of Limited Atonement and Irresistible Grace. Notice the code words of "elect," "specifically," "particular," "specific," and "accomplished."

> ... Jesus' death atoned only for sins of the elect. "He did not die for an anonymous, nameless group of people, but specifically he died for you and me who were chosen in him from the foundation of the world." ... "It was a very particular death. It was a very specific death. Not one drop of his blood was shed in vain. Upon the cross, Jesus accomplished all that he came to do. Upon that cross Jesus did not merely make us save-able, *[sic]* Jesus actually saved us."

He proceeds to bring the molecules of the universe into the sermon. He asserts that all of everything and the destiny of that all was decreed by God.

> ... "every molecule in this universe was pre-scripted *[sic]* by God in this eternal, sovereign will." That includes details such as "the means by which we would come to hear the gospel and come to a saving faith in Christ" and "when we would be born in history and who our parents would be and where we would grow up, what our gender would be, who would live next door us, who we would go to school with." "There are no accidents in our life."

Since it is impossible for him to know if there might be someone hearing him that is elected and that is predetermined to be regenerated and then given the gift of faith in that very service, he concludes his sermon with what he believes is a sincere invitation.

> "You may say I don't know if I was chosen, I don't know if I was predestined," he said. "You may know that you are chosen and

> you may know that you are predestined if you will believe upon his Son, the Lord Jesus Christ."

There is always that *if* in the preaching of the Calvinist. While I concede that the Calvinist was sincere in his invitation, since he does believe that only the elect could respond, I believe that the way that he phrases his invitation is disingenuous.

> "You may know that you are chosen and you may know that you are predestined if you will believe upon his Son, the Lord Jesus Christ."

If he said what Calvinism actually teaches, he would phrase the invitation thusly, "*If* you are predestined to believe, you will believe; and then, if you persevere until the end of life, you will know that you were chosen, elected, predestined, when you arrive in Heaven."

Once more, I call attention to the declarative invitation. Once more, I emphasize that I concede his sincerity. Once more, I must state that the invitation is inconsistent as it was worded.

> You may know that you are chosen and you may know that you are predestined if you will believe upon his Son, the Lord Jesus Christ.

The context of the invitation translates "if you will believe" to a message in code. "You may believe upon the LORD Jesus *if* you were predestinated by the determinative discriminative choice of God the Father that you are to be regenerated at this time in this place so that at this precise conjunction of time and events you might receive the believing grace that will regenerate you so that you might be enabled to have the faith to recognize that you are one of the elect and you will be equipped to persevere unto the end. You will believe *if* you are one of the elect and you will not believe *if* you are not one of the elect. There is nothing that you can do about it one way or the other."

That is impossible to describe as an invitation for whosoever will to come. Such an invitation has stringent qualifiers imposed that eliminate the *whosoever* and denies the ability to respond to any individual, unless that person is one of the fortunate elect *and* the time is that which was predetermined by God.

APPENDIX 8

AUTHORITY

The immediate criticism leveled against anyone who would dare to challenge any aspect of Calvinism is that of being ignorant of Calvinism due to a failure to read *firsthand* the proponents of Calvinism.

In researching material for this book, an internet search led me to a letter written by Dr. Marc Monte that answered criticism against his stand on the issue of Calvinism. A pro-Calvinism website[213] posted the following letter Saturday, February 16, 2008, with this introduction:

> I listened to a sermon a while *[sic]* back on Calvinism. ... Well, I had disagreements with the preacher, so I left a comment on his sermonaudio.com page. I don't remember the name of the sermon, but it was by a guy named Marc Monte. He sent me an email response. Here it is:

---

[213]http://byhisgrace.heavenforum.org/t100-marc-monte-on-Calvinism

The webpage is listed as being the responsibility of “Matthew, Administrator,” with no other information available online. It is a forum dedicated to the advocacy of Calvinism. I commend Matthew for placing Monte’s complete comments online and to post them with only the tepid swipe by “Mike” that labeled Pastor, educator, and author Monte as *a guy*. That is milder terminology than that which often arrives.

Dr. Monte consented to the inclusion of his letter in this work. His response to “Mike” expresses, with gentleness and kindness, the frustration that those of us who speak against Calvin and his loyal followers constantly endure. We are challenged as to our personal knowledge and as to our proficiency with original sources—usually with more of a bite than the words: *a guy*.

Monte’s letter answers the censure regarding his lack of credentials to be one able to criticize Calvinism and does so kindly, wisely, and firmly.

> Dr. Marc G. Monte, Senior Pastor
> Faith Baptist Church Avon
> 7090 U.S. Highway 36, Avon, IN 46123
>
> Dear Mike:
>
> Thanks for posting a comment about my Calvinism series. You state that I should study Calvinism from a non-biased standpoint. How would someone do that? If I read Calvin. I get his biased viewpoint. If I read his opponents, I get their biased viewpoints. An unbiased study of Calvinism is logically impossible.
>
> I have, however, read both sides of the issue. My chief pro-Calvin source for reformed doctrine has been Loraine Boettner. He is considered a standard authority on the Reformed faith. I have also read several detractors from Calvinism.
>
> However, the greatest contradiction to Calvinism is the Scriptures themselves.

The Bible describes a God Who is sovereign and yet allows man to exercise free will. Mans' exercise of free will cannot thwart God's sovereignty, but God is not responsible for mans' wrong choices. Calvin's view of God is that God is so small that He had to ordain everything in order for everything to turn out His way. Calvin's God is the ultimate micro-manager, responsible for both good and, ultimately, evil.

The Bible presents a God whose plan will be accomplished, but who can accomplish His plan in spite of man's attempts to thwart it. (A simple overview of eschatology illustrates this. God's plan is to establish His kingdom. Satan's plan is to thwart God's kingdom. Though Satan will work overtime to accomplish his plans, God will ultimately win. Calvinism seems to indicate that God is ultimately behind the acts of Satan, ordaining the evil of the Evil One, somehow to His (God's) glory. That, my friend, is confusion.)

Suppose for example that you told your children not to drink beer. Then you forced them to drink beer by opening their mouths and pouring it down their throats. Then you got angry and punished them for drinking beer. Would your children be confused? You bet they would be! Could that be considered abuse? Sure! Calvinism teaches essentially the same thing about God.

The Biblical view of God may be illustrated thusly:

Life is a chess game between me and God (or you could say the "world" and God or the "devil" and God, whatever). God knows ALL of my moves before I make them (His foreknowledge). In fact, God knows infinitely every move that will be made and every move that could be made. God does not force me to make any move, but He does know all of my moves. I am therefore responsible for every move I make. I make every move freely, of my own will. However, guess who wins in the end? That's right—God! God's sovereign victory in the accomplishment of His will is absolutely assured NOT because He ordained every move, but because He knew every move I would make.

Read the Bible with this illustration in mind, and you will see multiple examples of God's working providentially according to his foreknowledge. (The story of Queen Esther is a prime example.)

Now, one more thought about Calvinism. As a theological system, Calvinism is very difficult to understand and is based on logical extensions from questionable interpretive premises. Its complexity as a theological system gives me pause because the Apostle Paul warned us about being beguiled away from the "simplicity that is in Christ." The complexities of Calvinism indicate to me that Calvinism is not the Gospel, but a man made aberration from it. Just chew on that for a while.

Finally, my position against Calvinism is not a condemnation of the many fine preachers who are adherents to its theological positions. I also realize that there are degrees of Calvinism, just like anything else. I am a student of many of the fine Calvinistic preachers on sermonaudio.com. (I am currently listening to a series by Cornelius Van Til—not exactly a card carrying Arminian!)

My concerns about Calvinism stem from the fact that the reformed movement is experiencing a revival of sorts that is transferring its doctrines into formerly non-Calvinistic churches and schools. The resulting intellectualism and elitism has

> had a chilling effect upon soulwinning and evangelism. (Such is not always the case, but such is typically the case.) It is my hope that Christians think Biblically—submitting neither to Calvinism nor Arminianism as theological systems. I prefer Paul to St. Augustine any day!
>
> Thanks for your comment, and thanks for listening to sermonaudio.com!
>
> Dr. Marc G. Monte
> Senior Pastor

While the response by Monte seems reasonable and sound to a non-Calvinist, it will be inadequate to the Calvinist solely because it does not yield to the superiority of the system reared on Augustine and Calvin. The typical response of the Calvinist to a rejection of any Point of Calvinism by an appeal to Scripture is to counter with quotations from Calvin or another Calvinist authority. The pattern is so consistent that the conclusion is properly drawn that the cloudy reasoning of Calvinists takes precedence over the clarity of Scripture.

This relatively standard response to any dismissal of Calvinism identifies the issue that separates most non-Calvinists from the majority of Calvinists. The question is always "What is the authority for beliefs?" Historically, the Bible has been the sole and final authority for all matters of faith and practice for Baptists. It is not a matter of what Augustine, Calvin, Spurgeon, Warfield, Grundem, Piper or any other Calvinist has written. Individually or collectively, those men are not the end-all-discussion authority. The only genuine consideration is "What does the Bible say?"

Unless the dissenter demonstrates a super-exemplary personal proficiency with the *Institutes of the Christian Religion,* and to the multiple *Commentaries, Letters,* and *Tracts* of John Calvin his testimony is rejected as being nothing more than the "unworthy ramblings" of a doctrinaire uneducated Arminian.

The citation of Scripture is instantaneously discounted as having neither merit nor value, because, to the Calvinist, any Scripture without the interpretation of Calvinism remains a code waiting to be deciphered. *Sola Scriptura, Scripture alone,* was the verbalized battle cry of the Reformers; however, what was meant by Calvin was "Scripture *with my understanding* alone." For the Calvinist today, the secret, special definitions of what are otherwise common words, contained in the writings of Calvin, Augustine, et al, are required to unlock the hidden treasures of Scripture, meaning Calvinism.

I suppose that Dr. Monte should be grateful, because in the days of Calvin, the rejection of the belief system that he espoused secured more than the mild epithet "a guy." Dr. John T. Christian, a solid Baptist historian, reminds us that Calvin's deadly influence reached even into England:

> The influence of John Calvin had begun to be felt in English affairs. His books had appeared in translations in England. He was responsible in a large measure for the demon of hate and fierce hostility which the Baptists of England had to encounter. He advised that "Anabaptists and reactionists should be a light put to death" (Froude, History of England, V. 99). He wrote a letter to Lord Protector Somerset, the translation was probably made by Archbishop Cranmer (Calvin to the Protector, MSS. Domestic Edward VI. V 1548), to the effect: "These all together deserve to be well punished by the sword, seeing that they do conspire against God, who had set

> him [the Lord Protector] in his royal seat."[214]

As Servetus was to discover, living, or visiting as was his situation, in Geneva during the time of Calvin's religious rule was very *hazardous to one's health* should the citizen or visitor insult the teachings of Calvin by saying that infant baptism was a "doctrine of demons." Servetus died a fiery death, with the approval of Calvin.

Calvinists universally reject this charge by offering excuses of varying quality to cleanse John Calvin of complicity; yet, the facts of the event remain. The testimony of history indicates that Calvin engineered the outcome of the trial.

After a lengthy attempt to provide a vindicating rebuttal of all of the charges of malicious complicity leveled against Calvin for the death of Servetus—even contending that Calvin pled for "a lighter method" of death, the following paragraphs conclude the article "Calvin and Servetus" by William Wileman.

> Three hundred and fifty years after the death of Servetus, a "monument of expiation" was erected on the spot where he suffered death at Champel, near Geneva. It bears the date of October 27th, 1903; but the unveiling ceremony was postponed until November 1st. On one side of this monument are recorded the birth and death of Servetus. On the front is this inscription:
>
> Dutiful and grateful followers of Calvin our great Reformer, yet condemning an error which was that of his age, and strongly attached to liberty of conscience, according to the true principles of the Reformation and of the Gospel, we have erected

---

[214]http://www.pbministries.org/History/John%20T.%20Christian/vol1/history_15.htm

this expiatory monument. October 27th, 1903.[215]

If there is no guilt to be assigned, then why would a "monument of expiation" be erected **by dutiful and grateful followers of Calvin** *condemning* what is condescendingly referenced as merely *an error of his age*? To that question, there seems to be no answer offered.

The inscription reads that it is an "expiatory monument." One cannot make atonement for an action that is being presented as only an "error of his age." To do so is offering an excuse with the intended purpose of mitigating, if not condoning, that deed. The very existence of the monument testifies to the culpability of Calvin in the active participation in the death of a man solely for what that man believed.

Whether Servetus was a heretic or not is immaterial. Servetus was killed because he taught something that John Calvin opposed. The facts of that record cannot be changed. Calvinists do not deny the event; they expiate it, while they attempt to excuse it.

The death of Servetus was, after all, only the path of a raindrop decreed before the foundation of the world.

---

[215]http://www.banneroftruth.co.uk/pages/articles/article_detail.php?457

APPENDIX 9

CALVIN'S FINAL WORDS

I find the following document[216] to be severely depressing. John Calvin, considered one of the great theologians of the Reformation, demonstrates in his final written words that he personally has no settled assurance that he himself is one of the elect. He was a student of the Scriptures; but, in his dying hour, he was unable to pillow his head on "He that hath the Son, hath life." (I John 5:12)

> In the name of the Lord Amen.
>
> In the year 1564, and 25th day of April, I, Peter Chenalat, citizen and notary of Geneva, do witness and declare, that I was sent for by that excellent character, John Calvin, minister of the word of God in this church of Geneva, and enrolled citizen of the same, who, being indisposed in body, but sound in mind, said he was desirous to make his testament, and to express the judgment of his last will; and requested me to take it down, and write what he

[216]http://www.reformed.org/calvinism/index.html?mainframe=/calvinism/calvin_will.html

should dictate and declare by word of mouth; which I profess I immediately did, and wrote down word by word as he pronounced and dictated, without omission or addition, in the following form, dictated by him:

In the name of the Lord - Amen.

I, John Calvin, minister of the word of God in the church of Geneva, finding myself so much oppressed and afflicted with various diseases, that I think the Lord God has determined speedily to remove me out of this world, have ordered to be made and written, my testament, and declaration of my last will, in form and manner following:

First, I give thanks to God, that taking compassion on me whom he had created and placed in this world, he not only delivered me by his power out of the deep darkness of idolatry, into which I was plunged, that he might bring me into the light of his gospel, and make me a partaker of the doctrine of salvation, of which I was most unworthy; that with the same goodness and mercy he has graciously and kindly borne with my multiplied transgressions and sins, for which I deserved to be rejected and cut off by him; and has also exercised towards me such great compassion and clemency, that he has condescended to use my labor in preaching and publishing the truth of his gospel.

I also testify and declare, that it is my full intention to pass the remainder of my life in the same faith and religion, which he has delivered to me by his gospel; having no other defense or refuge of salvation than his gratuitous adoption, on which alone my safety depends.

I also embrace with my whole heart the mercy which he exercises towards me for the sake of Jesus Christ, atoning for my crimes by the merits of his death and passion, that in this way satisfaction may be made for all my transgressions and offenses, and the remembrance of them blotted out.

I further testify and declare that, as a suppliant, I humbly implore of him to grant me to be so washed and purified by the blood of that sovereign Redeemer, sited for the sins of the human race, that I may be permitted to stand before his tribunal in the image of the Redeemer himself.

I likewise declare, that according to the measure of grace and mercy which God has vouchsafed me, I have diligently made it my endeavor, both in my sermons, writings, and commentaries, purely and uncorruptly *[sic]* to preach his word, and faithfully to interpret his sacred Scriptures.

I testify and declare that in all the controversies and disputes, which I have conducted with the enemies of the gospel, I have made use of no craftiness, nor corrupt and sophistical arts, but have been engaged in defending the truth with candor and sincerity.

But, alas! my study, and my zeal, if they deserve the name, have been so remiss and languid, that I confess innumerable things have been wanting in me to discharge the duties of my office in all excellent manner; and unless the infinite bounty of God had been present, all my study would have been vain and transient.

I also acknowledge that unless the same goodness had accompanied me, the endowments of mind bestowed upon me by God, must have made me more and more chargeable with guilt and inactivity before his tribunal.

And on these grounds I witness and declare, that I hope for no other refuge of salvation than this alone - that since God is a Father of mercy, he will show himself a Father to me, who confess myself a miserable sinner.

Further, I will, after my departure out of this life, that my body be committed to the earth in that manner, and with those funeral rites, which are usual in this city and church, until the day of the blessed resurrection shall come.

As for the small patrimony which God has bestowed upon me, and which I have determined to dispose of in this will, I appoint Anthony Calvin, my very dearly beloved brother, my heir, but only as a mark of respect. Let him take charge of, and keep as his own, my silver goblet, which was given me as a present by Mr. Varanne: and I desire he will be content with it. As for the residue of my property, I commit it to his care with this request, that he restore it to his children at his death. I bequeath also to the school for boys, ten golden crowns, to be given by my brother and legal heir, and to poor strangers the same sum. Also to Jane, daughter of Charles Costans and of my half-sister by the paternal side, the sum of ten crowns. Furthermore, I wish my heir to give, on his death, to Samuel and John, sons of my said brother, my nephews, out of my estate, each forty crowns, after his death; and to my nieces Ann, Susan, and Dorothy, each thirty golden crowns. To my nephew David, as a proof of his light and trifling conduct, I bequeath only twenty-five golden crowns.

This is the sum of all the patrimony and property which God hath given me, as far as I am able to ascertain, in books, movables, my whole household furniture, and all other goods and chattels. Should it, however, prove more, I desire it may be equally distributed between my nephews and nieces aforesaid, not excluding my nephew David, should he, by the favor of God, return to a useful manner of life. Should it, however, exceed the sum already written, I do not think it will be attended with much difficulty, especially after paying my just debts, which I have given in charge to my said brother, in whose fidelity and kindness I confide. On this account I appoint him executor of this my last testament, with Laurence de Normandie, a character of tried worth, giving them full power and authority, without a more exact command and order of court, to make an inventory of my goods. I give them also power to sell my movables, that from the money thus procured they may fulfill the condition of my above written will, which I have set forth and declared this 25th day of April, in the year of our Lord 1564.

John Calvin.

When I, Peter Chenalat, the above mentioned notary, had written this last will, the same John Calvin immediately confirmed it by his usual subscription and hand-writing. *[sic]*

On the following day, April 26th, 1564, the same tried character, John Calvin, commanded me to be called, together with Theodore Beza, Raymond Chauvet, Michael Cops, Louis Enoch, Nicholas Colladon, James de Bordes, ministers and preachers of the word of God in this church of Geneva, and also the excellent Henry Scringer, professor of arts, all citizens of Geneva, and in their presence he hath declared and testified that he dictated to me this his will; in the words and form above written.

> He ordered me also to recite it in their hearing, who had been called for that purpose, which I profess to have done, with a loud voice, and in an articulate manner.
>
> After thus reading it aloud, he testified and declared it to be his last will and testament, and desired it to be ratified and confirmed.
>
> As a testimony and corroboration of this, he requested them all to witness the same will with their hands. This was immediately done by them on the day and year above written, at Geneva, in the street called the Canons, in the house of the said testator.
>
> In proof and witness of this I have written and subscribed, with my own hand, and sealed, with the common seal of our supreme magistrate the will above mentioned.
>
> P. Chenalat.

I chose not to interrupt Calvin as he gave his dying words. I repeat what I wrote earlier: John Calvin, on the very doorstep of eternity, could only testify that he *intended to persevere* the rest of his life and to *implore* God that He would grant that John Calvin *might be* one of the elect. The final words of John Calvin are unlike the Apostle Paul's last testimony.

One may hope that John Calvin believed better than he wrote or expressed himself and that he did indeed find himself in Heaven.

APPENDIX 10

LUTHER AND ANABAPTISTS

In the 1907 revision of Short History of the Baptist, Henry C. Vedder, certainly not considered a radically opinionated Baptist and definitely not a Baptist successionist, wrote of the agreement between the followers of the RCC and the followers of Luther that labeled Anabaptists as those to be persecuted, even to the death. The event is known as the Diet (assembly) of Speier, which is also spelled Speyer. This Diet is well documented because from it the term Protestant rose.

Veddar provides four chapters discussing the persecution by Protestants of those that they designated Anabaptists. The records of the oppression of those outside of both the RCC and the reformation movement are not denied by any reputable historian. In 2010, the assembly of the Lutheran World Federation issued a formal, public apology for the conduct of their ancestors.[217]

---

[217]http://www.mennohof.org/php/whats.happening/documents/2012%20Winter%20Reunion%20web%20copy.pdf

The following paragraphs from Vedder summarize the participation of Martin Luther and the RCC in that persecution.

> The Anabaptists of this period were the only men of their time who had grasped the principle of civil and religious liberty. That men ought not to be persecuted on account of their religious beliefs was a necessary corollary from their idea of the nature of the church. A spiritual body, consisting only of the regenerate, could not seek to add to itself by force those who were unregenerate. No Anabaptist could become a persecutor without first surrendering this fundamental conviction; and though a few of them appear to have done this, they ceased to be properly classed as Anabaptists the moment they forgot the saying of Christ, "My kingdom is not of this world."
>
> It remains to tell the disgraceful story of the treatment of the German Anabaptists. Luther began his career as a reformer with brave words in favor of the rights of conscience and religious liberty. At Worms he said: "Unless I am refuted and convicted by testimonies of the Scriptures or by clear arguments (since I believe neither the pope nor councils alone; it being evident that they have often erred and contradicted themselves), I am conquered by the Holy Scriptures quoted by me, and my conscience is bound in the word of God: I cannot and will not recant anything, since it is unsafe and dangerous to do anything against the conscience." But later, when the Anabaptists took precisely this position, Luther assails them with exactly the arguments brought against him at Worms, which he so boldly rejected:

---

http://metrolutheran.org/2010/09/lutheran-church-builds-bridges-works-toward-healing-with-mennonite-neighbors/

If every one *[sic]* now is allowed to handle the faith so as to introduce into the Scriptures his own fancies, and then expound them according to his own understanding, and cares to find only what flatters the populace and the senses, certainly not a single article of faith could stand. It is dangerous, yes terrible, in the highest degree, to hear or believe anything against the faith and doctrine of the entire Christian church. He who doubts any article that the church has believed from the beginning continually, does not believe in the Christian church, and not only condemns the entire Christian church as an accursed heretic, but condemns even Christ himself, with all the apostles who established that article of the church and corroborated it, and that beyond contradiction.

There was a similar change in Luther's opinions regarding the treatment proper for heretics. In his address to the Christian nobility of Germany (I520) he said: "We should overcome heretics with books, not with fire, as the old Fathers did. Ii there were any skill in overcoming heretics with fire, the executioner would be the most learned doctor in the world; and there would be no need to study, but he that could get another into his power could burn him." The same ideas are set forth in the tract on Secular Magistracy (I523): "No one can command the soul, or ought to command it, except God, who alone can show it the way to heaven ... It is futile and impossible to command or by force compel any man's belief ... Heresy is a spiritual thing that no iron can hew down, no fire burn, no water drown. Belief is a free thing that cannot be enforced." Luther even retained these sentiments, at least in the abstract, as late as I527, for in a treatise written in that year against the Anabaptists, he said: "It is not right, and I am very sorry, that such wretched people should be so miserably murdered, burned, and cruelly killed. Every one *[sic]* should be allowed to believe what he pleases. If his belief is wrong he will have sufficient penalty in the eternal fire of hell. Why should they be made martyrs in this world also? ... With the Scripture and God's word we should oppose and resist them; with fire we can accomplish little."

Yet such excellent sentiments as these did not prevent Luther from advising John, Elector of Saxony, to restrain by force the Anabaptists from propagating their doctrines within his domains. A decree issued by that prince in I528, on the plea that the Anabaptists were seducing simple-minded folk into disobedience to God's word, by preachings and disputations, through books and writings, commanded that "no one—whether noble, burgher, peasant, or of whatever rank he may be, except the regular pastors ... to whom is committed in every place the care of souls and preaching—is permitted to preach and baptize, or to buy and read forbidden books; but that every one who learns of such doings shall make them known to the magistrate of the place where they occur, in order that these persons may be brought to prison and justice." It was made the duty of every one to seize and deliver such offenders to the court; and whoever should fail to do so, did it at peril of body and goods. Whoever received such persons into their houses or gave them any assistance should be treated as abettors and adherents. The Protestants are therefore entitled to the distinction of beginning the persecution of the German Anabaptists.

We cannot wonder that the Catholics followed this example. At the Diet of Speyer, in I529, when the German princes and

> representatives of the free cities presented their famous protest, in which, in the name of religious liberty they claimed the right to force the reformed faith upon their unwilling Catholic subjects, while they spoke also a faint-hearted plea for the Zwinglians, they had no good word for the Anabaptists. The Diet at this session passed a stringent decree against these people: "All Anabaptists and rebaptized persons, male or female, of mature age, shall be judged and brought from natural life to death, by fire, or sword or otherwise, as may befit the persons, without preceding trial by spiritual judges. Such persons as of themselves, or after instruction, at once confess their error, and are willing to undergo penance and chastisement therefore, and pray for clemency, these may be pardoned by their government as may befit their standing, conduct, youth, and general circumstances. We will also that all of their children according to Christian order, usage, and rite shall be baptized in their youth. Whoever shall despise this, and will not do it, in the belief that there should be no baptism of children, shall, if he persists in that course, be held to be an Anabaptist, and shall be subjected to our above-named constitution.[218]

Phillip Schaff in his highly regarded eight-volume *History of the Christian Church*, reports on the involvement of Luther in the persecution of those identified as Anabaptists and who were decreed not to be recognized as Christians, even while he speaks of the RCC as "true Christendom."

The following citation from Schaff confirms this persecution and, indirectly, identifies the primary

[218]Vedder, Henry C., *Short History of the Baptists* ,1907 edition, 161 –164.

doctrinal issue that denied the Anabaptists the recognition of being called Christians. The Anabaptists (the word means *re-baptizers*) rejected infant baptism and recognized only the baptism of a believer. To the Reformers, this insistence was a belief worthy of death. That doctrine remains an unbreachable wall of separation that stymies the ecumenical movement. To surrender that doctrine is to cease to be Baptist.

> Nor did Luther or any of the Reformers and sensible Protestants doubt that there always were and are still many true Christians in the Roman communion, notwithstanding all her errors and corruptions, as there were true Israelites even in the darkest periods of the Jewish theocracy. In his controversy with the Anabaptists (1528), Luther makes the striking admission: "We confess that under the papacy there is much Christianity, yea, the whole Christianity, and has from thence come to us. We confess that the papacy possesses the genuine Scriptures, genuine baptism, the genuine sacrament of the altar, the genuine keys for the remission of sins, the true ministry, the true catechism, the Ten Commandments, the articles of the Creed, the Lord's Prayer. ... I say that under the Pope is the true Christendom, yea, the very *élite* of Christendom, and many pious and great saints."[219]
>
> But the Anabaptists had their martyrs as well, and they died with the same heroic faith. Hätzer was burnt in Constance, Hübmaier in Vienna. In Passau thirty perished in prison. In Salzburg some were mutilated, others beheaded, others drowned, still others burnt alive. Unfortunately, the Anabaptists were not much better treated by Protestant governments; even in Zürich

---

[219]http://www.ccel.org/a/schaff/history/7_ch05.htm

several were drowned in the river under the eyes of Zwingli. The darkest blot on Protestantism is the burning of Servetus for heresy and blasphemy, at Geneva, with the approval of Calvin and all the surviving Reformers, including Melanchthon (1553). He had been previously condemned, and burnt in effigy, by a Roman-Catholic tribunal in France.[220]

... the second Diet of Speier was convened in March, 1529, for action against the Turks, and against the further progress of Protestantism. The Catholic dignitaries appeared in full force, and were flushed with hopes of victory. The Protestants felt that "Christ was again in the hands of Caiaphas and Pilate."

The Diet neutralized the recess of the preceding Diet of 1526; it virtually condemned (without, however, annulling) the innovations made; and it forbade, on pain of the imperial ban, any further reformation until the meeting of the council, which was now positively promised for the next year by the Emperor and the Pope. The Zwinglians and Anabaptists were excluded even from toleration. The latter were to be punished by death.[221]

---

[220]http://www.ccel.org/a/schaff/history/7_ch06.htm
[221]http://www.ccel.org/a/schaff/history/7_ch08.htm

APPENDIX 11

GLOSSARY

Once theology was considered the queen of sciences, *regina scientiarum*, and philosophy was known as the handmaiden to theology, *philosophia ancilla theologiae.* The rise of the age of skepticism eroded the positions of both theology and philosophy and in this present age of skeptical political correction, neither is accredited as science. However, because they are legitimate sciences, both theology and philosophy have their own dictionaries. Words will have special applications in theology and in philosophy; however these applications always are consistent with the basic meaning of the word.

In particular, theology[222] is the attempt to explain Biblical Christianity in an organized logical sequential method. No valid book of theology is intended to replace Scripture. The language of theology will require a theological dictionary for understanding the technical terminology that has developed over the centuries.

---

[222]Cults have their own theologies, which must be understood as entirely distinct from Biblical Christianity.

The words that are used in Scripture *and* in Biblical Christianity are explained sufficiently in the *M-WD*. However, the meaning of the words of Scripture do not always correlate with the way those words are used by individuals professing to be Christians.

If the Pope, who is elected and seated by the College of Cardinals of the Roman Catholic Church, cannot speak authoritatively as to what each of the professing communicants of the Roman Catholic Church actually believe, it must be obvious that no Baptist preacher would ever be able to say all Baptist believe *thus and so*.

Correspondingly, this Baptist pastor does not represent that he is so brazen as to claim that *all Calvinists uniformly adhere* to precise definitions of the terminology of Calvinism that they use. However, the specific tenets that essentially identify the philosophy of Calvinism are so well established and so generally recognized as to be codified in the TULIP. The terminology that is used to explain the TULIP is relatively uniform through the ranks of Calvinism.

Calvinism, being the philosophical approach to theology that it is, through necessity, acquired its own distinctive language. The tongue of Calvinism must be rightly understood if it is to be interpreted in the light of Scripture. The words of Calvinism have their own distinctive meanings. Unless the reader is familiar with the specialized definitions that John Calvin and his followers have assigned to certain words, the reader is at a serious disadvantage and is exposed to error that he cannot recognize in its camouflaged verbal garment. To be blunt, common words have unique meanings when used in the Biblical or theological contexts by Calvinists.

This glossary is limited to those words that are related to the TULIP and is certainly not exhaustive. I have gleaned through a number of Calvinist writ-

ings to determine fair and correct definitions; for that reason, I believe that these definitions are accurate, but I do not wish to promote them as authoritative.

Remember that these are the definitions for terms that reflect how those words are used in Calvinism.

All:

> This word is assigned the definition of the elect in those passages of Scripture that concern the Gospel invitation and the extent of the atonement. The same assignment of special definition is made for the word *world.*

Atonement:

> This is result of the sacrificial death of the LORD Jesus that purchased and provided all of the graces that will insure the effectual calling and that will convey the faith, repentance, justification, perseverance, and glorification to all of the elect.[223]
>
> This word is often modified by an adjectives such as particular, special, limited, definite, saving, etc.

Decree:

> This term is the edict of God that determines a specific act will be accomplished. It is often used to speak of the eternal life that is conferred on one of the elect.

Determinism:

> This is the belief that everything that could ever occur was determined and then decreed before the foundation of the earth as to how and when that event will be and there are no alternatives possible.

---

[223]http://www.spurgeon.org/~phil/dabney/5points.html

The adjective exhaustive is generally used to remove doubts as to the extent of that which is determined.

Doctrines of Grace:

This phrase is used synonymously for the belief system that is identified as Calvinism or Reformed.

Election:

This is the decision that God made before creation that determines which individuals from among humanity will be saved and which individuals will be lost.

The adjectives unconditional, effective, sovereign, etc. are used.

Faith:

This is the gift that God gives to the elect when (after) He regenerates the individual chosen person. In Calvinism, this order is established in a very specifically arrangement:[224] (1) regeneration, (2) the gift of faith, (3) and the gift of repentance.

Grace:

The word has the meaning in Calvinism of an ability, a power, a force, a working principle that God conveys to the elect.

Additionally, Calvinists often attach to the word grace one of various qualifying adjectives that by its use implies grace being a

---

[224]"That repentance not only always follows faith, but is produced by it, ought to be without controversy (see Calvin in Joann. 1:13). For since pardon and forgiveness are offered by the preaching of the Gospel, in order that the sinner, delivered from the tyranny of Satan, the yoke of sin, and the miserable bondage of iniquity, may pass into the kingdom of God, it is certain that no man can embrace the grace of the Gospel without retaking himself from the errors of his former life into the right path, and making it his whole study to practice repentance. Those who think that repentance precedes faith instead of flowing from, or being produced by it, as the fruit by the tree, have never understood its nature, and are moved to adopt that view on very insufficient grounds." Calvin, *Institutes*, Book Three, chapter 3, 478.

power: atoning, elective, irresistible, persevering, regenerative, saving, etc.

Dr. John MacArthur states that "Grace is God's sovereign initiative to sinners ... Grace is the power of God to fulfill our New Covenant duties."[225]

> But here's what I propose—let's start by laying down a *biblical* definition of grace with this simple question:
>
> *What is grace? Grace* is a terribly misunderstood word. Defining it succinctly is notoriously difficult. ... Someone has proposed an acronym:
>
> GRACE is *G*od's *R*iches *A*t *C*hrist's *E*xpense. That's not a bad way to characterize grace, but it is not a sufficient theological definition. ... Grace is not a dormant or abstract quality, but a dynamic, active, working principle:
>
> "... Grace is God's sovereign initiative to sinners. ... Thus we could properly define grace as the free and benevolent influence of a holy God operating sovereignly in the lives of undeserving sinners.[226]

Dr. John Piper defines grace as:

> "Grace is not simply leniency when we have sinned. Grace is the enabling gift of God not to sin. Grace is power, not just pardon."[227]

Predestination:

This is the understanding that God chose some to eternal life before Adam was created. Technically, this would be understood as Single Predestination. Double

---

[225]http://www.gty.org/Resources/Articles/A317

[226]http://www.oneplace.com/ministries/grace-to-you/readarticles/what-is-grace-10339.html

[227]http://kindredgrace.com/grace-is/

Predestination presents God as having predestinated a particular number to eternal life and all others to perdition.

Preterition:

This is the act of passing over by God of those that He chose not to elect to salvation or eternal life. It is the act of His not choosing to chose a particular individual to be one of the elect.

Providence:

The Calvinist understands this to be the outworking of the predetermined plan of God for all things. To the Calvinist, providence is not the watchcare of God; rather it is the will of God being implemented to completion.

Regeneration:

This is the act of God whereby the individual is brought out of his dead spiritual condition and given the life to which he was elected. Having been regenerated, the person is enabled to receive the gift of faith whereby he may believe.

Reprobation:

This is the word used to describe the fate of those that are the non-elect and are therefore eternally condemned. It means to be foreordained to damnation according to the *M–WD*.

Total Depravity:

This is the natural condition in which all men find themselves. It is understood to be Total Inability, meaning that no individual possess by nature the capability or the capacity to do anything that is acceptable to God. In order for a man to be able to please God, man must be given that ability in regeneration.

Will of God

Calvinists describe the will of God with terminology that is rather consistent without regard to time or culture. There are two broad divisions in the will of God: the Reveled Will and the Secret (or Hidden) Will. Calvinists do not identify a Permissive Will; however, some Calvinists do speak of the Will of Disposition, which speaks of that which pleases God.

Revealed will:

This is also called the Perceptive Will, meaning that it is knowable to humanity. This is what God has declared in Scripture that He commands man to do.

Secret will:

This is also identified as the Sovereign Will, the Hidden Will, and the Disposing Will. This speaks of what God has determined that He will do, but which He has chosen to kept hidden from humanity and angels.

Whosoever:

This word is understood to encompass only those that have been regenerated. It does not include the non-elect, who will not be regenerated, or the elect that have not yet been regenerated.

This listing is not intended to be exhaustive. It should be considered only as a cautionary attempt to help readers understand how to interpret Calvinistic writings by using Calvinist definitions.

INDEX

A

B

C

D

E

G

J

L

P

R

S

T

ABOUT THE AUTHOR

Dr. Jerald Manley is married to Julie Hudson; 2014 will be their 50th Anniversary. They have three children and four grandchildren. He has been preaching since 1958 and pastoring since 1962. He has been in his present pastorate since 1975. He has a B.A. from Bob Jones University, a M.DIV. from Louisiana Baptist Theological Seminary, and the Doctor of Divinity conferred by Pensacola Christian College.

He is the founder and editor of *The Baptist Heritage.* He has written *When Sorrows Come, Confusion at Calvary, Resource of Weights and Measures for the Authorized Version, The Song of songs, which is Solomon's, What the Dead Man Wrote, Between the Valleys, Avoid My Mistakes*, etc.

89604136R00222

Made in the USA
Lexington, KY
31 May 2018